THE
KABBALAH
OF
LIGHT

"Catherine's done it again, assembling the hidden ingredients of mindfulness and brewing them in a cauldron of ancient and early medieval Hebraic mystery wisdom. An excellent guide whose magic we have yet to fathom and of which, through the book's many exercises, we might finally catch a glimpse."

RABBI GERSHON WINKLER, AUTHOR OF *MAGIC OF THE ORDINARY*

"Catherine Shainberg's new book is serious, delightful, and tinged with the magical, as is the author. It is a creative effort, filled with wonderful practices and exercises to raise the great Leviathan from the depths of the unconscious so as to awaken our creative imagination and life force. Shainberg's readings into biblical and Kabbalistic myth are wonderfully creative."

MELILA HELLNER-ESHED, AUTHOR OF *A RIVER FLOWS FROM EDEN*

"*The Kabbalah of Light* is an audacious endeavor to present the esoteric wisdom of the Jewish mystical tradition as the science of letting the unconscious speak. The guidance in this book is to lead one to spiritual enlightenment and psychic well-being, the experience that Kabbalists call *dveikut,* cleaving to the divine, the highest rung on the ladder of dreams."

ELLIOT WOLFSON, MARSHA AND JAY GLAZER CHAIR IN
JEWISH STUDIES, UNIVERSITY OF CALIFORNIA, SANTA BARBARA

"In this brilliant book, Catherine has given us a great gift. Not only is this work dazzling in its depth and beauty, it is also eminently useful and practical. Catherine guides us on a grand journey, a voyage of self-discovery. There lies buried treasure—the riches of a more fulfilling transformed life, illumined by the golden sunlight of divine revelation."

KEVIN MELVILLE JENNINGS, PAST CONTRIBUTOR OF
THE DAILY SCOPE FOR VOGUE.COM

"In her thrilling new book, Catherine Shainberg's treasure trove of playful and profound 'inductions' will guide you to plunge deeper and deeper into the innermost realms of your soul. What a gift this book is to all seekers of light and delight. *The Kabbalah of Light* is mind-expanding. It's fun and fabulous!"

DIDI CONN, ACTRESS AND PLAYWRIGHT

THE
KABBALAH
OF
LIGHT

Ancient Practices to
Ignite the Imagination
and Illuminate the Soul

CATHERINE SHAINBERG, Ph.D.

Inner Traditions · Rochester, Vermont

Inner Traditions
One Park Street
Rochester, Vermont 05767
www.InnerTraditions.com

Text stock is SFI certified

Note to the reader: This book is intended to be informational and should not be considered a substitute for advice or therapeutic counseling from a professional psychologist, who should be consulted by the reader in all matters related to his or her psychological health and particularly with regard to any symptoms that may require diagnosis and attention.   Cataloging-in-Publication Data for this title is available from the Library of Congress

ISBN 978-1-64411-474-2 (print)
ISBN 978-1-64411-475-9 (ebook)

Printed and bound in the United States by Lake Book Manufacturing, Inc. The text stock is SFI certified. The Sustainable Forestry Initiative® program promotes sustainable forest management.

10 9 8 7 6 5 4 3 2 1

Text design and layout by Priscilla Harris Baker
This book was typeset in Garamond Premier Pro, with Futura, Grand Cru, and Legacy Sans used as display typefaces

To send correspondence to the author of this book, mail a first-class letter to the author c/o Inner Traditions • Bear & Company, One Park Street, Rochester, VT 05767, and we will forward the communication, or contact the author directly at **schoolofimages.com.**

To my students past and future
Without whom I would be mute

Contents

PART III

Raising the Leviathan

*The Serpent of the Deep, Your Superconsciousness or,
as the French Like to Call it, Your Sur-nature*

✳

List of Exercises

PART II

Taming the Leviathan

13 Healing: Will It Be Leprosy, Wellness, or Wholeness?

PART III

Raising the Leviathan

14 The Heart-Centered Way

Preface

Without leaps of imagination or dreaming, we lose the excitement of possibilities. Dreaming, after all, is a form of planning.

GLORIA STEINEM

I have always been fascinated by the subconscious. At first I didn't know what the word meant—but I knew I was more interested in following what my imaginary friends were doing than what was happening around the dinner table. In fact, I saw no difference between the angels and fairies that populated my world and my little friends I played with in Hyde Park. It was my mother who persistently reminded me to pay attention to the real world and not to dream my life away.

I developed many strategies to remain aware of what was happening around me, so I was able to accomplish the many tasks that were required of me at home and at school. But at the same time, I couldn't ignore the goings-on in my other world. It took me years to understand that most people simply lived in the real world and paid scant attention to the other world. To me, this was a terrible loss. The flow of my imagination was varied and quick, and endlessly entertaining. It also educated me. A large dry leaf could be restored to the soft green of early spring, the leaf still attached to its branch, and the branch to a centuries-old tree whose wisdom I could hear booming in my inner ear. Colors glistened, and voices sang. Souls required me to accompany them to their heavenly rest. And homeless ladies (there was one who

lived in a vacant lot opposite our house, and I waved to her every evening) needed a cocooning of light to stay warm at night. I lived a life of
richness and beauty I couldn't get enough of. I devoured fairy tales and
mythological stories. Voices spoke words in my ears that I generously
transmitted to my playmates. This led to my being accused of lying and
then punished. I soon learned not to communicate what I heard and
saw. I became secretive and mute about my inner world, but its lure was
too powerful.

When it came time to go to college, I opted out of practical solutions
(my mother urged me to go to l'École Polytechnique, a prestigious engi-
neering school, where I would meet lots of nice boys) and went to study art
history at the Sorbonne in Paris. There I revived, somewhat. The colors on
the canvases ignited colors within me, and soon my imagination was running wild. I wanted to study how images change people, but my thesis professor explained to me that I was there to become a scholar. As he put it,
there were two types of people, those who live and those who watch other
people live. Art historians watch other people live. I stood up and told him
I was one of those who lived. I walked out on a career that seemed at the
time the only way forward for me if I was to navigate the real world.

After floundering for a while in jobs that didn't suit me, I decided
to apply to American universities. I did well and got a full scholarship
to Harvard, but in 1971 I gave it up to follow my inner voice. The voice
said: Go to the Middle East. I did. I went all over the Middle East.
I was intending to go to Harvard to study the use of imagery in the
political dialogue of Arab-speaking countries, so the voice made sense.
But then the voice began making no sense: Go to Israel, it said. I had
never been attracted to Israel or to the Jewish people. In fact, I knew
next to nothing about them. My mother was anti-Semitic, as were many
"pieds-noirs."* And I was a by-product of her belief system. Thus far
I'd had no reason to question her prejudices and had lived in a happy
oblivion of nonconfrontation.

The voice woke me up: Go! My mother thought I was crazy and
that I was going to Israel to annoy her. My father, being a journalist, was
more tolerant. But still, giving up a scholarship to Harvard? He tried to

---

*The name French people living in Algeria were called.

talk me out of it. To this day, I wonder what internal compulsion made me disregard his kindly and reasonable advice.

This reminds me of the inscription "Know thyself" that was written in the pronaos* of the Temple of Apollo at Delphi. One can imagine two guardians of the sacred gates, swords raised, crying out: Do you know yourself? I had no idea who I was, what I wanted, nor what the voice meant. But there it was. I was committed to my inner world, and I was giving up a higher education to go pick fruit on a kibbutz in the Negev desert.

Two years later, during the Yom Kippur War, a friend and I were serving as night sentries. To pass the time under the starlit sky, Yoav read me excerpts from the Hebrew Bible. I remember most poignantly the passage where a voice speaks to Abraham. "Lekh lekha!" There are two ways of translating this: Go! Or go to yourself. Abraham (or Abram as he is called before God makes a covenant with him) is asked by the voice to leave his father's home in the fertile Mesopotamian Valley and to venture forth into the desert. Where to? There are no signposts in the desert. "Where I will show you," comes the answer. I was in a similar no-man's-land, lost somewhere in a dusty desert with the sounds of tanks rumbling by, waiting to be shown.

In the Hebrew language are many hidden signposts—not stone gates like the gate at the pronaos of Delphi, but written gates. The words *olam* (world) and *ne'elam* (hidden) have the same Hebrew consonants. We call them roots. When two words have the same roots, they are connected in their deeper meaning. You can imagine these two words as the two guardians of the gate. One says: You are a world unto yourself; the other: that world is hidden! You want to cross our threshold? Beyond awaits the great unknown. That night, listening to Yoav's voice reading the Bible, the guardians let me cross the threshold into the sacred inner space where a whole world of secret knowledge is hidden.

What was I doing in the middle of nowhere, among a people I didn't belong to, listening to a disembodied voice reading the ancient stories? We were so close to Sinai that during the day we could hear the cannons roar. What if the Egyptians reached our kibbutz? And what

---

*Also known as a forecourt.

was it that invaded me during those nights? Inner spaces were opening up, a seething world of emotions, impressions, déjà-vu, a violet ocean of expanding contracting chaos, filled with the *tohu va'bohu** that I later learned was the beginning of creation.

I had been sitting for two years in a darkness of intention, not understanding why I had traded an amazing opportunity to be, literally and figuratively, in the desert. This was the first inkling that the darkness was lifting, but I didn't know how or why I felt this way. I was moved, but my thoughts were in turmoil. Finally I consciously accepted that my mother was wrong: The rational mind didn't know everything. A deeper or higher mind was at work orchestrating my destiny. I was confused, angry, and unsettled, but a wiser part of me trusted that all this confusion was not in vain.

A few weeks after the end of the war I encountered a French man who lived in Jerusalem and who, in pronouncing the unknown name "Colette," sent me rushing to fulfill the destiny my subconscious self intuited. I describe my meeting with Colette Aboulker-Muscat, who was to become my Kabbalah teacher and spiritual mother, in my first book, *Kabbalah and the Power of Dreaming.*†

A year after my meeting Colette, my aunt came to visit. I took her to meet Colette, and to my amazement, the two ladies fell into each other's arms. They had gone to the same school in Oran, Algeria, where they grew up, as had my mother. My mother at the same school as Colette? In fact, she lived across the street from her! The voice had led me across the seas and all the way to the door of a lady who, while definitely not accessible to my conscious mind, was known to my subconscious mind. How was that possible?

I will tell you more about how this amazing story unfolds in chapter 9. You will find out how my all-knowing subconscious spanned eight hundred years to link my present incarnation to Colette's ancestors.

What if I hadn't listened to the voice? My story would have

---

*Genesis 1:2, tohu va'bohu, without form and void. In other words, emptiness and desolation.

†Published by Inner Traditions in 2005.

continued, of course, but would I have discovered my true calling and life's work? Would I have experienced the radical joy and wonder that would suffuse my life from there on? I believe that I would have fulfilled my mother's dreams, but not my own. I know that my life would have felt incomplete and meaningless. Listening to the voice, to the stories Yoav read me, and then meeting Colette, something hidden deep within me exploded, and a flood of hitherto unknown knowledge burst onto the screen of my conscious mind.

Who was Colette? To me she was one of the great loves of my life, my teacher, my spiritual mother, my home. When I was first introduced to her, I had no idea that she was a teacher. She sat me in front of her, looked me in the eyes, and said, "What do you want?" To my utter surprise, unrehearsed and unexpected words came out of my mouth: "I want you to teach me how images move and transform people." This is what I had been pondering since childhood. She smiled and said, "I have waited for you a long time!"

Thus began my apprenticeship. I was required to be there every morning at 7:30 a.m., my dreams written and fully illustrated (I painted them). She would listen to them, then ask me to close my eyes. She guided me with precision and mastery into my subconscious realm. The first induction she gave me was to draw a circle in the sky. I did, and thousands of white birds burst out of the circle, followed by a great and powerful blue angel who told me his name was Pursel. I was mesmerized.

Colette was one of the most notable female Kabbalists living in the land of Israel at the time. To the many who came from all over the world seeking consolation and enlightenment, she was a revered spiritual teacher. For those of you who wonder about a woman teaching Kabbalah, it is true that Ashkenazi rabbis* required those studying Kabbalah to be men, over forty years old, and married. No women were allowed to plunge the depths. But Colette was from a Sephardic family,† so no such restrictions applied. Her grandmother had been a famous teacher to the

---

*Ashkenazis were originally Jewish settlers in northern and eastern Europe. Today an Ashkenazi is one who follows Ashkenazi practices and customs. The rules for teaching Kabbalah have been loosened, and there are contemporary rabbis (even orthodox ones) who teach Kabbalah to women and people under forty.
†Jews living around the Mediterranean sea.

rabbis and Jewish community in Algiers. Her granddaughter was simply following in her footsteps.

Colette was the last lineage holder of her family's ancient Kabbalistic tradition, a tradition that dated back to the thirteenth century, but was said to go back to the patriarchs and prophets who roamed the land during biblical times. Her direct ancestor, through her mother, was Rabbi Yaakov ben Sheshet of Gerona, Spain. She also claimed descent from Rabbi Yitsḥaq Saggi Nehor, known as Isaac the Blind, the first man to coin the word Kabbalah. Isaac the Blind lived in the South of France where he taught and founded an academy of learning and Kabbalah called Posquières* which remains, to this day, in the memory of Jews, a great beacon of wisdom and radiance.

Shema, listen, says the main Jewish prayer. The people listened. "And the people *saw* the voices."[1] It is possible that Yitsḥaq Nehor was called The Blind not because he had lost his eyesight, but because, like the biblical patriarch Isaac, he listened with inner ears and saw with inner eyes. The Sheshet family's transmitted knowledge had to do with listening, with vision, with dreaming, and with activating the subconscious to reveal its secrets.

When one reads the Bible, one is struck by the fact that every story starts with a night dream, a daytime vision, or clairaudience. The sayings of the prophets of Israel occupy a third of biblical texts. How did the prophets learn? A midrash† tells us that after Isaac was saved from his father Abraham's knife by an angel, he went off to study at the academy of Shem and Ever. Academies such as these were later called academies of the *bnei ha-nevi'im,* the sons of the prophets.[2] They were learning to consciously develop prophecy.

My mother tried to stop my dreaming, but I had been born a dreamer. Dreaming was far too compelling to give up. I had followed it, but I had become exhausted. Colette restored my joy and trust in the power of dreaming to lead me to myself. Who was I? I was going to find out, and the truth was grander and more magnificent than I had ever dared hope for. I was going to find out that dreaming is a royal road to enlightenment, and that our subconscious holds the key to our true meaning and destiny.

---

*Today it is called Vauvert.
†The legends that serve as exegesis to the Hebrew Bible narrative.

Introduction

Brain researchers estimate that your unconscious database outweighs the conscious on an order exceeding ten million to one. This database is the source of your hidden, natural genius. In other words, a part of you is much smarter than you are. The wise people regularly consult that smarter part.

MICHAEL GELB

This book is about the unconscious. Later I will call it the subconscious. There is a reason for this, which I will explain shortly. How is it possible to write a book about something that, if we take its name at face value, is unknowable? As I am writing, I am using words, a conscious language related to the activities of a much more recent brain development called the neocortex. But at the same time, many of my body functions are operating sub rosa, unbeknownst to my conscious mind. We have two brains, two different ways of processing our reality. Our more ancient brain is referred to as our reptilian brain. The two brains are like fire and water. Why has the unconscious received such a bad rap? This antagonism is not new. Joseph's brothers, the Hebrew Bible relates, wanted to kill him because he was a dreamer.* The ancient Greeks portrayed Apollo, the sun god, as transpiercing with his arrow

---

*See Gen. 37. Joseph was the son of the patriarch Jacob and his wife Rachel. Dreams come from the unconscious.

of light, the womb-like darkness of the cave of the Pythia,* keeper of messages from the unconscious. Thereafter Apollo, the clear light of the conscious mind, ruled over Delphi.

The conscious mind is naturally antagonistic to the unconscious. It prides itself on its precise observation and objectivity. It likes to separate, analyze, categorize. It uses its powerful logical thrust to establish scientific proof of things that it calls "facts." This chair, this table, the sea are facts of the reality we live in. Facts depend on hypotheses, such as the types of questions we ask ourselves, and the points of view from which we perceive and examine them. Our dearly held certainties may shift and change when new questions and new hypotheses emerge. Ask Albert Einstein if the table is really solid, and he may say that also being pure energy, it is both a solid and not a solid at all. The sea is blue, but the ancient Greeks saw it wine red. Blue was not a "fact" in the time of Homer. The world was geocentric until Copernicus proved otherwise. A scientist will describe the rose as having a stem, thorns, leaves, petals, pistils, coloring, and scent, which are different aspects of a totality of experience, which only the unconscious gives access to. The unconscious has no hypotheses; it is a cauldron of swirling experiences. Tap into it, and up pops a dream image. The unconscious deals only in revelation, and revelation, being an experience, is, by definition, true. If I turn a corner and am suddenly faced with a blazing sunset over the ocean, my heart moves not to the "fact" of the sunset, but to the wondrous experience. The conscious mind deals in facts, the unconscious deals in truth.

To get to the truth of what you really want, you're going to have to tap into the unconscious. The unconscious runs the show, and this is a "fact" verified by many tests conducted by experimental psychologists and researchers. Some researchers go so far as to say that the unconscious runs 95 percent of our body functions. It is a "fact" that our carefully analyzed and agonized choices are mostly decided by the unconscious. Our creative innovations rise up, fully formed from the unconscious, and yet most of us have no clue how to access this great power. Unlike the conscious mind, the unconscious cannot be worked out, analyzed,

---

*Pythia was the priestess of the Oracle at Delphi. She was said to channel the God Apollo and utter prophecies in his name. Many made the pilgrimage to Delphi to consult her.

or pinned down; it can only be received. It will come in whatever form it chooses. Kabbalah, which means "receiving," is the science of letting the unconscious speak.

To learn who you are, to discover your hidden motivations, and to speak to your body and cells, you will have to leave behind what you perceive as the safe shores of the conscious mind. Can you trust the unconscious? There lies the rub. Most of us don't see its value because we confuse our visions with fantasy. But fantasy is the contrary of "true imagination," as William Blake liked to call it. Fantasy is a product of your conscious mind seizing upon your brain's capacity to make images and twisting them to suit its purpose. Suppose you desperately want to believe this very handsome man (or woman) who is married to your best friend is really interested in you. You fantasize about the person's overcoming many obstacles to come to you, including getting rid of his or her partner. You visualize the person finally embracing you, and now both of you are riding off into the sunset. This has nothing to do with the truth. Unfortunately, many of the visualizations taught today trade in fantasy. You are told what to see. While that may be entertaining, it is not transformative.

The unconscious is the source of all creativity. How to tap into your creativity, dialogue with your images, and trigger transformation is the subject of this book. There is a methodology to it that is as precise as anything science pertains to be. The Celts' image for this work is a naked blade lifted above dark waters by a mysterious woman called the Lady of the Lake. The waters, you may have guessed, are the waters of the unconscious. The sword illustrates the jolting, the sometimes cutting truths of the images that pop up at the surface of the unconscious. If you wish to return to the Garden of Eden, you must face the revolving sword of the angel guarding its gates. Don't worry, you will not be cut by the sword or, as the Greeks saw it, turned to stone by your Medusa truths. Like the hero Perseus* you will learn to disarm and, more saliently, to transform those aspects of yourself that you don't like.

---

*Perseus was a Greek hero who beheaded the monster Medusa. Anyone who gazed upon Medusa turned to stone. Perseus used the mirrorlike surface of his polished shield to guide his sword when he cut off her head and put it in a black bag.

But the Celts' powerful image of a sword above waters speaks to the cutting edge of truth that the unconscious wields against you. What better way than to tackle your images head-on, and respond to their necessity to ignite the creative shift! You will become the warrior, hero, gallant knight, or lady of your life story.

✳

When Sigmund Freud coined the words "unconscious mind," he may not have realized that the concept of a vast unconscious part of ourselves, submerged like an iceberg beneath the surface of what we commonly call the conscious mind, has existed since time immemorial. The ancients were well aware of an unconscious realm populated by dangerous or godlike characters, fierce animals, hybrids of all sorts, and mind-boggling obstacles. What Freud understood as the unconscious mind was a store of memories, repressed emotions, and other mental complexes that remained trapped in a no-man's-land and could negatively affect our everyday life and behavior. He believed that these repressed emotions and memories should be brought to conscious awareness in order to be cured. He interchangeably used both "unconscious" and "subconscious," until he finally settled for the word "unconscious." Today psychologists are still debating the differences between the two, but the word "subconscious" is rarely used. The preferred term is "unconscious" for all of our "other than conscious processes." Yet I propose to you that the term "subconscious," coined by French psychologist Pierre Janet (1859–1947), is more accurate. Janet believed that there was a storehouse of information below our conscious mind that could be accessed through focused awareness. We will see more about the subconscious further on.

The ancient world had many names for the realm that lies below our awareness. They called it the other world, the world of the dead, the Happy Isles, Olympus. Heroes' journeys involved crossing the "val" to the other world: *Perce la vallée*, pierce the valley, is the meaning of Perceval's name in the Arthurian legends.* An Ivri, or Hebrew, is the

---

*Perceval was a Knight of the Round Table and the hero of *Perceval, the Story of the Grail* by Chretien de Troyes.

one who crosses over. Shamans the world over speak of journeying out of their bodies to seek hidden knowledge and wisdom. Alchemists had a funny way of illustrating their relationship to the unconscious: a man sitting in a vast cauldron, a fire burning under the pot. Likewise in China, the oldest book in the world, the I Ching, has a hexagram named the cauldron. Here is what the hexagram says: "The image suggests the idea of nourishment. . . . The supreme revelation of God appears in prophets and holy men." In other words, without resisting, sit in the cauldron of natural forces, and the information from your unconscious will rise up in you, nourishing you, and flooding you with prophecy and holiness.

Do we really need to travel out of our bodies, or do we simply let the unconscious rise and submerge our conscious minds, thus giving us access to hidden knowledge? Here is another way it is described: "And God hovered over the *p'nei tehom* (the face of the abyss),"* and created the world in seven days. Read p'nei tehom as God's unconscious realm. Can we, like God, hover over the void of the unconscious and bring forth new creations? We do it every night when we dream. Kabbalists call this maneuver the plunge—*yeridah*†—the drop of the conscious mind into the unformed substance of the unconscious mind to elicit new formations.

Since Freud, much has changed in the world of psychology. Psychology has gone through many incarnations, and different schools have developed. But today a new discipline has arisen in response to criticisms that psychology is but a soft science. Psychology has become experimental, and social psychologists are scientists who, among other things, set up experiments to demonstrate the influence of the unconscious mind on the conscious mind. A great many scientific studies—many that have been replicated—show without a doubt that our rational mind is deeply influenced by the unconscious. The new discipline is aptly called the "new unconscious." It is based on a two-tiered model of the brain. We could see it, suggests Leonard Mlodinow in his 2012 book *Subliminal,* as two railway systems with interconnected lines that crisscross and sometimes share stations. He goes on to

---

*Recall Genesis 1:2, tohu va'bohu, without form and void.
†See Gershom Scholem, *Major Trends in Jewish Mysticism.* The Merkabah mystics described themselves as "descenders to the Merkabah."

describe many scientific experiments that make it "abundantly clear that within this two-tiered system, it is the unconscious tier that is the more fundamental." The unconscious responses that are triggered in our bodies when we are threatened happen *before* our conscious mind gets involved. No animal species could have survived on this planet without those instantaneous unconscious responses to existential threats. As we have already mentioned, some scientists are suggesting that as much as 95 percent of our entire cognitive functioning happens beyond our consciousness. Think of what that means: The unconscious in you runs the show. Wouldn't you want to know what the unconscious is all about? But unless you turn yourself into a shaman, a prophet, or an alchemist, how will you gain access to it? Given that most of you think these people are mad monks or lunatics, you won't.

Freud has said our unconscious mind is full of repressed emotions, dark memories, and knotted complexes. Social psychologists have proven, in numerous experiments, that our reactions are governed by categorization, stereotyping, and prejudice embedded in the unconscious. But where is the pure survival response of the wild animal? If the unconscious hides only the roots of mental illness, neurosis, and prejudices, where do the holy men and prophets get their inspiration? This puts into question the concept of the two-tiered model. A duality, an opposition between the two functions, conscious and unconscious, is a trap from which we cannot escape. Which one is better? We live in a world where the prevalent view is that conscious thinking is reasonable, sound, and sane, whereas the unconscious mind can trick or influence us negatively. This is far from the pure survival power of the unconscious. What are we missing? Seeing the mind as two-tiered will bias our thinking as much as our prejudices and stereotypes do; in fact, it also is a stereotype. Was there ever another model?

Imagine that you are on a frail boat sailing across a vast ocean. What happens in your boat—the tiller, the sails, the ropes, your own body, your sense of observation—are all contained within the hull of the boat, and above it in the clear light. We'll call the boat your conscious mind. If you are a modern sailor, below the boat may be much flotsam and garbage. In fact, our oceans carry amalgamations of toxic floating garbage as vast as continents. Equate the garbage with your repressed memories, traumas, complexes, stereotypes, prejudices, expectations, and claims, and you'll see why it's so important not to confuse the garbage with the ocean. Let's call this mass of polluted waste your subconscious. Below the garbage, in the as yet unpolluted waters, is the home of the myriad diversity of marine life, aquatic plants, and corals, and the great beasts of the depth. At the deepest part of the ocean, the old story goes, lies hidden the great serpent, Leviathan. Raising the Leviathan is what happens when, having cleared the subconscious of its garbage the subconscious and the conscious minds meet in an explosion of light, a revelation. This co-creation is what I call the manifestations of the third mind, the superconscious.

To think of the mind as comprising three levels fits what ancient stories tell us about heroes exploring the three levels of Earth, the underworld, and the sky. Descending from the Earth level into the underworld, the hero Herakles meets Cerberus, who guards the entrance to the underworld. To be sure we don't miss out on the deeper meaning of the myth, the story tells us Cerberus has three heads, three levels that Herakles must master (which he does with his bare hands) to ascend to Olympus, the heaven of the Greek gods, and become immortal, a god or a star in the firmament. Osiris, Isis, and Horus are the Egyptian trinity, Father, Mother, and Son, the active, the receptive, and the holy breath that must be mastered to reach enlightenment. The same theme reemerges in the Christian trinity of Father, Son, and Holy Ghost. Jesus of Galilee dies and is resurrected in three days. In medieval times Dante's journey takes him through hell and purgatory to paradise. The Tarot's High Priestess wears the three-tiered crown to remind us that this is what we must aspire to. To escape the imprisonment of duality we need the movement *through* illustrated by the number *three*. Call these three levels the conscious, the subconscious, and the superconscious. In the myth of Noah's ark, God, infuriated by the villainy of people on Earth, sends a great Flood to annihilate them. He warns Noah, whose name means "rest" or "comfort," to build an ark, a place of refuge against the chaos and subsequent flooding of the people's untamed unconscious forces. According to midrash, the ark has three levels, one for the beasts, one for the refuse, and one for the humans. Each level must be tamed, cleared, or visited for creation to reemerge, whether in the form of a new world, a new life, or a transformed personality. In either case, insight from the superconscious—in a brilliant flash zigzagging past the refuse into consciousness—can change the course of one's life.

Leviathan, we are told, is the flash of insight. He rises at the call of the holy ones, the ones who dare to plunge. His scales spark colors radiant with rainbow hues and brilliant white. He offers himself up, like truth, on a platter for the sages' delectation. The Leviathan's scales of rainbow light are reminiscent of the flaring multicolored brilliance of the Holy Grail, or of the alchemists' philosophical stone. It is he—the body-mind that "knows"—that rises up in response to threats to your survival, whether external or internal. When Leviathan rises, the place is flooded with light. And God said, "Let there be light, and there was light." Here is no place for anything UN-conscious. Keep using that word and your mind will subliminally hear "unconscious" as meaning unreachable, even by focused awareness. And since the subconscious is so powerful, this will block the light from rising.

Because the subconscious and the superconscious often appear together in a mixed state, I am choosing to use the word **subconscious** from now on to refer to both. The aim, of course, will be to clear the subconscious garbage to reveal the **superconscious** in its clarity and give it free range to act in our favor, for our survival, and for our joy.

Like the heroes of old, the restful ones, the holy men and women who dare, can you also plunge into the underworld where creation is awaiting the jolt of your presence to emerge, like the great beast from tohu va'bohu? How do you provoke the information hidden in the magma of the chaos? My goal here is proving to you that you can do what the old ones did. This book will guide you through the swamps, jungles, and deserts of your inner subconscious landscape. Like Herakles, you will find the tools and resources to deal with your Nemean lion, your Augean stables full of excrement, your Stymphalian birds screeching in your ear. You will learn to respond to the necessity of the images that surface in your mind, thus clearing the path for the superconscious to emerge. Will you find the light? Yes, you will. This is a tried and true path to enlightenment, based on the knowledge of thousands of years of studying the plunge, and verified by many initiates' successes in attaining light and what Jewish sages call *dveikut,* the cleaving of the self to the divine.* This Kabbalah of dreaming† is also called the Kabbalah of light or Saphire®.‡ Saphire is unique among other forms of Kabbalah, in that it limits its practice to the imagination and visualizations to access higher levels of consciousness. Whereas other schools use letters and chanting or mediations on the void, Saphire only works with dreams, day visions, waking dreams, and guided imagery exercises to climb the ladder to dveikut. While the practice incorporates Jewish concepts, you do not need to be a Kabbalist or even Jewish to do this practice; everyone dreams.

What does this book offer you? Food for both your conscious *and* your subconscious minds. You will be led step-by-step through the methodology and tools to tap into your subconscious, thus satisfying the needs of your conscious mind. Simultaneously, through practicing the visual exercises you will find in this book, you will be plunged into the wondrous experience of your subconscious mind. There are no words, save a poet's, that can come anywhere close to describing the experience of the inner light. I will not even attempt to express its power and wonder. Each of you has a unique version of the interior world, like an individual signature the world has been waiting for. By activating your inner vision, you make your outer world more real, alive, and exciting. Try the exercises, and you will fall in love with your creative power to transform yourself and—oh, surprise—to change your world.

---

*Elevated mystical states reached through ascetic methods practiced in Kabbalistic circles throughout the Middle Ages and Renaissance, and later among the Hasidim.

†There are many different forms of meditative practices in Kabbalah. See *Jewish Meditation: A Practical Guide* by Aryeh Kaplan for a general outlook on the different varieties that exist.

‡The name I gave the method to distinguish it from other imagery methods. I picked Saphire because when Colette was chosen as a young child to be the next lineage holder, her two grandmothers marked the occasion by giving her a sapphire. See *Life Is Not a Novel,* by Colette Aboulker-Muscat, Vol. 2. I do not know the reason for the sapphire, but it is said that King Solomon gazed into sapphire tables to gain wisdom. Also worth noting: The throne in Ezekiel's vision is described as being in the likeness of the sapphire stone, and in Ex. 24:10 God's feet stand on the likeness of a pavement of sapphire.

In the time-honored practice of plunging, methodologies have varied slightly. Shamans put more emphasis on rituals, fasting, chanting, or drumming. In their mystery rituals, the Greeks liked to embody their gods' myths, employing theatrical illusions, rituals, and mirrors. Tibetan Buddhists use very rigorous and specific forms of visualizations of the Buddhas. The Sufis still practice the movements of the dhikr dance to induce mystical visions and heart-to-heart devotion to the teacher, representative on Earth of the perfect man. The founder of the Christian Jesuit order, Ignatius of Loyola, trained his priests in the imitation of Jesus of Galilee, using visualizations he called Spiritual Exercises. Jewish, Sufi, and Christian saints and mystics all over the world, throughout time, have plunged into waking dreams to imagine their emotional connection to world alignment and to the first man before the fall. And of course, the Kabbalists, whose methods we will be exploring together, use visualizations, chanting, movements, permutations of letters to restore the Garden of Eden on Earth. All masters of dreaming use parable, allegory, and metaphor to unveil the hidden mystery of the interior world, ne'elam, behind what the Hebrew masters call the olam, or world of reality.

Practicing your imagination as prescribed by the Kabbalists is not difficult. It requires very little time; just a minute or two every morning and night will suffice. You need nothing but a place to sit and be quiet. Close your eyes, and follow the inductions in the book; they act as a window opening into your subconscious. The subconscious response is instantaneous and free-flowing. Contrary to the Tibetan practices, the Kabbalists do not fixate on an image, but see it and let it go. It is in the exploration of many different perspectives of the interior that a fountain of creativity bubbles up, and paradoxically, a solidification of light takes form within you. Unblocked and gushing up toward the blue skies, your fountain of creativity connects your three levels and you to the whole universe. You will never again feel abandoned or alone.

Imagine sitting at your desk, lethargic before a difficult report you've been agonizing over, and slowly drifting into a half sleep. Suddenly from behind a bush, a leopard springs at you, roaring and sporting its sharp canines, smelling of beast, black spots vibrating. Wild, strong energy courses through your body. Subversive ideas flash through your mind. The leopard is an experience that shakes you awake. Where does it come from? You're not in a jungle. Or maybe you're in the jungle of your subconscious. As your eyes turn inward, the subconscious magma coalesces into a revelation. You may not mentally understand your image, but the powerful experience energizes and enlivens you. Now you are furiously writing, and your ideas are unexpected and fresh.

The Hebrew Bible tells us that on the seventh day, God stopped creating in order to *la'asot,* to make.[1] In other words, stir the pot, but then stop to let the food cook to perfection. When you stop agonizing over your report—through sleep, rest, or simply entering into an empty state of mind—your creative magma can coalesce, and it will manifest one aspect of you, the leopard springing to the task. "The soul never thinks without an image," says Aristotle, and your leopard proves his point.

But don't fixate on your leopard. Don't turn him into a mascot or an archetype. He has played his part in your creation adventure. Let him go. You can trust that the creative flow will coalesce into another image, just as potent and full of creativity, to deal with another challenge you're facing.

The subconscious, as one student put it, is a "massive oceanic riddle." We're going to jump into this oceanic riddle and start playing with the myriad forms, colors, textures, numbers, puns, patterns, and emotional subtleties. "Close your eyes, breathe out three times, slowly counting from three to one. Turn your eyes into the darkness of your body. What happens?"—"I'm going down a mysterious tunnel, down, down, until I reach a closed door."—"Do you want to open it?"—"Oh, yes, I'm so curious! When I open the door . . . I step into a world of light, gemlike, and this warm loving feeling envelops me." Doesn't this remind you of the hero Aladdin of *One Thousand and One Nights*? He too explores his inner cave and finds it filled with treasure. The more you venture into your subconscious looking with eyes wide shut,* the more you activate your DreamField™† and "make" or manifest yourself

---

*A reference to Stanley Kubrick's 1999 film *Eyes Wide Shut.*
†A term of my own coinage for teaching this concept.

in the endlessly creative mode of your soul. The more, in other words, you grow your superconsciousness.

When your conscious mind turns toward your subconscious mind, like two lovers, they activate each other, creating together a world of joy and magic. Bereft of its companion, your conscious mind lives in linearity, its daily routine of toil and trouble, its obstacles, its painful ending in death, become more and more stifling and exhausting. The conscious mind lives in the manifest world, olam. But turned toward its partner, the subconscious, it begins to loosen its ties to causal effects and looks instead below the story line to patterns, light effects, shifts in emotional texture. The hidden world, ne'elam, the sub rosa country of its partner, the subconscious, rises to the surface of your consciousness. "I see a temple, flanked by a column on the right, and a column on the left. In the center is a clear reflective pool, and in it are five pink flamingoes! Their pink is so brilliant my heart starts to pound. I'm filled with wonder." Life becomes a "many splendored thing,"* a love affair, telling you to "follow your bliss."† But if you say to yourself, "I can't leave my husband; we have health insurance, the house, the children, the plush life . . ." the pink flamingoes in their reflective pool vanish, and so do joy, wonderment, and love. Can you look into the eyes of your inner beloved and accept that by following your images you will find a creative way out of the mess of your life? Or will you tuck your dreams away into a drawer, never to revisit them?

Let's go on a treasure hunt, for indeed that is what Kabbalists call it, the Sod, the treasure. If you tap into the treasure trove of your ne'elam, you will find the new configuration your soul is crying out for. Your images will anchor you in the new configuration, and grow your courage to pursue your dreams. Soon you will experience the way opening up easily and without pain. But don't believe me, why should you? Take the plunge, and verify for yourself. Have I convinced you to at least dip your eyes in? Will you follow me on this journey into your reunion with yourself?

✳

---

*A reference to *A Many Splendored Thing,* Han Suyin's 1952 novel.
†This phrase was coined by mythologist and writer Joseph Campbell (1904–1987).

The Leviathan story being about the subterranean movements of your psyche and their transformations will guide you. It guided me, as I didn't choose to write this book; it chose me. The inner voice said I was to write a book about "Raising the Leviathan." I didn't question the voice, as I have learned to always follow the promptings of my subconscious. But I had to learn about the Leviathan, and his story told me what I was being asked to write about. The great beast of the deep, Leviathan, is our subconscious, the creative magma we are asked to raise to consciousness and tame into form in our work as co-creators with God.

Like a dream, the myth presents what appear to be contradictory statements.

We are told Leviathan has neither beginning nor end. "His tail is placed in his mouth"[2] and he is "twisting around and encompassing the whole world."[3] Here he represents the basic unity underlying the whole universe. His name means "the wreathed one," entwining the many different strands of an underlying reality that is energetic, unseen, and subconscious.

"Were it not that he lies on the deep and presses down upon it, it would come up and destroy the world and inundate it."[4] In essence, separating clearly the conscious mind from a subconscious oceanic inundation is necessary for our survival and sanity. For God said, "Let the waters beneath heaven be gathered into one area, and let dry land appear."[5] We need both our conscious mind and our subconscious mind to work in tandem.

The one inundation we know of happened in Noah's generation "when the Earth became corrupt before God" and He allowed "all the fountains of the great deep (to) burst forth"[6] and flood the dry lands, drowning all those who had not listened to their subconscious and had become corrupted. In Noah's story we are told how to avoid the inundation. Build an ark, enter it, and turn your eyes within. Like Noah, whose name means "rest," rest within yourself, dream.

We are also told that the inundating waters rose up boiling hot, as (I am putting the two stories together: Nowhere else are boiling waters talked about except in Noah's story and in the Leviathan story) a Leviathan untamed, filled with fear and rage, "sends forth from his mouth a heat so great as to make all the waters of the deep boil."[7]

On this fierceness of the sea monster, his untamed emotions "HaShem will bring punishment with his harsh, great, mighty sword, upon Leviathan, the bar-like [male] serpent, and upon the twisting [female] serpent, and he will kill the great fish in the sea."[8] For Leviathan is not meant to be linear or entangled. We must cut ourselves from purely linear thinking, (the bar-like serpent) and from our emotional or mental entanglements (the twisting serpent) to reincorporate the larger reality that is holistic and phenomenological (the serpent who bites his own tail).

He was created to rise and "frolic with" God.[9] Surrender to the promptings of the subconscious, play in its ocean with all the forms that bubble up. This is what God meant your life to be like, effortless and fun.

Thus when the Leviathan transforms his emotions "he ascends. In his wake, a path shines. Nothing on Earth can compare to him, he was made to be without fear. He looks down on everything elevated. He is the king over all the haughty."[10] The Leviathan is our kundalini, the powerful divine feminine energy that Jews call Shekhinah. By instigating the raising of the Leviathan, we connect Earth and sky.

And God offers the sweetness of the Leviathan's transformation, his transfigured flesh as a "feast for the righteous in the time to come."[11] Following the path of the Leviathan brings enlightenment.

This is a journey back to the pure light of Eden, where human and God gaze into each other and become one. This can only be accomplished by dreaming.

✳

The book is divided into three parts.

The first part deals with the methodology of tapping into the subconscious, the different ways that you can "cross over," get answers to your questions, and return safely from your voyage. It also shows you how to dialogue with your images, dealing, as you go, with the obstacles in your path. This is called *tikun*, "correction," and is your most effective tool for transformation and growth. As the subconscious responds, you will learn to recognize what the signs of transformation are. You will experience how the subconscious is the source of all creativity and leads directly to manifestation.

The second part is about using the power of the subconscious to better manage your life. The subconscious is the ground of your being. It is an oceanic mass as vast as the universe. Its currents, whirlpools, swamps, and storms are what the Bible poetically calls Leviathan, the great beast of the deep. His thrashings to and fro are a manifestation of your untamed emotions and memories that need to be acknowledged and weeded out. To quiet the movements of the Leviathan and learn to tame our beast is the aim of all those who wish to become wise. Your wounded child, your fixed complexes, your ancestral patterns, your relationship blocks, your time issues—all your healing will depend on what is happening below the surface of your conscious mind. How your subconscious moves will show you whether it is troubled or peaceful. The premise of this book is that all starts with the subconscious. Attempting to change yourself by changing your conscious mind or behavior will not work. The root of your blockages, belief systems, and pernicious behaviors is in the subconscious. You must first change the subconscious. When you do that, the vast oceanic mass of movements, your Leviathan, will become rhythmic and peaceful. The waters will become translucent. Each chapter will deal with one of the issues mentioned above.

The third part of the book is bringing to light the superconscious, the soul, the blueprint you came into this world with. I call this work Raising the Leviathan. Through a technique that we will examine called the Life Plan, through prayer and through dveikut, cleaving to the divine, you will flip over from being blinded by the conscious mind to being exalted by the intrinsic magnificence and beauty of creation. I hope that by the end of the book, you will have transformed so much, that like the holy ones, you will be able to commune with the flesh of the great beast of the depth and know the joy that an illuminated consciousness brings.

I wish you joy of the plunge. May you play and frolic in the waves of the oceanic subconscious and learn to trust and become fast friends with the mysterious source of all creativity.

How to Practice the Exercises

To help you to experience and work with your subconscious, you will find, in every chapter, a number of guided imagery exercises that you can practice on your own. These exercises are meant to be done quickly. They should take no longer than one to three minutes, unless otherwise indicated. Do them once, and don't repeat for three months, unless advised otherwise. Exercises called "formal" are to be practiced every day in the morning or evening as indicated, for twenty-one days from the new moon onward, for men and for women in menopause. For the younger women, practice them from the end of one menstrual period to the beginning of the next. Formal exercises build new habits. You practice them as indicated for only one cycle. If you desire to continue a formal practice, vary the exercises. Practice a different formal exercise each cycle. In this way, your subconscious doesn't get bored but has time to catch on to the rhythm and incorporate the images.*

At first, learn to do your exercises sitting, back straight, hands and legs uncrossed like an Egyptian pharaoh. As you become more proficient, you will be able to do the exercises, standing or lying down, eyes open or closed. But to start with, find a quiet space where you'll be undisturbed for a few minutes. Sit up straight, with your arms and legs uncrossed so as not to mix the energies. Close your eyes. Slightly open your mouth, and breathe out slowly through your mouth, seeing the number 3. Breathe out, and see the number 2. Breathe out, and see the number 1, tall and clear. Why do we breathe out? We empty our

---

*See Learn More at the end of this book.

body of the carbon dioxide, the gaseous refuse in the body. When we are empty, the breath comes in on its own easily; you have nothing to do. We count from 3 to 1 as a light self-hypnotic induction. All it takes is three exhalations to reach the depth of the subconscious.

Most of the exercises are very short and give you thirty seconds to a minute or two to look through the metaphoric window into the subconscious created by the words of the induction. When you go fast you have no time to indulge in fantasy. Breathe out, look through the window, see what you see, and open your eyes.

Notes on Terminology

If you don't resonate with the word "God," please feel free to substitute whatever word feels right for you. For instance, you could use "universal consciousness."

Throughout the book I use the words "male" and "female" to represent archetypal energies rather than types of people. For instance, a man can be female in sensibility, a woman male in intellect. When speaking of couples, I am not exclusively speaking of the classic male-female coupling; couples of all sexual orientations follow the same inner male and female tensions. In the subconscious realm switching genders is common. If you are a woman in real life, you may see yourself as a male in the dream world, and vice versa, a man may see himself as a woman. These shifts occur until we have learned to balance male and female energies in ourselves and become one, like the androgynous Adam before the exile from Eden.

PART I

The Leviathan, Great Beast of the Deep

Fishing in the Ocean of the Subconscious

*Call Me and I shall answer you, and tell you great tidings,
and obscurities that you did not know.*

JEREMIAH 33:2

There are simple ways of tapping into the subconscious. The methodology I will be describing in the next chapters requires nothing from you but a paper, a pen, and a firm intention of piercing through the veil of our everyday reality. The subconscious is elusive. You must let it know you are pursuing it with neither violence nor possessiveness. Sometimes it comes as a little child you can't fool with false protestations of love. Sometimes it comes as a woman, and she won't respond well to bullying, PowerPoint presentations, logical proofs, or statistics; she wants to be seduced, adored, and revered. Visualize a sunset. Scientific analyses concerning its many-colored splendor are not preeminent to your mind. You are immersed and enchanted. How refreshing is that?

The subconscious is also the receptacle for all your pains, fears, angers, resentments, and envy. It will show you your monsters and ghosts, your fogs and dark holes, your bogs and illusions, but it will also give you magnificent tools to overcome the obstacles that block the flow of its imaginal ocean. In its varied forms and rapid transformations, the subconscious is both its own diagnostic and its cure. It is ever in movement, and when you can accept that "change is the one thing that never changes,"[1] it stabilizes you while gifting you with fireworks of light and joy.

While the methodology is simple, you will be asked to step back, wait, stay awake, and be attentive. Give it your respect and devotion, precisely what you so desire from your own family and peers. Watch the mystery, and respond with excitement, gratitude, wonder, and awe! The subconscious will "open sesame,"[2] and reveal its treasures.

1

The Mystery of Dreams

Whatever a man does in the day, his soul testifies against him at night.

ZOHAR 92A

"Truth is a pathless land."* To access the truth of the superconscious, we must, each and every one of us, find the pathless land. How do we drop into it? We are faced with the impossible task: "Go where I will show you." But where? The abyss between our conscious mind and our subconscious appears insurmountable, yet we constantly receive glimpses, elusive signposts, and alluring tidbits. Most of them appear to us in night dreams, others in daytime clips or sound bites. To start exploring how we tap into the subconscious, we will begin where accessing the subconscious occurs naturally and nightly. I am speaking about our night dreams.

Since night dreams are a universal phenomenon, we can speak about our dreams without appearing foolish or eccentric. Why do we dream? Does tapping into our subconscious have important beneficial effects on our health and balance? What physiological function do dreams have? The pop-ups of our night dreams beg the question: What are they trying to tell us? Do we need them for our survival? And if so, why do they configure themselves in these incomprehensible ways? Gifted with

---

*So declared twenty-one-year-old Indian philosopher Jiddu Krishnamurti in his speech to the Theosophical Society as he refused to become their messiah.

21

these strange unfolding images that we don't understand, what are we supposed to do with them?

Dreams are a phenomenon common to humans and other mammals. Sleep laboratories have shown that we all dream, especially, scientists believe, during rapid eye movement (REM) sleep. Some modern scientists have suggested that dreams are the glut of our brain processes. "We dream to forget,"[1] say Francis Crick and Graeme Mitchison, and our dreams are simply garbage on the way to being discarded from memory. Professor Allan Hobson and his colleague Robert McCarley see dreaming as the result of a sudden barrage of stimulation just prior to REM that the higher brain then attempts to make sense of.[2] Their activation synthesis theory has since been disproved, leaving room for other theories, such as the memory consolidation theory of dreaming (we dream to remember) and the expectation fulfillment theory of dreaming (dreams are the arousal, de-arousal process of an emotion whose expectation the brain fulfills through the unfolding of images). This is a far cry from Freud's wish fulfillment theory of dreams, which was predicated on their symbolic meaning.

A study of the biological function of dreams shows us that there are many physiological processes involved in the act of dreaming. Breathing patterns, blood flow to the brain, and brain activity change during REM sleep. Many scientists prefer to think that dreams are simply biological processes with no conscious or psychological meaning. If so, we could say the same of our thought processes: They are nothing more than biological activity. Subtracting meaning from our lives by reducing every activity in our bodies to biological functions doesn't serve us. Would a piece of meat (biological matter) be interested in studying the meaning of dreams? Since our consciousness is alive and asking questions, we have to assume that within or beyond the piece of meat (our biological processes) something else is happening. A dualistic approach—we're either biological matter or embodied souls—sends us back to concerns common to philosophers and theologians of the Middle Ages. And while the seventeenth century scientist and philosopher René Descartes* searched for a way to link these two

---

*René Descartes (1596–1650) was a French philosopher, mathematician, and scientist. In his 1641 text *Meditations on First Philosophy* he expounds on the dualism of mind and body.

seemingly irreconcilable activities—the body that worked like a machine, and the soul/consciousness that was nonmaterial—through the pineal gland, he was still caught in a duality. Today we are not looking for the physiological seat of the soul, but our thinking has not evolved beyond warring opinions. Scientists group themselves squarely in the biological camp and believe that the body has no consciousness. "What is at stake here is a theory of dreams that is scientifically valid," says Dr. Hobson, and he proceeds to discount the psychoanalytic dream interpretation. The real problem is not who is right or wrong, but framing the issue within a duality. What we need to do is break out of that confinement. Instead, could we not say that consciousness arises out of biological processes—or vice versa, that biological processes arise out of consciousness? Could both be true?

In *DreamBirth* I point out that dreaming is not limited to REM stages of sleep.[3] While REM may contain peak moments of dream activity, in fact we are always dreaming. Dreaming is a survival faculty of the brain. Again, Descartes famously said: "I think, therefore I am." What people forget is that he dreamed this statement. Maybe he meant that any form of consciousness should be called thinking. In this sense, is there any difference between thinking and dreaming? They are both forms of communication that employ different languages. Can we compare hearing "I love you" to being kissed? We engage in both verbal and sensory exchanges. The sensory exchanges are read on our mind's screen as 3D images synergistic with all our senses. Verbal exchanges are abstract concepts. They used to be descriptive of sensory exchanges, but today, the link between our bodies and verbal concepts grows more and more tenuous. Which came first? Brain imaging on humans shows that in REM dreaming, our limbic system, a more ancient brain structure (not as ancient as the reptilian brain, though we know that reptiles dream) is highly active. Thinking in words developed much later with the appearance of the prefrontal cortex. Today we are trained to prioritize verbal information at the expense of experiencing.

Dreaming is another word for experiencing. Experiencing the world around us, and also inside of us, means that we process the world through our senses. Through our senses, we feel, hear, see, smell, and taste. This is not information, but in-**form**-ation, coming directly from apprehending **form**. This vast container of experiences that we, like the alchemist, sit in and are made of, is alive in a matrix of knowing that I call the DreamField. How do we know that all experiences and their 3D images, sensations, and emotions are contained within our brain matrix? One of the models of the brain is that we discard unnecessary parts of our memories and keep only that which is necessary to our survival. Maybe we put them to sleep, stored away for future use. We do know that memories are clustered together by form and similar patterns. We will return to this when we study the language of the night dream. But does it mean that we forget and discard? Memories of long forgotten experiences will surface at unexpected moments, under the effect of a rare stimulus. Where were they hidden all this time? What did our brains do with them while we were apparently totally unaware of them? Or are our brains simply consoles reading in-FORM-ation coming from the cells of our bodies? Does memory of experience truly disappear for good? "I never forget anything," said one friend, to which another replied, "How do you know?" We can never know. But we can learn to watch them surface. Here are three exercises to watch the subconscious surface.

Exercise 1
· · · · · · · · · · ·
Awake while Falling Asleep

Close your eyes. Breathe out slowly three times, counting from three to one. See the one tall, clear, and bright.

Lying in your bed before falling asleep, relax completely, feeling your limbs and trunk become heavier and heavier.

Breathe out. Stay awake while watching yourself falling asleep. You will begin to feel that you are floating. If you remain conscious while falling asleep, you will experience a flood of chaotic images. Don't try to make any sense of them, just observe until sleep takes over.

· · · · · · · · · · ·

Maybe you've had a similar experience while lying on a massage table. This phase of chaotic images flooding your rapidly disappearing consciousness is called the hypnagogic stage. This dreamlike stage can also surface when you have had a terrible shock, and the world suddenly makes no sense. You are crossing the veil, as did Perceval, but you haven't yet learned to do this consciously and to hold these images steady in your mind's eye. Don't try just yet. But sit a moment with yourself and do this next exercise.

Exercise 2
. . . .
Looking into Your Body

Close your eyes. Breathe out slowly three times, counting from three to one. See the one tall, clear, and bright.

Feel your body just now. Turn your eyes inward. What do you observe: constriction or expansion, light or dark, density or pulsation?

Breathe out. What feelings do you have?

Breathe out. What question do you want to ask it? Does it respond? If it does, what does this say about your body?

Breathe out. Open your eyes.
. . . .

Your body is not what you think it is. When you turn your eyes inward to look into your body, your body starts shifting and doing things you never thought it could. Your body is not solid, nor is it fixed, as you believed. Its boundaries are more fluid. When your consciousness pays attention to your body, your body starts reconfiguring. It is porous and can stretch, contract, dissolve, and remake itself. The key is the interface between your consciousness and your body.

Exercise 3
. . . .
Enter Your Thumb

Close your eyes. Breathe out slowly three times, counting from three to one. See the one tall, clear, and bright.

Bring your eyes into your body, and down your right arm into your thumb. Be totally in your thumb. Only your thumb exists, and your consciousness occupies your thumb. What is happening to your experience of your thumb?

Breathe out. Bring your consciousness back into your whole body.

Breathe out. Open your eyes.

· · · · · · · · · · ·

You are the observer affecting the observed: Your watching is the dialogue your body needs to respond and to change. If you are able to totally bring your consciousness into your thumb and nothing else exists for you at that moment except your thumb, your thumb will start growing. It will become pulsating energy, then light, and will grow larger. "The body organizes and incorporates experience," says Stanley Keleman in his wonderful book *Your Body Speaks Its Mind*.[4] Or you fix your body by your way of looking at it. It will adapt to how you see it, talk of it, or think about it. If you believe your body has fixed boundaries, it will adapt to your belief system. It will conform to the stories you tell yourself. Your individual DreamField and your larger familial and generational DreamField (experiences of the family stories and patterns) are the tapestry or network around which your body takes form. Looking at a body is like reading an open book, if you are alive to what it is trying to tell you.

You also have a cultural DreamField, a national DreamField, a universal DreamField. Carl Jung called our universal DreamField the collective unconscious. Others have called it the Akashic records. All these different dreamfields are interacting networks of experience, cauldrons of images that make us who and how we are. Your subconscious is a container, impressed by the experiences it is filled with. It has no power to change those impressions. Because it is part of your subconscious, your body cannot change itself unless you consciously look into your body and allow it to show you its dreaming. Your experiencing body interacting with your conscious looking is your dreaming.

Since our dreaming is the ground of our being, it is even more imperative for us to understand our dreaming. If only 5 percent of us is conscious, how do we interact with the other 95 percent? How do we know that we are connected to the collective unconscious or to the Akashic records* since they are both said to be unconscious? The mystery of tap-

---

*This term is used by theosophists and anthroposophists to indicate an encoded nonphysical compendium of human knowledge, past, present, future.

ping into your subconscious starts by turning your eyes inward to look. We have two ways of doing this: in the daytime with guided exercises such as the three you have just experienced, or with your night dreams. We will talk more about guided exercises in the chapters that follow, but in this first chapter we will focus primarily on night dreams.

❋

Most rabbis will tell you that God thought the world into being. I once had the audacity to tell a great Talmudic scholar that I thought God had dreamed the world into being. "God thought the world into being!" he emphatically declared, then turned on his heels and marched away. If you agree with him, you're in good company! And I promise you, I won't take it badly. But being a dreamer, an Ivri or passer-over,* I am made in the image of God. I am His mirror image. All mirror images are dreams. If I step into the mirror and stand in God's shoes (not that he has any), looking out at myself, I am His dream come true. I come back through the mirror into my body, and I read in Genesis: "God hovered over the p'nei tehom. And God said, 'Let there be light.' And there was light."† I am a product of this light. Mirroring God, how do I do what He does? When I go to sleep, this is exactly what I do. I hover over the subconscious, and I create light.

Have you ever wondered how this inner illumination works? The sun's rays do not penetrate inside your body, and there are no electric bulbs to illuminate the space within. Inside of you it is dark. And yet, each time you turn your eyes inward, light goes on and forms appear. The Kabbalists call this light the "light of creation" to differentiate it from the light of the sun. They say that God created with this light, but that it was too strong for the vessels that held it, and they shattered. (So,) Then He created the sun and stars‡ to channel the light so that we could be shielded from his naked light and not be destroyed. It is said that only Moses, the greatest of biblical prophets, had a clear mirror reflecting the pure light of God. We are not Moses, but our work is

---

*See the Introduction.
†Once again, recall Genesis 1:2.
‡Gen. 1. God creates light on the first day, but the sun, moon, and stars only on the fourth day. Kabbalists call the light of the first day the light of creation.

to slowly acclimatize our eyes to the true light. We start with one sixtieth of this light,[5] the light that we create, like God, by looking into the darkness. Think of it: Each time you turn your eyes inward, you create more light. Of course, unless you consciously pay attention to its appearance, that light won't stay. If, on the contrary, you make turning inward a conscious practice, the more you look in and create light, the more light coalesces within you. I am talking of a very practical concrete technology of creating light and becoming in effect "enlightened."

Dreaming is not only one of the great paths to enlightenment, it is your path to manifestation. God looks into the chaos and creates light, and out of this light, forms emerge. Adam is taught to do the same as God. He calls out the names of the animals, and the animals appear. If you want to learn to manifest, you must call for what you want. But what if you don't know what you want? Abraham heard the voice saying, "Go!" But he didn't know where he wanted to go. He did know that he and Sarah, his wife, were barren and so far hadn't been able to create "something." If you call for creativity, turning your eyes inward to create the light, the light will take form, and you will be shown the form your creativity is meant to take.

The subconscious is mute. It will only "speak" to the one who asks a question, in the same way that you can't access a computer program until you click on it. If I'm anxiously awaiting news about publishers, and this question is foremost in my mind, my subconscious will happily produce a response.

> *I dream that I am in an Egyptian tomb, and that the walls are covered with repetitive paintings of the god Anubis grinning at me. All of the Anubis figures are holding my book in the crook of their arm, pointing to it with the index finger of their other hand.*

The next morning, I checked which publisher sported the Anubis logo. It was Inner Traditions. I called my agent and dear friend Jane Lahr and said, "I dreamt last night that Inner Traditions would publish my book. Can you contact them?" Following the dream brings manifestation: In 2005 Inner Traditions became the publisher of *Kabbalah and the Power of Dreaming.*

We all dream, whether we like it or not. But are we conscious of our questions and anxieties? Most of us are not, which doesn't stop the dreams from popping up. Dreams will respond to an anxiety, a need for clarity, a worry about the past or the future, or what is happening in our life just now, or simply "protests from various parts of our bodies that the conductor is not managing the orchestra well." Our pains, anxieties, or longings call forth our night dreams. As we sleep, we hover over the great chaos of images and experiences that is the caldron of our subconscious. Our questions call forth an answer, which is our dream. Mirrors show us our reversed selves. In the same way the dream doesn't show us our everyday reality, but a different, "reversed" version of it. The great law of attraction says that like attracts its mirror image. One of the many errors people make is that they think they can force the subconscious to give them what the self-conscious ego wants. We cannot become a millionaire simply because our ego wants it. If we ask our subconscious about becoming a millionaire and it shows us a tent instead of a palace, we know we were not meant to become a millionaire. It is not in our DreamField. We cannot force our dreams to produce what we want. But we can ask our dreams to give form to our longing. "Mirror, mirror on the wall, who is the fairest of us all?" And the dreaming answers the truth, "Snow White is more beautiful." It is not your vanity that is beautiful, but your snow-white soul, says the dreaming mirror to our inner stepmother. We might not like what we see and hear in our dreaming, but the subconscious can only show us the truth.

In the Hebrew language dream is called *halom;* the consonants H L M are the root of the word.* Imagine these three consonants as the roots of a great tree. As the tree grows, each blossom unfurls a different word, always using the same three consonants. A different permutation of letters, such as *lehem,* L H M, creates a different meaning, but one that is nevertheless connected by the same letters. Lehem means "bread." What is common between dream and bread? You must throw

---

*There were no written vowels in the Torah until the Middle Ages; prior to that, they were transmitted orally.

a little yeast in the dough to make the bread rise, and then you put it in the oven. With the dream, your question is the yeast, and your body is the oven or crucible. The question calls forth the different ingredients of the dream that are mixed together and baked in the oven of your sleeping body. When you awaken, your dream is cooked! Dream and bread have in common that they both rise.

By asking a question, you have begun the dialogue with your dreams. Dreams are forms of communication. When you understand this, you will realize the great power you have. You can "incubate" a dream by asking a specific question; think of it as fishing. You load your hook with juicy bait and throw your line into the ocean. The right fish for the bait will emerge to swallow the hook. Through your question you stir up the subconscious. Further along we will discuss the process of dream incubation, but let's not get ahead of ourselves.

The first question should be: Do you remember your dreams? If you don't—or even if you sometimes do—you must evince the desire to remember them. Most people find dreams intriguing, so that should help you. It is all in the intent. People often say to me, How can I work with you when I don't remember my dreams? I always answer: Bring me a dream next week. They invariably rise to the challenge and have a dream to show me when they next come to see me.

I hope I have said enough to intrigue you, and that you are willing to put a bit of time and effort into remembering your dreams. The first thing you must do is prove to your subconscious that you are serious about wanting to remember your dreams. Do this by getting a DreamBook. Find a journal whose cover or paper is aesthetically pleasing to you. On the first page, write "DreamBook." On the second page write tonight's date. Leave the book open on your night table with a pen beside it. You have manifested your intention to remember your dreams.

If during that first week your intent is strong, you may find yourself waking up a few times during the night remembering fragments of your dreams. Write them down in your DreamBook. As you become accustomed to remembering your dreams, your deep sleep will return, and you will not be troubled with waking up during the night. If you are healthy and vibrant and don't take sleeping pills, you will easily learn to remember your dreams. You need a good flow of hormones to dream. This is why dream recall is stronger in children and younger people, and especially strong in pregnant women. My Chinese doctor calls the hormone pills he gives his older women patients "dream pills." If your dream recall is still difficult, try this ancient Tibetan practice: Imagine a small ball of bright red light, and put it into your thyroid* before falling asleep. Or you can massage your adrenal glands,† in your mind's eye with the following exercise.

Exercise 4
. . . .
Adrenal Rainbow

Breathe out three times slowly, counting from three to one. See the one tall, clear, and bright.

See a rainbow in the sky after a rainfall.

Breathe out. Stretch your arms out toward the rainbow; see them elongating and elongating. With both hands, grab the rainbow and bring it into your body to place over your two adrenal glands.

Breathe out. See your two adrenal glands becoming one wide band of colors.

Breathe out. Sense the flow of hormones from the band of colors streaming through your whole body as colored light. What color do you see? How does your body feel now?

Breathe out. Open your eyes.
. . . .

We have four periods of REM at night, each period longer than the last as morning approaches. As you approach consciousness, your self-conscious mind starts interacting with your subconscious mind and putting some order into the chaos of images that arise. Your dreams are an interaction between the subconscious and the conscious mind. The subconscious throws up a jumble of images, and the conscious mind arranges them into some semblance of order. When we awaken, what we remember is a sequence of images. This sequence may not appear to be logical but

---

*An endrocrine gland in the front of the neck, below the Adam's apple. It secretes important hormones.

†Endocrine glands, situated above the kidneys that produce important hormones.

does have some kind of story line. That is what you will write down in your DreamBook. Your morning dreams are more important than your dreams of the middle of the night, because this interaction is more active.

Memories are in the body. This is why you should remain in the same position you slept in as you wake up. If you move, the dream is likely to disappear. If it does, simply return to your original position. Keep your mind empty of all thoughts, and remain still. If the dream doesn't resurface in a minute or two, create a clear space in the back of your mind, a receptive emptiness. Dream fragments or the whole dream may reappear as you stand under your shower, or at some unexpected moment during the day when your mind is relaxed. Welcome them, and quickly write them down in your DreamBook. By doing so, you are telling your subconscious that you are attentively listening and wanting to hear more.

You are the fisherman. You have thrown in your bait. Now sit, wait, watch, and listen. If you catch a golden fish in your line and net, when it begs for its life, don't drop it back in the sea like the old fisherman did in Alexander Pushkin's fairy tale.[6] Ask it to reveal to you the powers that are hidden in the subconscious. What does your dream mean? What is it trying to tell you? "Dreams not interpreted are like unopened letters,"[7] warn the Talmudic sages.* Perceval, a legendary knight of King Arthur's Round Table known for his "good boy" acquiescence, when shown the Holy Grail in a vision doesn't ask, What does this mean? For this he is sent back to the beginning and must, through hard labors of the soul, reacquire his right to be shown the source he disrespected in his first vision. You will be given dreams. Your work is to ponder and decipher them. But don't worry, there is a way in.

Here is a Talmudic story that will guide you in.

Four rabbis decide to visit the Garden of Eden. They enter into a state of intense meditation and ascend to the Garden. The first rabbi, Ben Azzai, gazes and dies. The second, Ben Zoma, gazes and goes mad.

---

*The Talmud is the central text of Rabbinic Judaism, a compendium of religious laws, commentaries, and legends. There are two Talmuds. The most commonly used is the Babylonian Talmud, written between the third and sixth centuries CE. The Jerusalem Talmud was written in Galilee in the fourth century CE.

The third, Elishya ben Abuyah, named Aher (other), gazes and loses his faith. Only Rabbi Akiva enters in peace and leaves in peace.[8]

In Hebrew, the Garden is called PRDS,* pronounced "PaRDeS," which is the origin of the word paradise in English. Each letter represents one of the steps to deciphering the meaning of your dream:

> P stands for P'shat, the story line.
> R stands for Remez, the pattern.
> D stands for Drash, the question.
> S stands for Sod, the secret or treasure.

Do not worry. The death, madness, and heresy of the three rabbis are what could happen if you were to remain stuck on one of the three levels, but you won't. Think of your search for the meaning of your dream as setting out on a treasure hunt. You don't want to get caught on the surface level of the story (P). The glittery reflections are just an illusion. You don't want to be seduced into playing with patterns (R). Patterns are useful to sort out the story line, but if you stay there, they become food for gossip (this one is connected to that one because they both wear the same T-shirt, and that one is connected to the second one because their T-shirts are pink!). Asking what all this means is fine, but beginning to doubt that this means anything at all (D) is not. Keep your eyes steadily affixed to your goal, the secret or treasure (S) you seek, and you will be able to avoid the three dangers on your way to the truth.

Not all dreams are the same. Some dreams are clues to the next part of your life's journey. Other dreams fall straight into the source, and like the hero Perceval, you are given a glimpse of the treasure. But like him you may not be able to grasp it. We will examine what the different kinds of dreams are in the next chapter and how they fit into a rising ladder of dreaming that leads to enlightenment. First we must accustom ourselves to recognizing the story line, the pattern, and the main question of the dream. If we succeed, the golden fish or secret treasure will jump. This is what is called revelation. Revelation brings greater clarity and power. The dreamer will be shown what the next step is.

---

*"Pardes" is a loan word in Hebrew from Persian.

Dreams always talk to us about Now. They are not interested in the past. They only go to the past to clear out knots and entanglements that block the flow of dreaming. In fact, in dreaming, there is no past or future. Dreaming is always in the now. What I see is what is. I can only see one thing at a time. The knot from the past is here today, and that is what the dream shows me. It gives me the opportunity to undo the knot and to clear the DreamField. Night dreams are there to help you to do just that. Spending a little time writing them down and then trying to untie them is immensely worthwhile. It is your Ariadna's golden thread.* Opening your dreams leads you eventually to the source, the Holy Grail, the paradise we all—albeit unconsciously— search for. DreamOpening®† is the gateway to the happiness, joy, health, and abundance we are all longing to obtain here on this Earth.

Before we begin the process of what I call DreamOpening, let's establish ground rules. The dreamer is precious. The dreamer intuitively knows what rings true to their soul. We must respect the dreamer and recognize that we are not interpreting their dream or dictating to them what the dream means. We are opening it up to its different facets. "There were twenty-four interpreters of dreams in Jerusalem. Once I dreamed a dream and went around to all of them, and they all gave me different interpretations, and yet all were fulfilled."[9] The dream is like a diamond. Each interpreter will illuminate a facet of the diamond, but none alone will master its whole meaning. In the story of the golden fish, the fisherman's wife wanted to be the mistress of a better tub, a better home, then a palace, but when she asked to be mistress of the sea (read, mistress of the subconscious) the golden fish swam away, and all her powers were lost. The old fisherman and his wife returned to their original poverty and were stripped of the golden abundance they had benefited from. You must never kill the hen (or the fish) that lays the golden eggs. You will never know scientifically or otherwise where wisdom comes from. You can only respect it, bow to it, and follow its advice as best you can.

---

*Greek myth of the golden thread that Ariadna, Princess of Crete, gave the Athenian hero Theseus so he wouldn't get lost on his way back from killing the Minotaur, the half-man, half-bull monster kept in the Labyrinth.

†Another term of my own coinage.

• • •

It is more enlightening to open a dream in a company of dreamers. Ten dreamers is a good number. But you can open your dreams yourself, or with a dream companion. Choose your dream companion or company carefully. A dream companion should never look you in the eye when opening your dream. They should say: "As the secondary dreamer of this dream, this is what I feel." They should not unilaterally attempt to interpret the dream's true meaning. By saying unequivocally this is what your dream means, they would be imposing their point of view and fixing the dream. Always return the dream to the original dreamer, asking what resonates for the dreamer, and respecting the dreamer's understanding of their own dream. Dreams are openings into the very delicate vulnerable movements of the psyche. We must tread carefully. The Talmud also says: "All dreams follow the mouth."[10] This means that the way you choose to verbalize your opening will affect the original dreamer. Always find a way to state the truth of what you see and understand in a way that is life affirming and can lead to positive outcomes. Never give a negative DreamOpening. Instead, always pursue the dream thread that leads towards goodness. In this way, you follow the truth of the body that strives for balance and for life. Dreams are another way your body communicates with you about survival. They warn us of dangers and may lead us through the valley of death, but they always illuminate a way out. Even if the dreamer produces a nightmare in which they are killed, they awaken with the knowledge that they are in danger and must do something about it. In chapter 2 we will discuss how the dreamer can respond to the necessity of their dream. Think of dreams as an important part of your evolutionary process.

To reach paradise, or at least the way to a greater harmony and peace within, let us examine how to work with the four levels of a DreamOpening.

P'shat, the story line

Dream sequences don't appear to our consciousness as a bundle of nonsense. They have a more or less understandable story line. Although the story line might not make logical sense (one moment I am walking upside down up some spindly stairs going toward the sky, the next I am crouching in a basement deep in the earth), it still appears as a linear progression. Write your dream as you remember seeing it. When you write your dream down in your DreamBook, avoid short cuts. You want your reader—your dream companion or company—to be able to "see," to follow in their mind's eye, the sequences of images that you describe.

A man is walking down a street when he hears a truck's tires screeching behind him.

Can you see this image? What is missing in the description? What does the man look like? What kind of street? Is it day or night? How do you know it's a truck? What kind of truck? These questions could result in your writing your dream down as follows:

I watch from the right sidewalk as a man in a black trench coat crosses to the left sidewalk. It is nighttime, and he doesn't see the approach of a white truck that suddenly brakes to avoid hitting him. I hear the screeching of its tires.

Describing in detail the images that you have experienced is a discipline. It will teach you to become more precise and grounded in your body and in everyday life. For instance, it can help you to identify what you have forgotten to explain to your friend, and is causing a nasty misunderstanding between you, or what is missing in an employee's report of an incident at work. Being precise in what you see and how you communicate what you see is a skill you will soon learn to value. We call this aspect of the P'shat* level of DreamOpening *clarification*.

The second part of the P'shat level of dream opening is *day residue*. Day residue is about finding out which part or parts of the dream belong to reality and which to dream material.

---

*Pronounced "Pe-shat."

I watch from the east sidewalk near my house at 73 Fifth Avenue, as a man I don't know, wearing a black trench coat, with a tag that says FREEDMAN on its back, is crossing to the west sidewalk. It is night, and he doesn't see the approach of a white truck that speeds down Fifth Avenue from north to south, and suddenly brakes to avoid hitting him. I hear the screeching of its tires.

My school is located at 73 Fifth Avenue, which makes this detail of the dream less impactful. It is not dream material, but material transposed from my everyday reality into the dream. Freudians would call this detail "day residue" from everyday reality and would spend a lot of time identifying why you brought this daytime residue into your dream. For us, "There can be no dream which does not contain meaningless matter,"[11] and residue from everyday reality has less to say about transformation than dream material. Dream material is what your subconscious throws up from its depths when stimulated. It is in the plummeting into the subconscious and the return to consciousness that transformation occurs. This is what we will focus on.

Remez, the pattern level of the dream

Every story line has a pattern. We will note without judgment the patterns in our dreams. All we seek to do here is identify patterns; we are not yet trying to understand.

Pattern can be a map. The east, west, north, south orientations of the dream are patterns that we note.

Pattern can be opposites: man and woman (I am a woman). Black (coat) and white (truck); night and white truck.

Pattern can be numbers: 73 is not a pattern, since it is the real number of my building. Nor is Fifth. But there are two people. Although the dream doesn't mention the number two, it is implied.

Pattern can be puns. Fifth Avenue is not a pun and doesn't sound like something else. But Freedman does. Is the man touting his freedom?

The language of forms works by analogy. It brings observed similarities together in the mind: a cigar, a zucchini, and a penis all have similar shapes. They are not symbols of each other, as Freudians would say; they simply have similar oblong shapes. Shapes have function: a bowl receives, a knife cuts through. These two shapes are not analogous, they are opposites (in terms of form). Physiologically, a man's genitals are outside, a woman's genitals are inside her body. They fit together like puzzle pieces. For example, a basketball fits into the hoop. The ball is the positive space, the hoop its negative space. Remember that the language of dreaming is about forms. These forms can be commenting on different levels: physical, emotional, mental, and spiritual. The dream doesn't make that distinction. It's energy and light speaking in forms. In the emotional realm, a victim calls forth its opposite, the tyrant. In the dream this could be illustrated by the ball going into the hoop, or by a tyrant punching his victim, who collapses inward. It's still the same dynamic form: Something goes into something else. The pattern of movement counts, but we won't know whether this is a physical or an emotional scenario or both. We must ask for the emotional context of the dream. Another clue will be the dreamer's response when we identify the pattern.

Learning to read patterns will give you instant access to what is really happening to your child when she comes home with a rambling story about classmates and a lollipop one of them stole from her. If you can identify the pattern, you're one step closer to figuring out what she's upset about and to resolving it. Here's a little exercise. This is a man who always returns back to two pet peeves of his: I hate my mother, and I hate the synagogue. Can you figure out the pattern? A good mother envelops you with love, a good synagogue serves as an embracing warm center. The pattern is pointing us to the next level of dream opening.

Drash, the question

What is the real question the dream is trying to figure out? This is the hardest level to home into. The dream has a motivating purpose; it is trying to resolve something. Let's go back to the man who hates his mother and the synagogue. While this was not a night dream, it was a repetitive motif he brought up every time he came to see me. You will come to see that there is little difference between a person's repetitive stories and their repetitive dreams. Your friends' repetitive stories are like bad dreams, and you must consider them as such. What was the real question here? What was the man looking for? Hating his mother suggested that she had rejected him. He equated the synagogue, where she went regularly, to his mother. In his mind they were one and the same. He had put them both in the same bag. The question was: Where can I find loving support in a trustworthy environment? Clarifying the true question of the dream is already pointing us to what I call "responding to the necessity of the dream."*

Sod, the secret or treasure

Here the dream companions pause and wait. If they have opened the dream appropriately (becoming the secondary dreamers of the dream, they have described what they feel about the dream, and what they feel its true question is), the original dreamer will be touched. His/her (the original dreamer) response signifies whether or not the treasure has been accessed, and the original dreamer feels relieved and enlightened.

Remember that you can open your own dreams. After writing your night dream in your DreamBook, underline the words that indicate the patterns, and then ask yourself what the real question of your dream is.†

Your dreams are like the daily briefings every president of the United States begins his day with. The daily briefing, your dream, tells you about national (internal) and international (external) security issues you are dealing with and warns you of impending dangers. If you neglect your dreams, those security issues could implode (health issues) or explode (difficulties in your daily life and relationships). You will be sent nightmares and other difficult dream messages to get your attention. In this chapter I have described the way to plunge into a dream's true meanings. In the next chapter we will see how we can dialogue with our dreams to begin working together toward maximum health and harmony. Our dreams are our best advisors. We must learn to engage with them in mutually beneficial collaboration.

---

*We will talk about this in chapter 2.

†See Learn More at the end of this book.

2

Tikun and a Ladder
to the Light

If one is disturbed by a dream he has seen, let him remedy
the dream in the presence of three people.

BERAKHOT 55B

Do our dreams bob up on the waters of the subconscious just because of some random impulse of the subterranean world or some anxiety of the moment? Or is there more: a story line, a theme, or even a continuum appearing over the course of many night dreams? As we hover over the p'nei tehom of our subconscious, watching our dreams appearing, do we, like God, say "That is good?"[1]* On the sixth day God calls all that He created *"tov m'od,"* very good![2]† Midrash tells us that Adam, God's ultimate creation, contains all His creation, which he mirrors back to God. Adam is pure light and color.[3] Subsequently he falls from translucence into a naked body, and his mirror becomes opaque. We are his descendants. How do we work with our dreams to return to being the pure mirror God created us to be, His dream come to perfection? If there is an unfolding process back toward tov m'od, the very good, our conscious participation in developing that purpose is necessary.

Ki tov.

†Tov m'od is pronounced "tov me-od."

Our dreams live in a timeless present that dissolves just as suddenly as it is experienced. How can there be a continuum? We might as well speak of squaring a circle. And yet I am suggesting that a dialogue, creating continuum, is possible. All dialogues imply a give and take in time. Can dialogue and experience live in the same universe? We can dialogue endlessly about our relationship, but the experience of love is something altogether different. It's timeless and revelatory, fresh as a gushing fountain. Fitting the dome of the sky on the square walls of the earth has been done in countless basilicas, never perfectly, but the effort has been well worth it. We feel grounded while also being uplifted by the soaring cupola above the square columns. We talk about our relationships (the square columns), and we live our relationships (the soaring cupola). Both movements are enriching. Ignoring one side of the equation will result in a drying up of options or feeling.

Is there a way to dialogue, to speak across (*dia*) the barrier? And if there is, what would we gain by doing so? We can stay on this side of the barrier and "analyze" our dreams. We can peruse dream dictionaries to tell us what images mean. This might feel more secure, but it is fruitless: You cannot analyze experience without bleeding it of meaning. You can't stay on this side of the barrier. But then, must you jump across the abyss? How do you dialogue in the land of nonsense and come back making logical sense? How do sense and nonsense interact? The answer lies in the interface. The self-conscious speaks in words (the square columns), and the subconscious speaks in images (the cupola). It is the mix of these two languages that we must learn to integrate. The poet is best suited to that task. His words speak images and experience. Hearing the voice of the poet, revelation comes as it came to the Hebrews at the foot of Mount Sinai. "And the people *saw* the voices."[4] How we will be using words to tap into the subconscious and "see the voices," and how those images will, in turn, elicit descriptive words—words that are based in actual inner body experience—will be discussed in chapter 3. Meanwhile, *seeing* the voices, we can enter into the experience and interact with the images. **We dialogue by responding to the necessity of the images**, a work that is called "tikun," rectification/correction. The aim, you will remember, is to return to being a true mirror of God.

Dialoguing with the dream is a subversive action that has been disenfranchised time and again. "Here comes the dreamer, come now and let us kill him,"[5] say his older brothers on seeing Joseph, the epitome of the dreamer in the Bible. Many of us, like Joseph's brothers, have wanted to kill our dreams or ignore their relevance. The brothers shove the dreamer into a pit, another way of saying that they shove their dreams into oblivion.

Joseph is seventeen when he has two seminal dreams:

> "Listen to this dream I had: we were binding sheaves of grain out in the field when suddenly my sheaf rose and stood upright, while your sheaves gathered around mine and bowed down to it."[6]

> He had another dream, and told it to his brothers. "Listen," he said, "I had another dream, and this time the sun and moon and eleven stars were bowing down to me."[7]

Looking at these two dreams you wouldn't be wrong in thinking that the dreamer has a bad case of narcissism. Joseph, the Bible tells us, was a vain young man. And yet both dreams are speaking about a future that has little to do with vanity, a future that is already preexistent and embodied in the present. "His brothers were jealous of him, but his father kept the matter in mind,"[8] because his father recognized the perfect symmetry and repetition of the two dreams, a sign of prophecy.[9] Here was his son's potential revealed—for a moment in perfect alignment but not yet earned—a blueprint of Joseph's soul, portending a possible future, like a seed containing its future flowering. We call these "great dreams." We are all great dreams in potential. Sometimes, like Joseph, we are gifted with a vision of who our soul knows we are. We will talk more about these types of dreams in a moment.

Since we are God's dream, we can consider our whole life as one long dream within which we have night dreams. This is the lens we will use to consider Joseph's life story: a dream within which night dreams occur and rectification is possible. Or more accurately, a myth. What is the difference between dream and myth? "Myths are collective dreams, and are not to be taken as literal. They are metaphors."[10] Joseph's story is not the story of a boy named Joseph, with all of its particulars; rather, it's the story of every boy. Myths and, as we will see further on, fairy tales, are common dreams shared by humanity through the collective subconscious. Contrary to a personal night dream, in the myth or fairy tale, all extraneous events have been eliminated, every hero or heroine is generic, and the application of the necessity is part of the storytelling modeling all similar scenarios. Joseph's name, from the root word YSF, means "the one who adds," that which is needed to transform and grow a life. Adding means answering the necessity of the dream. "To use yourself differently is the key to your salvation,"[11] and myth (or fairy tale) lays out that path, showing you how it's done. We will use Joseph's myth as an example of DreamOpening.

Since we are considering Joseph's entire life story as his dream, we apply the rules of DreamOpening to the story, and we consider that every part of the dream is a part of the dreamer. Thus, the jealous brothers are parts of Joseph. The brother parts of himself (jealousy, carelessness, envy, competitiveness, vanity) destroy his great dreams and send him into a pit where there is no water and no refreshing hope. "They cast him into a pit swarming with snakes and scorpions, beside which was another unused pit, filled with offal."[12]* Darkness, aridity, snakes, scorpions, and offal all offer the sensations of some awful fate. Then he is pulled out of the pit and sold into slavery. In other words, this is a nightmare. You can easily transpose that myth into the story of the boy next door who falls into a drug habit, becoming enslaved to his addiction. Finally, a better part of himself (in Joseph's story, this is Potiphar, the man who appoints Joseph overseer of his house) pulls out of his addiction to rebuild his life and get his house in order. Climbing out of the nightmare (the pit), Joseph begins a linear journey toward embodying the potential that was, for a moment, revealed in his two night dreams. Simultaneously, he also rises (out of the pit) like good bread or a "good" dream, in a vertical journey

---

*Offal is waste material.

toward freedom. Remember that "bread" and "dream" have the same letters, HaLoM and LeHeM.*

The brothers—the parts of Joseph that deny and destroy his "goodness"—tear at his robe of many colors, smear it with the blood of a wild animal (his emotions), and present it to their father Jacob as proof that his favorite son is dead. Imagine your dream brothers as your emotions. You are the angry, rebellious, rude, nasty teenager being predictably impossible with your father, letting your father know that you are dead to his advice and way of life. The robe of many colors is the kaleidoscope of your inner seeing. You were born with it, and it is every human being's inheritance. Tearing at the robe is an imaginal way of saying that you are sabotaging your most precious tool of transformation: your dreaming.

In the story, the work continues sub rosa—the subconscious cannot be fully extinguished. Joseph adds to the dream by following where the language of the subconscious takes him, and by responding to its necessity. He becomes the mouthpiece for the dream, a powerful role, as it is said, "The dream follows the mouth."[13] As a dream opener, opening the dreams of his fellow prisoners, the cupbearer and the baker,[14] it is Joseph who verbalizes the meaning of the dreams.† In so doing, he manifests the dreams' predicted outcomes: One will live, and one will die.‡ Curiously, it is the baker who loses his head. Again, the motif of bread! The bread of dreaming cannot be on the dreamer's head. Dreams are not mental but experiential, for "mythic image is the body speaking to itself about itself."§ The one who lives is the cupbearer who offers the wine of experience to the pharaoh.

To "interpret" a dream is an enormous responsibility we all

---

*See chapter 1.

†*Patah,* open, and *patar,* interpret, are homophones (sound the same but are written differently) and in gematria they are linked, like puns in a dream.

‡They both have a dream the same night. The cupbearer dreams that a vine has three branches that bud and blossom and produce clusters of ripe grapes. He squeezes the grapes into a cup and offers it to Pharaoh. The baker dreams he has three baskets of bread on his head but the birds are eating them out of the basket.

§Recall Genesis 1:12, Ki tov. God sees "that it is good."

undertake, mostly unaware of the power of our interpretations.*

But Joseph is protected, for he is guided by his connection to God. He asks, "Do not interpretations belong to God?"[15] Here is an interpreter who has learned to listen to God speaking through dreams. In other words, he has learned to listen to his subconscious. DreamOpening arises from the secondary dreamer (you are not the original dreamer) dreaming the dream.

Pharaoh, learning of his skills,[16] releases the dreamer from prison and gives him the power to use his dream skills for the "good."

Pharaoh has two dreams: one of seven years of plenty, one of seven years of famine. Joseph acts upon the necessity of the dreams: In the years of plenty he stores the grain needed to feed the people during the years of famine. He provides storage against famine. What kind of famine? "When all the land of Egypt hungered, the people cried out to Pharaoh for bread."[17] Joseph dreams of **wheat**† shafts when he is young and dispenses **grain** for bread when he is older. Read this as meaning that Joseph gathers **dream power** when he is young and dispenses **dream meaning** when he is older. Are you surprised when the story tells us that a **famine** in Canaan sends Joseph's brothers down to Egypt to look for grain? What the brothers find is their brother, **their lost self, the dreamer, who has the key to the grain or dream storage**. The brothers come to get the "bread of dreaming" they had previously lost, by aggressively separating themselves from their source of meaning. Reuniting the dispersed parts of themselves cures their famine. The dream story tells us that killing our dreams is not the answer. Allowing them to rise like good bread fills us with goodness and meaning. It is through following dreams and responding to their necessity that Joseph gains his power in the land, second only to Pharaoh.

Mythical stories, as well as dreams, have a way of leading us to deeper truths. We could also say they are dreams stripped of personal details and adopted into the collective subconscious. Here is another myth that tells us why and how the dialogue needs to engage. Perceval,

---

*By saying, "You're a stupid little girl; no man will ever marry you," you are programming your little girl to visualize and to bring upon herself this unfortunate fate.

†Words in bold show the patterns in the dream story of Joseph.

whom we have met before,* is traveling to see his mother, when he encounters the dying Fisher King and is invited to a meal at his manor. Beautiful youths and maidens carry strange objects through the dining hall. A young man holds a bleeding lance, a fair maiden carries an elaborately decorated cup. Perceval looks and wonders, but having been warned not to question his elders, he doesn't inquire. Upon leaving the manor, he learns that his mother has died. Later at Camelot, a loathly woman confronts him. She chides him for not asking the questions: Whom does the grail serve? And why the bloody lance? For, she says, **those questions would have healed the dying king.**

Whenever you listen to a story, be it your friend's story, a night dream, a myth, or a fairy tale, think of it as a dream that requires you to open it. That is its first necessity. All stories are dreams coming from the flow of your imagination, including those you tell yourself and those your friends tell you. Opening them as dreams will reveal their secrets. In the story line, the Fisher King is wounded, and only the question can heal him. We have already talked about fishing, throwing the line into the ocean of the subconscious to find the hidden treasure, Sod. We have spoken of asking a question of the subconscious and receiving a dream in response. Here the questioner must go further. Having received the dream, he must dialogue with the dream itself. This, says the old woman, is what will heal you. To do this, again, think of every part of the dream as an aspect of the dreamer. The dreamer Perceval, the wounded Fisher King, the bleeding lance, the grail, and the mother, all are parts of the dreamer, since the dreamer's subconscious creates the dream. Mythical stories, night dreams, and visions come from what our bodies tell us they are experiencing. "The human imagination is grounded in the energies of the body."[18] Listening to them, we are the secondary dreamers of this story. We become every part of the story. We know the Fisher King of our subconscious is wounded: Our intent to fish into the subconscious is compromised. At the end of the story, the mother—our *mare*, our ocean, our subconscious waters—who usually nourishes and sustains us, has died. The story is telling us that the dreamer has lost contact with his subconscious, his source of truth. He is at a dangerous cross-

---

*See Introduction.

roads, and our conscious mind must do something about it before it is too late.

The bleeding lance is showing us that someone has been hurt.
The grail is a vessel meant to contain, but to what purpose is still unknown.

As listeners of the story, are you not eager to find out? A child—Perceval is described as a simpleton, a good child—will ask the simple questions:

Whose blood is on the lance?
What is in the cup?

These simple questions are the necessity of the dream. The dream is asking us to pursue the unfinished business of the dream. When you wake up, you need to return into the dream and respond to the necessity the dream presents to you. After all, the dream is a part of you. Why would you distance yourself from what it's trying to tell you? Because it speaks in images doesn't make it less worthy of your attention.

Exercise 5
. . . .
The Drop of Blood

Close your eyes. Breathe out slowly three times, counting from three to one. See the one tall, clear, and bright.

With your index finger, pick up a drop of the blood from the lance. Lift it to the light of the sun.

Breathe out. What images arise out of this place of wounding? See the images. How old are you in those memories? Who is there with you? What is happening?

Breathe out. Accept the images. Ask the sun to clear the images by flooding them with warm golden light.

Breathe out. Put the drop of golden light on your tongue and swallow it, asking it to reintegrate its perfect role in the healthy functioning of your body.

Breathe out. Open your eyes.
. . . .

The subconscious will show you when the drop of blood is integrated into your DreamField. Answering the necessity of the dream, you have healed that wounded part of yourself.

And the grail?

Exercise 6
. . . .
The Grail

Close your eyes. Breathe out slowly three times, counting from three to one. See the one tall, clear, and bright.

You are in the manor of the Fisher King. A beautiful young woman shows you an ornamented cup she's holding. Approach her and look in the cup. What do you see?

Breathe out. If you don't like what you see, respond to the necessity of the images until the subconscious shows you images that feel good to you.

Breathe out. Open your eyes.
. . . .

The key to dealing with the subconscious is always to respond to its images, but never to force them.

I see a snake coming out of the grail cup.
What color is it? **Green.**
What kind of green? **Dark green.**
Do you like the color? **No.**
Ask the snake why it is here. **The snake hisses.**
Ask the snake what it is angry about. **It shows me not standing up to my boss, and not standing up to my father when I was a kid.**
Ask the snake how you can learn to do that. **It opens its mouth and shows me a radiant sun in its mouth. It blows the sun into my solar plexus. The solar plexus expands, and I feel very strong.**
Look at the cup now. What is in the cup? **A bright sun.**
Breathe out. Open your eyes.
. . . .

For each of you, looking into the grail will reveal something different and unique. The great wonder of the subconscious is that it speaks to you, in images, about the mystery of your soul. Remember to always respect your subconscious and let it reveal its images to you. By responding in the same language—images—and watching your subconscious unfold like a luminous flower, you will be filled with wonder and a sense of growing meaning.

When I was in Japan, I was introduced to Mr. Obata, the head of a martial arts lineage called Ying Yang. Mr. Obata teaches dreaming to his disciples as part of his strengthening process. Our work had much in common. I also teach dreaming techniques to strengthen my students. For instance, a strong solar plexus will protect and arm a student with the strength of will and magnetism they need to face the world. Mr. Obata explained to me that in his tradition, if you have a bad dream, you come to see the master. The master buys your bad dream and sells you one of his good dreams. He told me with pride that he is the undisputed expert at buying and selling dreams in Japan. A stock exchange for dreams? Presumably the master is able to transform the bad dream into a good dream, just as King David did, who dreamed the nightmares of his people every night. In Jewish tradition *hatavat halom,* amelioration of the dream, is still a common practice. If you have had a bad dream you must ask three friends to declare to you: "You have seen a good dream; it is good and may it become good and may the Merciful One transform it to the good."

In my ancient Kabbalistic lineage we answer the necessity of the dream every morning after writing the dream down. To fail to do so would be detrimental to your well-being. How do you recognize the necessity? Exactly as you would recognize the necessity in everyday life: If the door is open, go through. If it is closed, ask yourself if you want to open it. If the table is dirty, wash it. If there is a mirror, go look in the mirror. If there is a knot, untie it. If you see a closed book, read its title and open it. If your male and female aspects are fighting, find what needs to be removed or added to bring peace between these aspects. You will find more examples of necessity and repair when we deal with repetitive dreams. A dream is not fixed; it is engaged in a dialogue with you: It asks you to pursue the movement toward the good it points you toward. Imagine opening up a computer program, finding a virus, and doing nothing to correct it. It can't correct itself without your input, nor can the dream. Night after night it will repeatedly offer you the same images until you clear the virus. Not all dreams appear bad, but many are asking us to ameliorate them. Again, you do not arbitrarily change the dream to good. You read the images, follow where they lead you, and respond. You dialogue in images with the dream until the subconscious comes up with its own solution. This is an organic movement, intrinsic to the dreamer's own truth, and far more powerful. Your dreams, like your immune system, which they reflect, always strive for greater balance, greater goodness, and greater consciousness expansion. Knowing how to respond to the necessity of your dream images gives you tools you can use on your own. You will also find that responding to the necessity of your dreams teaches you to do the same in your waking life. You learn to not waste time, and to respond immediately, or as soon as possible. Seeing your own powerful transformations take shape in your mind's eye will give you the hope and the power to continue climbing the ladder of dreams.

✳

From the darkness of the pit to the light of supreme power, Joseph navigated a ladder of growth using his understanding of and amelioration of dreams. His father Jacob had forged the way. He too was a dreamer. A man on the run, Jacob lay down to sleep in the desert and dreamed a seminal dream. This dream models the ultimate goal of dreaming. Jacob sees a vertical path, a ladder ascending from Earth to heaven. At the summit of the ladder is God, the transcendent, the ultimate One. Angelic messages, dream forms, flow up from Jacob to God and from God down to Jacob, telling us that dreams are arrows of intent, a means of reaching the divine, and ways the divine has of speaking to us. The subconscious veils of Jacob's soul have parted, and Jacob's soul mirrors God. For a moment, "what is below is like to what is above."[19] God blesses Jacob and all dreamers who dare to draw apart the veils of the subconscious: "You will spread out to the west and to the east, to the north and to the south. All peoples on Earth will be blessed through you and your offspring. I am with you and will watch over you wherever you go, and I will bring you back to this land."[20]

The five levels of the soul ascend from the dense physical body to the subtle ethereal form. These are *nefesh*, the body and awareness of the physical sensations; *ruah*,* the spirit and emotions; *neshamah*,† the soul and intellectual understanding; *hayah*, the nullification of the ego and merging with the divine; and *yehidah*, the God consciousness of the first human, Adam haRishon.‡

Think of the levels like layers of clothing as a metaphor for layers of consciousness. As you drop your clothes one by one, you come closer to nakedness, the truth, reflecting the divine form. We will see that the five rungs of the ladder of dreams mirror the five levels of the soul. The work of dreaming that we will set forth allows you to reach closer to God consciousness.

The First Level: Nefesh Dreams

The Nightmare

The robe of many colors, as we have said, is the kaleidoscope of your inner seeing. You were born with it, and it is your inheritance. Its colors are those that light up your inner world when you look in. Going up the ladder of dreams is about restoring those colors to your inner life. If you have lost someone you love, or have known trauma, you will have experienced how color seeps out of your life, and the world turns gray. Mourners used to put on sackcloth and cover their heads with ashes. When we do not follow the inner dictates of our superconscious—which is our soul—our inner world turns dull and our dreams darken. We are looking at the garbage on the surface of the ocean that obscures the radiant colors of the superconscious.

In the case of the nightmare, the colors most often seen are black, red, or fluorescent, like acid green.

Remember that you are dealing with the inner world, where linearity doesn't exist. One night you may have a nightmare, the next

---

*Pronounced "ru-ach" (like "Bach").
†*Pronounced "n'shama."
‡The notion of levels of soul developed gradually in the Tanakh, then in the Talmud. The Hasidic sages spoke of five levels of soul.

you may have a dream in clear colors. Colors tell you where you are in the present moment on the ladder. Don't be disappointed. Joseph had two great dreams, and then he fell into a pit (nightmare). Coming out of it, he was a slave (slave to his baser instincts) and was tempted by a woman.[21]* In the subsequent turmoil, he lost his bright dreams again: He was put into prison (another pit). You will all go back and forth on the ladder until something consolidates and you "cleave" to the light. The Kabbalists call this dveikut. Joseph achieved dveikut when he forgave his brothers and gathered them all into his arms. We will talk more about dveikut subsequently. The aim of the dreamer, Maimonides tells us, is to become like a constellation or a star in the sky. As you have guessed, the top of the ladder is pure light. For a moment, as pure light, you are the mirror image of God.

The Talmud tells us that nightmares are our best dreams. They wake us up, shake us up, and remind us to pay attention. King David had nightmares every night so that he could clear his people's inner garbage. Like King David, you too must respond to the necessity of your nightmare if you want to ascend the ladder.

Exercise 7
· · · · · · · · · · ·
Protection in a Nightmare

Close your eyes. Breathe out slowly three times, counting from three to one. See the one tall, clear, and bright.

Look up into the blue sky. See where the sun is. Catch a ray of light, and wrap yourself in a cocoon of light. If needed, fashion weapons of light, such as a shield and sword.

(If it is nighttime in your dream, look up into the night sky and catch the light from the Milky Way.)

Breathe out. When you are protected, address the necessity of the dream.

Breathe out. Open your eyes.
· · · · · · · · · · ·

But what if you were to wake up from a nightmare and say, "It was only a dream!" as so many others have? Having dismissed your dream,

---

*Potiphar's wife.

you may find that your dream life becomes less vivid, or your dreams fade away.

Repetitive Dreams

As if tired of trying to shake you awake, your dreams will become repetitive. Like a broken record, they spew up the same message ad nauseam. Here are some examples of repetitive dreams:

> *I'm going to miss my train; I have to take an exam but haven't prepared; I've lost my wallet; my teeth are falling out; I can't find my house and search endlessly for other houses, none of which suit me; the toilets are clogged; I'm falling with no end in sight; I've lost my pants and am walking around naked.*

Need I continue? We have all been plagued with repetitive dreams. What our repetitive dreams tell us is that a big clump of refuse is obscuring our inner lens. Being stuck makes us anxious, and most repetitive dreams are anxious dreams. But there is hope, as the labors of Herakles (Hercules in Latin) show us. Some of his labors, such as cleaning out the Augean stables (clogged toilets), and getting rid of the Stymphalian birds* (monkey mind) are reminiscent of repetitive dreams.

Exercise 8
. . . .
Responding to the Necessity of Repetitive Dreams

Responding to the necessity of clogged toilets, flush them and clean them. For fallen teeth, plant them back in your gum, just as the dentist would do in real life. If you are late for a train, turn back the clock and see that you have all the time in the world.

. . . .

By responding to the necessity of your repetitive dream, you clear it out, and it won't reappear. By the end of his labors, when Herakles has

---

*In Greek mythology, the fifth and sixth labors of Hercules, divine hero.

conquered each of his tasks, he becomes a star in the sky. Dveikut happens for him too. He cleaves to the light.

Repetitive dreams have mixed and muddied colors. Khaki, mustard yellow, or purple-tinged gray are common colors for these dreams.

Busy Dreams

Paying no attention to your nightlife, or simply being too busy with your everyday reality to sink into deep sleep, brings on busy dreams. Busy dreams are shallow dreams. Your dreams flounder around, looking for meaning. "Too many dreams and nonsense."[22] They may resemble closely your everyday busyness: running around, endlessly shopping, endlessly traveling, endlessly turning around in the same space, endlessly scrolling on your phone.

Colors of busy dreams are mostly gray, dull, or mixed.

This is what you do with busy dreams.

Exercise 9
· · · · · · · · · · ·
Clearing Busy Dreams

Close your eyes. Breathe out slowly three times, counting from three to one. See the one tall, clear, and bright.

Imagine that you are seeing your busy dream on a screen. With your left hand, sweep the images of the dream out of the screen to the left.

Breathe out. Breathe in the blue light from the sky through your nostrils into your mouth, filling your mouth with blue light. Blow the blue light on the screen, seeing the screen becoming blue and clear as a bright blue sky.

Breathe out.

Now watch your breathing, allowing your breath to find its own rhythm; knowing that when your breath finds its rhythm, what is out of place tends to return to be in place.

Breathe out. Bring your consciousness down into your chest. Watch your breathing, allowing your breath to find its own rhythm; knowing that when your breath finds its own rhythm, what is out of place tends to return to be in place.

Breathe out. Bring your consciousness all the way down into your abdomen. Watch your breathing, allowing your breath to find its own rhythm; knowing that when your breath finds its own rhythm what is out of order tends to return to be in order.

Breathe out. Let your consciousness flood your whole body, reaching the tips of your toes, your fingers, your hair, the edges of your skin and beyond. Open your eyes.

· · · · · · · · · · · ·

Nightmares, repetitive dreams, busy dreams are the first rung of the ladder. As we have said, their level of soul is nefesh, the animal soul level. We all have them, so don't feel bad. Remember that, like Herakles, you must tackle the task at hand and respond to its necessity today. If you do, you will find yourself much more often dreaming higher up on the ladder of dreams.

The Second Level: Ruah Dreams

The Clear Dream

The second rung up the ladder is the clear dream. We could also call it a clearing dream, because it shows you a way through the garbage of the subconscious. Your clear dream is asking you to perfect its work. It doesn't completely show you how to do this, but it indicates the way. It corresponds to the soul level ruah,* the breath. It is active. Your breath and your emotions are intimately linked. Your emotions change your breathing rhythm. You must make an effort, interact with the dream, and follow where the images lead you! If there is a closed door, open it, go through, see what is beyond. If there is a broken bridge, repair it and cross over. Always respond to the necessity. By doing so, your emotions will calm down. The clear dream is your friendly dream. It isn't frightening or boring. Most of our dreams are clear dreams.

The colors of the clear dream are the colors of our everyday life, clear, pastel, and natural.

The Third Level: Neshamah Dreams

The Great Dream

Now comes the third rung: the great dream. The soul level is neshamah. From here on you won't need to respond to a necessity as there will be none. It's as though the waters parted, and you can clearly see your superconscious. For a moment, having attained perfect alignment, you get to glimpse your true potential, as we saw happening in Joseph's dreams. The great dream shows you your neshamah, your soul, in all its intense and vivid colors. You never forget a great dream. Its impression is indelibly imprinted on your memory.

The colors of the great dream are vivid blues, deep emeralds, pure fire engine reds, and bright yellows. The purity of the colors and their intensity are striking.

The Fourth Level: Hayah

On the fourth rung your dream floods you with white light. This is hayah. Every image, if images are there, will be intensely white. You are returning to be like Adam before the expulsion from Eden.

The Fifth Level: Yehidah

There is a fifth level. Can you imagine it? It is called yehidah, union with oneness. For a moment you are the pure mirror reflecting God.

Dveikut is when, having done your clearing work, you finally cleave to the higher rungs of the ladder. Your dreams become pure light every night. When our imaginative faculty reaches a state of ultimate perfection, all images disappear. While we cannot will ourselves up the ladder, we now have tools to dialogue toward a greater good in ourselves. Respecting our dreams by:

> writing them down every morning
> opening the dreams
> responding to their necessity

engages the dialogue. Soon you will see a continuum appearing. If your clump of garbage relates to your father, night after night, the dreams will tackle that problem until the garbage is cleared, and you are free of it. If you are in a dream group, you will soon experience how one dreamer tackling a father problem triggers other dreamers to tackle their own father issues. A fascinating dance engages all participants until the father issue has cleared for all dreamers in the group.

✳

Bringing dreams or images up from the subconscious is useless unless each time we respond to the necessity of our images. The work of tikun (TKN: fix), rectification/correction, is the work of the tailor who fixes and assembles many pieces to create a perfect garment. Like Joseph, we have lost or damaged our inner garment, our robe of many colors. We have seen that we can correct it by adding in new pieces, and new colors. We can climb the ladder the slow way, through our night dreams, repairing our garment until our robe of multicolored light is restored to us. "In Kabbalah . . . we are taught that the consummately rectified "power of imagination" borders on the powers of prophecy."[23] But is there a faster way to engage in the work?

This next chapter will address just this question head on. Can we, instead of relying only on our night dreams, tap into our subconscious at will, during our secular time, and accelerate the work of tikun?

3

Incubation and
Saphire Imagery

*Either let me see it in a dream, or let it be discovered
by divination, or let a "divinely inspired priest/priestess
declare it, or let them all find out by incubation whatever
I demand of them."*

SECOND PLAGUE PRAYER OF MURSILI II

Can we become even more proactive in bringing up images from our subconscious? Can we, instead of relying only on our night dreams, tap into our subconscious at will, in our day-to-day activities, to accelerate the work of correction? If Joseph's life story is a dream, so too is our life story. Can we look at it as a dream, and deal with it accordingly, using tikun as a means of transformation and amelioration?

Like Joseph, the great dreamer of the Bible, we have a robe of many colors. Our robe of many colors is our dreaming. We dream all the time. That kaleidoscope of colors, shapes, sounds, smells, tastes, and textures we experience as we navigate the world is what feeds our ancient brain, our storehouse of experiences. Our storehouse is constantly replenished day and night and built up by our ongoing experiences. From the moment we are conceived until the moment of our death, we are accumulating experiences. Our brain doesn't wait for nightfall to begin absorbing through all our senses what we call image—the 3D language of all our senses working in synergy. Images are always available to us if we know how to tap into our subconscious.

What we know about images is that our experiences are nestled, like Russian dolls, into form within form. This in-**form**-ation isn't available for viewing until you induce it into motion. The double process of storage and induction is what I call dreaming. Your night dreams and daytime visions are the result of these two activities. The first activity—storage—happens subconsciously, without your active participation. The second—induction—requires a stirring of the subconscious soup. An unexpected jolt or shock may set off a dream or daytime vision. Or you may consciously induce a jolt to provoke a dream or vision. Induction is what we are going to be exploring in this chapter. There are two types of induction: the night induction that is called incubation, and the daytime induction that is specific to Saphire, the ancient Kabbalistic lineage I belong to.*

Incubation can be seen as "any act of intentional sleeping to produce dreams" or simply as a phase of creativity. Let us first look at the narrower definition of incubation, as it was practiced in classical Greece, and later across the ancient Mediterranean world. Most of the examples of dream incubation that have come down to us are pleas for healing. Asclepius, son of Apollo, was the god of healing. His temples, called Asclepions, were dedicated to the practice of healing through dream therapy. The most famous Asclepion in classical Greece was Epidaurus, but there were many others scattered around the peninsula. Since we do not have dream temples anymore, we will try to understand the steps used in the ancient world for incubation, to learn from them the best way to incubate our own dreams.

Pilgrimage to a temple required time, effort, and money. People came from all over the peninsula, often on foot, and the travels were long and

---

*The holder of the lineage is given a sapphire stone to serve as a reminder that the heavenly light is within. (See Colette's memoirs, *Life Is Not a Novel*, Vol. 2.)

arduous. At the temple, pilgrims were first required to go through an intense purification process called katharsis. On the physical level, this meant undergoing ritual baths and purges for three days, while eating a clean diet. If the complaint was of the mind, purging of the emotions was done through some form of art therapy. The second phase consisted of making an offering of an animal sacrifice. This was often the hardest part, since many supplicants lacked the funds for an animal sacrifice and were therefore precluded from the ritual. The third phase was the actual incubation process. The patient was brought into the temple to sleep, in the hope that proximity to the divinity would induce a divine visitation. The god often did appear in the supplicant's dream, or in a half-conscious vision, with advice and directions for healing. If the god did not appear in the dream but the supplicant had a dream, the dream was interpreted by the priest, and used to determine an appropriate treatment. A modern-day example of a priest-interpreter of dreams is Edgar Cayce, with the difference being that he did the dreaming for his patients, using dream incubation to read his patients' bodies, and then suggested a remedy.

Adapting the oneiromancy practices of the ancient Greeks to a modern context requires some thought. The pilgrimage, the sacrifice, the sleeping in a sacred place, are all steps that must be modified in a modern context. What do pilgrimage and sacrifice imply? A burning desire—a willingness to "sacrifice" your all—to get an answer. What do you want to know so urgently today that you are willing to dedicate all your time, energy, and resources to it? While most examples we have from the ancient world were requests for healing dreams, your questions can be more far reaching. Remember that a question implies a need for clarification, transformation, and new configurations. All sincere questions are valid here, and the pilgrimage can be within. A pilgrimage always suggests a direction: I'm going to Epidaurus, or I'm going to my dreamtime. Honing your question to a fine point is similar to choosing to set forth toward Epidaurus, albeit not as physically taxing. To make this inner pilgrimage successful, a fierce determination and focus are required. Your question must be simple, reduced to its barest elements. Your dreaming should be able to answer your question via a simple yes or no. Here is an exercise to help you whittle down your question.

Exercise 10
· · · · · · · · · · ·
The Question Banner

Close your eyes. Breathe out slowly three times, counting from three to one. See the one tall, clear, and bright.

Gather all the different strands of your question into your hands, and roll the strands up into a ball. See the color of the ball.

Breathe out. Throw the ball into the sky. Watch it disappearing into the blue sky.

Breathe out. On its return, see the ball unfurling like a banner over your head. What color is the banner? What image or words appear on the banner?

Breathe out. Open your eyes.
· · · · · · · · · · ·

If the question does not call for yes or no, try asking for a dream to narrow down the issues for you. You could use this formula: What is the advice of my dreaming on the true question concerning my issue? Your question is the arrow that stirs the subconscious soup and jolts it to respond.

Exercise 11
· · · · · · · · · · ·
The Flying Arrow

Close your eyes. Breathe out slowly three times, counting from three to one. See the one tall, clear, and bright.

Imagine that you are in front of a round mirror. Take up a colored crayon and write on the mirror, "Show me my true question."

Breathe out. See the letters becoming a flying arrow shooting straight into your dream world.

Breathe out. Ask to remember your dream as you wake up.

Breathe out. Open your eyes.
· · · · · · · · · · ·

Once you have your true question, what will your sacrifice be? You must offer the "beast" of your own time and attentiveness to the process. Your Asclepion may be your very own bedchamber, but it will be your fierce desire to stimulate a dream that will transform it into a sacred space.

Exercise 12

· · · · · · · · · · ·

Asking a Question of Your Dream

Lie in your bed, on your back, with your limbs uncrossed, and your eyes closed. Breathe out slowly three times, seeing the numbers from three to one.

Breathe out on zero, open your mouth, and blow the zero out, seeing it become a circle of light in front of you.

Breathe out. See your question appear in the circle of light.

Breathe out. See the light flooding the question until all the letters have turned to light.

Breathe out. Breathe in the light to illuminate and orient your dreamtime tonight.

Breathe out. Don't open your eyes; just let yourself sink into a deep but intentional sleep.

· · · · · · · · · · ·

Will your dreamtime answer your urgent supplication? Don't take my word for it. Why should you? You don't have the example of countless pilgrims who came before you, vouching for the process, who experienced a divinely inspired dream and returned cured. Many of you may not ascribe to God or even to the belief that there is something divine/creative within you that knows. You will have to suspend your critical mind and give it a try. My best advice to you is to be adventurous: Dare to spend the time exploring the possibility that there is a mystery within you (call it life) that can guide you to your answer. If you are rewarded with an answer, won't it have been worth your time? Confirming to yourself your dreaming mind's ability to deliver truthful answers grows your trust. The more you seek your own inner counsel, the more actively it will seek you out. If your night dream answers your urgent question, you can take a red pen and mark the box labeled "verification" in your DreamBook.

Taking seriously your desire to remember your dreams is of course, a necessary first step in the incubation process. Have your DreamBook open, write down tonight's date, and have a pen ready for your use. On awakening, write everything that you've seen. Don't omit any details.

Does your dream give you a clear answer? If not, return to chapter 1 and use PRDS, the four levels, to open your dream. If you still don't get an answer, then maybe your question wasn't properly honed. If you are seriously determined, go back to whittling down your question and try again.

Incubation in its larger sense is a phase of creativity that involves letting ideas sit and churn in the subconscious until some novel configuration emerges. You can envision your inner space as a pouch into which you drop your question. How are you going to signal to your subconscious that you desire an answer if your question isn't one of the urgent ones we've just discussed? Here is an example of how it works: I need to give a speech in six weeks, but I have no idea what I'll be talking about. I drop the question "What should I talk about?" into the pouch, or if you prefer, into the back of my mind (I always see it as the back of my neck), and create the urgency by giving the subconscious a date. For example: I need an answer in three weeks or on March 15. Does it work? As you probably know, the subconscious lives in timelessness. Past, present, and future are all jumbled up. Why would the subconscious answer you in three weeks, or even more specifically, on March 15? Where is the interface between subconscious timelessness and linear consciousness?

The subconscious acts like the programming in your computer. Unless you consciously or accidentally open a specific program, the program will forever remain hidden. Your conscious mind or a jolt must initiate the movement. Your subconscious cannot show itself unless stirred to do so by anxiety (the induction behind many dreams) or asked to do so by an urgently felt question. If the question is not urgent today but may be in three weeks, timing will act as the induction. Timing is the key to the meeting here: If I want to meet my friend tomorrow, I must ask, where and when? Space and time are the two essential coordinates of meeting. Without defining space and time, the meeting won't happen. It is the same with the conscious and the subconscious. The space, we know, is the inner space already spoken of. Now we must establish the timing.

Exercise 13

· · · · · · · · · · ·

Timing Your Answer

Close your eyes. Breathe out slowly three times, counting from three to one. See the one tall, clear, and bright.

Imagine that you have a question you need answered in three weeks' time. Imagine writing your question on a piece of paper and folding the paper three times into a triangular shape.

Breathe out. Write on it the date at which you need your question answered. Drop it into your dreaming pouch.

Breathe out. Deliberately forget your question, letting it sink out of sight into your dreaming pouch. Program yourself to continue forgetting it for the three coming weeks.

Breathe out. Ask to be informed of the answer in three weeks' time.

Breathe out. Open your eyes.

· · · · · · · · · · ·

You cannot know for sure that this will work unless you take the risk of trusting your dreaming. The answer can come in many different ways, so keep your eyes and ears open. You may have a night dream or walk into a bookstore and a book calls out to you. When you pick it up, it is the answer to your question. Or someone says something that triggers your creative insight, or you see a sign on a billboard, and suddenly, eureka! The answer is clear and unequivocal. We call this phenomenon synchronicity.

✳

Creativity and truth are linked in the subconscious. The sign of creativity is a knowing, a certainty that this is right! This is the truth! The artist simply *knows* he's using the right color. The physicist *knows* this is the right direction to explore. The dreamer sees and does not question what she sees. The experience is often called intuition. Intuition acts as a powerful revelation, opening up a whole new set of experiences. I am often asked: How do we know this is not fantasy? How do we know we are not being fooled to believe what we want to believe? Fantasy is not revelation; it doesn't deal with truth. Fantasy is a distorted use of the imagination by your left brain to serve a foregone conclusion. The desire to be a superman, a superhero, with big muscles and the ability to knock down any obstacle in the way; or a downtrodden woman who is finally recognized for her inner charms by a rich man who carries her away on a white horse. Am I mixing metaphors? You know it's a fantasy, because the story gets more and more exaggerated, like the latest Hollywood blockbusters. Fantasy exhausts, whereas revelation brings renewal, freshness, and joy. Revelation is always unexpected. How to trigger it consciously is our issue.

The sign of a creative mind is the leap, the ability to find unexpected links between apparently disparate elements. "There is nothing new under the sun,"[1] says Solomon, the wisest of men. But we can play with all the forms we do have. There is an inexhaustible cornucopia of possible new configurations. We often hear that many people can reason, but few are creative. Is that true? Creativity can be activated. The ability to *know* is a gift all men and women have been endowed with but most adults have lost. As children we all have it—we play, we invent, full of joy and vivaciousness—until we are reined in by linear thinking. Now, as adults, how can we recover our lost joy? How do we open the floodgates of creativity? "The true sign of intelligence is not knowledge, but imagination," says Einstein, and he should know. He *saw* himself riding a beam of light when he was a child. His insight was the impetus that led to the theory of relativity.

Like Einstein, we do not have to go to sleep to access our creative subconscious. Many people have had sudden flashes of insight, but what brought them on? Is there another way to incubate, one that doesn't require falling asleep? Can we ignite the flash of insight at will, and instantly? We know that honing our question will stir the subconscious to answer us in dreams or even during the daytime if we apply some pressure, such as timing. What other, more immediate pressure can we apply?

We have seen that many shamanic traditions and mythic stories speak about "the crossing." You cross every night when you fall asleep. But unless you've done the work of staying lucid while dreaming, a work we'll address, you fall asleep and lose consciousness. Can you come close to the crossing and not lose consciousness? Gaston Bachelard, a twentieth-century French philosopher called this half-state—not quite awake, not quite asleep—*rêverie*. We could call it daydreaming. Rêverie or daydreaming is not fantasy. Unlike fantasy, rêverie has no preconceived goal, except that of letting go of one's critical thinking. Suppose that you are a poet and are stuck on a line of your poem: Decide to take a nap with the intent of catching the hypnagogic images and words that arise from the chaos of dreaming. Make sure not to fall asleep, but to stay half lucid on the border between sleep and nonsleep. Many creators have used this technique to trigger their creative inspiration. They write their poems, start their novels, find mathematical answers and responses to burning questions, all at the very edge of sleep and wakefulness. Or they take a wandering walk in nature, eyes un-focused, body relaxed. Rêverie will arise spontaneously and, like the night dream, will answer your question, whether it is inchoate or formulated. Make sure you have a notebook at hand. Like Einstein whose daydreaming jump-started his creative journey, do not dismiss your rêverie, and let it guide you to new adventures. You have already taken the first step toward rêverie in performing the exercises in this book by counting 3-2-1 backward.

Exercise 14
· · · · · · · · · · ·
The Dream Catcher

Lie down with a pen and notebook nearby. Close your eyes. Watch your breathing, allowing your breath to find its own rhythm. Relax every part of your body, as you do at night when falling asleep.

Let yourself sink into half sleep, but with the intention of staying just at the horizon between consciousness and dream. Hold the intention that when the first images arise, you will wake up and remember them.

Immediately write down in your notebook what you saw and heard.

Then breathe out, and let yourself sink into sleep again with the same intent: You will awake as soon as the first images arise.

Once again, immediately write in your notebook everything you saw and heard.

Then, if you need more "information" from your dreaming creative pool, start all over again.

· · · · · · · · · · ·

Rêverie is a very powerful tool that will take you on unanticipated journeys into the subconscious. Always make sure you don't drift off into fantasy. Fantasy has a masturbatory quality to it and doesn't refresh you. Rêverie does; it gives you a jolt or surprise.

Imagine Abraham's surprise when he hears a voice he recognizes as his God's voice saying terrible things to him: "Please take your son, your only one, whom you love—Isaac—and get yourself to the land of Moriah; bring him up there as an offering."[2] Is it possible that the dream voice can order such evil? A story in which a divine voice orders the killing of one's own son can only provoke horror and repulsion. Yet Abraham answers: *Hineni*, I am here, I trust the inner calling, I will go. Mount Moriah is three days away, a pilgrimage to the Holy of Holies, the sacred space where the future temple of Solomon will one day be built. As Abraham tells the two young men who had accompanied him and Isaac: "Stay here by yourselves with the donkey, while I and the lad will go yonder (*ad ko*)."* The donkey is called *hamor*, from the root word *homer*, meaning clay or matter. Stay here with the clay or matter, in the literal world, while we go ad ko, beyond, to that unknown that is hidden from our daily reality. To go beyond, one must die to all forms of literal understanding, to linear ties and rationality. One must drop all claims, expectations, and hopes of ever truly understanding the truth of the subconscious ocean that is the core of our being.

Abraham lifts his knife to kill the creative form he put such intent into bringing to life, his beloved son Isaac. Abraham makes his sacrifice in the name of the creative God: Something must die for something new to emerge.

To give you a more concrete example, it is as if, having written my book, I erased it because I can sense that a new configuration, a different way of writing is calling me.

---

*Gen. 22:5; I owe thanks to Rabbi Gershon Winkler's interpretation of ad ko.

Exercise 15

· · · · · · · · · · · ·

HaShem Yireh

Close your eyes. Breathe out three times, counting from three to one, seeing the numbers. See the one tall, clear, and bright.

Imagine that you are Isaac, tied to the logs of the sacrificial fire. You realize that you are the sacrifice. What are you feeling?

Breathe out. Go beyond, ad ko, to the other world, and learn what you need to learn.

Breathe out. Return, bringing with you the insight you were given.

Breathe out. Open your eyes, seeing your insight with open eyes.

· · · · · · · · · · · ·

Isaac wasn't killed. An angel stopped Abraham's arm, and a ram was substituted for Isaac. Isaac was sent by his father, figuratively speaking, to the school for prophets and dreamers, the Academy of Shem and Ever,[3] which, we are told, is "in the world to come"[4] or, for our purposes, in the world ad ko. Then—and here we must marvel—Abraham calls the site HaShem Yireh, the Lord is seen! You too, in the exercise, have hopefully seen a new configuration. This is what we call revelation: a new creation.

What do we learn from this controversial story? To get to the beyond, we must die to homer (matter), the rational literal world. How do we accomplish that? By a shock, such as is described in Isaac's story when his father raises a knife to slaughter him. That doesn't make sense. This story continues to confound all the interpreters of the story. And yet, can we get ad ko without a shock? The shock breaks open the pattern, and all the images are free to configure differently. You can't force creativity. You throw all the broken pieces into the cauldron, and the tides send back a new configuration.

Saphire imagery is like that. It creates a little shock, a jolt, an unexpectedness that opens up the possibility of a new configuration. I often give the example of this famous zen koan:

Exercise 16

· · · · · · · · · · · ·

The Zen Koan

Close your eyes. Breathe out three times, counting from three to one, seeing the numbers. See the one tall, clear, and bright.

Hear and see the one hand clapping.
Breathe out. Open your eyes.

· · · · · · · · · ·

This koan is so obviously shocking to the rational mind that most people opt out. So let's try a softer jolt.

Exercise 17
· · · · · · · · · ·
The Key to a Lock

Close your eyes. Breathe out three times, counting from three to one, seeing the numbers. See the one tall, clear, and bright.

Imagine that you've just been given a key. What does the key look and feel like in your hands?

Breathe out. Find the lock to which the key belongs. Is it a door, a casket, or something else?

Breathe out. Turn the key in the lock, what do you find? What happens?

Breathe out. Open your eyes.

· · · · · · · · · ·

Here are some answers given by students:

The key goes into the lock of a big wooden door. I open it and step into a magnificent garden.

The key opens a casket, and in it I find a quill. I've always wanted to write but never dared to!

The key opens my heart, and it starts to shine, I feel so happy!

· · · · · · · · · ·

The shock can be that for a moment you lose your rational mind.

Exercise 18
· · · · · · · · · ·
Losing Your Head

Close your eyes. Breathe out three times, counting from three to one, seeing the numbers. See the one tall, clear, and bright.

Imagine that you're walking in a tall forest. You lose your way.

Breathe out. Grow taller and taller until your head is above the tree canopy. Breathe out. Stretch your neck even longer to spy above the trees your way out of the forest. Suddenly your head is too heavy for your neck and falls off.

Breathe out. Return to your size, and run after your head. Screw it back on perfectly.

Breathe out. Walk out of the forest. What do you see? What has changed for you?

Breathe out. Open your eyes.

· · · · · · · · · · ·

Or the shock can simply mean taking a different point of view.

Exercise 19
· · · · · · · · · · ·
The Flying Carpet

Breathe out three times, counting from three to one, seeing the numbers. See the one tall, clear, and bright.

Sense, see, and feel an entangled situation you are in with other people in your family, or with friends, or at work.

Breathe out. Imagine that in your DreamBody, you step onto a flying carpet. It flies off, and now it's floating above the situation you've been having a problem with. Look down at yourself and those involved in that situation, seeing the entanglement.

Breathe out. Stretch your arms down, and move the people or yourself into new positions. Repeat this until the situation feels more resolved and peaceful.

Breathe out. Fly off on your magic carpet to visit different parts of the world or different people.

Breathe out. Return to the situation you were dealing with. Look down at it from your flying carpet. What do you feel now? Is there another adjustment you wish to make? If so, stretch your arms down, and reposition the people or yourself until you're satisfied.

Breathe out. Your magic carpet returns to the ground. Step off it and reenter your body on the ground. What does the situation feel like now?

Breathe out. Open your eyes.

· · · · · · · · · · ·

Since it is bodywork, creativity (right brain nimbleness), like muscles, must be exercised. Let's say you're interested in exploring your emotional reactions to change. Here is a series of exercises that will stimulate your creative abilities when faced with change.

• • •

This class was written, many years ago, by my teacher Colette.

Exercise Class
. . . .
From Twilight to the Rainbow

Before each exercise, breathe out three times, counting from three to one, seeing the numbers. See the one tall, clear, and bright.

After each exercise, breathe out, and open your eyes.
. . . .

1) Look at the twilight and the slow disappearance of the sun behind some hills until the total disappearance of the sun. Sense and feel the differences in your emotions.
. . . .

2) Look at the multicolored twilight when the sun is sinking at the horizon of the sea. How are you reacting? What do you feel?
. . . .

3) Imagine that you are in front of a threshold. What do you do? Are you jumping over it, crossing over quietly, or standing without moving?
. . . .

4) See yourself as the hero crossing the threshold on the edge of a radiant sword.
. . . .

5) See and know that you are between one state and another. Feel the uncertainty and the ambivalence inhabiting you. Describe them.
. . . .

6) See and live the ending of one sort of life and the beginning of another as entering a new cycle.
. . . .

7) There is no bridge and no sword over the abyss. Wear a bright colored turban. Feel the courage, the decision, and the energy to jump over the abyss.
. . . .

In response to these kinds of jolt inductions, sensing, seeing, feeling in images will help you to develop your resilience and fluidity. Going through multiple practice runs of these kinds of inductions exercises your creativity, preparing you to deal with whatever shocks your real life will present you with. Think of this as similar to a yoga practice. Learning the postures has made you strong and aligned. Someone knocks into you on the subway platform, but your yogic experiences of strength and alignment kick in. You don't fall. You realign yourself instantly and without difficulty. The Saphire practice deals with all four of your bodies: physical, emotional, mental, and spirit. You get knocked down—betrayed by your best friend or over-looked in the workplace—and instantly a creative solution appears from the subconscious soup to realign you. Because you have practiced "plunging," when faced with a real shock, you will instinctively tap in, and the creative solution will pop up. I call this Saphire practice an **aerobics of the soul**. In the face of multiple induced small shocks, your subconscious will rise up to the occasion and show you that you are smarter, tougher, and more creative than you realized. Saphire imagery will reveal to you who you are, what you feel, and what you truly think.

Please don't confuse Saphire imagery with visualization. What most people call visualization is, in fact, imitation. I imitate my mother's hand movements or my father's expression. I imitate my skiing teacher's moves. I follow the voice that tells me to walk down a golden path and turn right to see an altar flanked by two angels. I'm still in visualization. But if I'm asked what each angel says, I've moved from imitation to revelation. Try it.

Exercise 20
• • • • • • • • • • •
The Two Angels

Breathe out three times, counting from three to one, seeing the numbers. See the one tall, clear, and bright.

Sense, see, and feel, following a golden path until you come to a crossroads.

Breathe out. Turn right and see an altar flanked by two angels. What does each angel look like?

Breathe out. Ask each angel for advice. Hear what each angel tells you or shows you.

Breathe out. Look at what is now on the altar.
Breathe out. Open your eyes.

. . . .

Visualization helps with relaxation. It helps with simple tasks you want your physical body to do. Showing the body precisely how to repair itself is the surest path to simple healing. When it comes to complex health problems such as cancer, where more than the physical body is involved, the emotional, mental, and spirit bodies must be accessed. You can't do that with visualization. You must access the creative force within you to reconfigure the whole situation. This requires a little shock or jolt.

You are a creative being in the process of creating yourself. You started off as a single cell and developed into this complex network of creative form building. With age, like Isaac, you will auto-destruct and die. That too is a creative process. When in Genesis, on the sixth day, God creates man, He says, tov m'od, that too is very good. The sages tell us tov m'od means that death enters the equation. Creativity requires a death to renew itself. We will die and be reborn in a new configuration. This is hard to accept, but the work of revelation is there to prove to you that creativity always renews itself. If you practice Saphire imagery, you will learn by experience that you are a creative being. Trust that each time you tap into the ocean of the subconscious, a new aspect of you will emerge. It's like painting your house, changing the furniture, or sporting new clothes; you will feel renewed and refreshed. It will still be you, but the clock has now traveled backward: you look so much younger, happier, and lighter! Is imagination the famed fountain of youth?

4

The Creative Act

God wills man to be a creator—his first job is to create himself as a complete being.

RABBI JOSEPH B. SOLOVEITCHIK

The Kabbalists see the world bathed in Consciousness. They call it immanence and give it a female name, Shekhinah. She is the receptive pool—the fluid-filled vacuum—the mirror image of her mate, the transcendent God whose desire creates this world in His image. In a secondary play of mirrors Adam haRishon, the first human, is male/female, hybrid, like God and his consort Shekhinah, and inside Adam haRishon resides all God's consciousness or thoughts that create this world. The word thought in Hebrew is *mahshavah*. The translation leaves something to be desired. Mahshavah is not so much an abstract thought, as a weaving* of different strands of thinking, creating a pattern or matrix. We could say that all six days of creation are the matrix, the DreamField of *mahshavot*† woven within Adam. Adam has no form. Adam is an infinity of intertwining lights, colors, sounds, dissolving forms. He/She is as vast as olam, the created world. "Adam

---

*There are many ways the same message is communicated in the dreaming. For example, Leviathan means to twine, to join. He is "wreathed, twisted in folds." He is part of the weaving.

†Plural of mahshavah.

extended from the Earth to the firmament . . . from one end of the world to the other."[1] As we have seen, olam, world, and ne'elam, concealment, have the same root letters, A-L-M, which makes them related. For Adam haRishon, the passage from ne'elam to olam is a simple matter of breathing out with intent, expressing desire through sound. Adam names the beasts that are within his/her DreamField, and they become manifest.[2] It is only after the fall, when God fashions clothes out of animal skins to cover Adam and Eve's nakedness, that olam and ne'elam are separated. The weaving is concealed (ne'elam), and what we see is the revealed outer world, olam. Our bodies are on display, whereas our DreamField, like mist, appears and disappears in night dreams or visions. It is very tempting to conclude that body is all there is. But what do we lose in the process?

"In pain (etsev) shall you give birth,"[3] says God to Eve after giving her animal skins to cover her nakedness. Etsev also means "grief," "sadness," and "anxiety." Creation for us humans in this fallen reality is accompanied by all the furies of existence, pain, grief, sadness, fear, and anxiety. Our emotions are the surface skin of the ocean we have to transpierce and dissolve for our superconscious to emerge. They are the spark that sets in motion our creativity. Our pain leads us inward to seek what we haven't found in the outer reality. Turning our eyes inward is the first movement back to creativity.

✳

To illustrate what our task is, let's return to the three-tiered model of consciousness presented in the introduction: the self-conscious, the subconscious, and the superconscious. Imagine them as three concentric circles. The inner circle, closest to us—the self-conscious—is the smallest circle, yet seems to take up much of our consciousness. The second circle is the subconscious. It is infinitely expandable, containing all our experiential memories, both personal and genetic, past and future. The largest but most removed of our circles is the superconscious. The superconscious is our basic blueprint, at the center of which, radiating, or immanent to it, is our soul made in the image of God. But we don't see much of it, because it is obscured by the subconscious and the self-conscious. And yet without it, how do we know who we really are?

To recapitulate:

The self-conscious is our mental body (commonly called left brain). It is active through the neocortex, our most recent human brain development. It believes in linear time, cause and effect, and reason. It is analytical. It works like a binary system. It thinks in words.

The subconscious is our emotional body (right brain). Located mostly in the limbic brain, it deals with creative processes, forming and dissolving, and with experience. It works by analogy. Its language is sensory, and when fully developed, it speaks in images.

The superconscious is traditionally located in the pineal gland, which Descartes, who was the originator of this idea, called "the seat of the soul" or the bridge between soul and body. Recent research shows that the pineal gland, when active, emits a sapphire blue light. A sapphire blue light also shines in Noah's ark, which is not just a boat having three levels but, if read as a dream, is his body illuminated by the pineal gland. Noah's name means "rest" or "comfort." Our superconscious is our feeling body, the mysterious source of rest, comfort, peace, love, mercy, joy, and compassion.

When all three levels of consciousness are simultaneously awoken, the slumbering Leviathan will rise, "throwing out flashes of light, its eyes radiant like the rays of dawn,"[4] and you will see your illuminated consciousness. The big bang of creativity is its most resplendent and mysterious manifestation.

As we have said before, think of your self-conscious mind as your boat. How can you, the captain, the observer (self-consciousness), be in control of your boat if you know nothing of the storms, erratic currents, and vast patches of garbage cluttering the surface of the ocean? Below the surface is a treasure trove of beauty, forests of variegated shapes, and beasts of many hues. At the bottom of the ocean, like a great foundation stone, lies your all-knowing soul, the tabernacle and power center of your being. Wouldn't you like to get to know it? To bring up to consciousness the creativity that lies hidden in the depth of your being?

In Kabbalah creativity is called *hokhmah*, wisdom, the first flash of insight, the dot in becoming, whose initial movement speeds outward to become a line, then a form, and eventually the totality of manifestation. "Wisdom shall be found in nothingness."[5]

If so, how do we learn to tap into nothingness? And like Adam and Eve before the fall, how do we return to creating and giving birth effortlessly and without pain? What are the maneuvers needed to clear the way back to where we are told that only "God understands the way thereof, and He knoweth the place thereof?"[6] Is this hubris? Or is this the true challenge we are presented with on incarnating? Going through the three layers of consciousness, we will need to dissolve the fixed constructs on which our daily reality is built; sweep away pain, sadness, fear, anxiety and all the emotional blocks that obstruct the way; and mend the interconnectedness between all three layers of consciousness. Can returning to a larger view of who we really are restore our Adamic fluidity, allowing our soul's creativity to leap and play in the waves of the subconscious ocean?

✳

Let's start with the self-conscious mind. It is a most precious commodity, since it allows us to use reason to bring order into the confusion of our lives. That doesn't mean sweeping the confusion under the rug. When the self-conscious takes over and rules, without even attempting to give space to the other levels of being, the result, as we've seen, is pain. A midrash* illustrates this.

> God made the two great lights, then, without so much as an explanation, the two great lights became "the **great** light for ruling the day, and

---

*A midrash is a Jewish mode of biblical interpretation that adds new elements to the canonical stories, in the same way that association will add to the narrative of a dream.

*the **small** light for ruling the night, as well as the stars." Where does that contradiction come from? The midrash says that the moon said to God, "Sovereign of the Universe! Is it possible for two kings to wear one crown?" God answered. "Go then and make yourself smaller."[7]*

Is the moon jealous of the sun? Can this be a case of sibling rivalry, of two lights, two brains fighting for the same crown? Or is this male/female competition (the sun in Hebrew, *shemesh,* is male, the moon, *levanah,* female)? And does God the father, in frustration, punish the moon? Or does He, like Apollo the sun god, with a burst of pure left-brain light, shatter the right brain's visions and voice rising out of the cavernous darkness? What is certain is that, using the language of metaphor, the midrash acknowledges competition between the two brains and recognizes that the left brain shines brighter. The moon, we are told, is reduced to one-sixtieth of her former radiance, both her visions and her voice diminished and devalued. Today that discrepancy continues unabated, and reason and science have all but killed the visions and voice from the depths. But as a modern midrash points out, the dangers of the sun are not negligible. "The sun will parch the earth, bring dehydration, burn the skin of those exposed, cause cancers to erupt on human flesh." Whereas the moon "ever-changing, ever-watched, ever-admired, ever-mysterious, dazzling the moonstruck lovers, will comfort those who gaze upon her."[8]

We are living in a parched world of reason. Fixed belief systems have immediate consequences. They block the creative abilities and healing powers of the DreamField. Therefore, the first rule for developing creativity is getting the sun to shine upon the moon; in other words, getting the self-conscious to "hover over the chaos" of the subconscious.

Here is the story of a man with pulmonary fibrosis whose breathing had greatly deteriorated. The doctor, wanting to take his oxygen levels, poked again and again at his arm in vain, attempting to catch his artery. Could it be that pain and fear kept the artery concealed? I asked permission to do an exercise, and the patient accepted.

Exercise 21
· · · · · · · · · · ·
Talking to Your Body

Close your eyes, count slowly from three to one.

As you count, feel your arm relaxing, feel it getting heavier and heavier.

It feels longer and weightless.

Ask the artery to show itself.

· · · · · · · · · · ·

The artery immediately popped up, and the doctor was able to take her blood sample.

Thank your artery.

Open your eyes.

· · · · · · · · · · ·

This story shatters our preconceived notions of the body being just flesh. By observing the arm relaxing, we see it change from flesh to energy (elongation, weightlessness) and, furthermore, being conscious and responsive (the artery appears). A physical situation blocked by a rational belief system (sun: the body is only flesh) was transformed by turning the eyes inward to observe the subconscious reality of the arm (moon: the body dreams, and the body is energy), giving credence to the saying that "the moon will comfort those who gaze upon her." Does this allow us to apply the rules of quantum theory, which states that "the greater the amount of 'watching,' the greater the observer's influence on what actually takes place"?[9] Does "the observer affecting the observed reality" apply to consciousness? Notable physicists such as David Bohm and Roger Penrose and renowned neuroscientist Karl Pribram came to believe so, and coined the term "quantum mind." We will see example after example of the self-conscious mind looking into the subconscious mind and affecting the observed reality.

Here is another case. A man came to see me because he had taken his accounting exams nine times and failed. He didn't want to give up.

Exercise 22

· · · · · · · · · · ·

Mirror Left and Right

Close your eyes. Breathe out slowly three times, counting from three to one. See the one tall, clear, and bright.

In a mirror to your left, see the image of your failure.

Breathe out. Lift your index finger to the sun, fill it with light, bring it down to the mirror, and cut the image in two. Sweep the two parts of the image out of the mirror to the left.

Breathe out. Bring the mirror to your right. See yourself in the mirror holding up your diploma with your grade written in large letters or numbers.

I see 80.

Breathe out, knowing that you can trust your own eyes.

Open your eyes, seeing this grade with open eyes.

· · · · · · · · · · ·

This young man took the exam and got exactly the grade he had seen in his imagery. He achieved his lifelong dream of becoming an accountant by observing his dreaming. Seeing the grade, his anxiety was assuaged, and he was able to do what his dreaming had always told him he could do.

Looking into the dreaming dissolves pain and clears situations that cannot be cleared by reasoning. A young man came to see me after 9/11. His friend had called him from one of the towers and said, "I'm going to die; I love you." Since his friend's death, he hadn't been able to sleep, or eat, or look at his pregnant wife.

Exercise 23

· · · · · · · · · · ·

Sweep to the Left

Close your eyes. Breathe out slowly three times, counting from three to one. See the one tall, clear, and bright.

What is the image you see (when thinking of your friend's death)?

I see the tower collapsing.

Breathe out. Sweep the image off to the left.

Breathe out. What do you see now?

I see my pregnant wife.

Breathe out. See her belly growing, and growing. See her giving birth.

Breathe out. Catch the baby in your two hands as it's coming out of its mother's womb.

Breathe out. Look at your baby, smile, and see your baby smile back.

Breathe out. Open your eyes.

· · · · · · · · · · ·

This young man went home, slept, ate, and was able to be present with his wife again. A few seconds of pause were enough to restore the flow of imagery that had been arrested by his trauma.

All life situations—whether physical, emotional, or mental—can be improved by this switch toward dreaming. You will not always conquer all difficulties, but you will transform pain and sadness.

If you think I'm the lone voice in the desert calling you back to your dreaming, you are wrong. To retrace old truths that we may have forgotten, let's look at two versions of the tarot, an ancient and a modern deck. We'll concentrate on two Major Arcana cards, the Empress and the Emperor. In the Rider-Waite deck, which was published in 1910, at the tail end of the Victorian era, the Emperor sits on a throne, facing forward, wearing armor. He is framed by a wilderness of desert and rock. His Empress sits on cushions, surrounded by nature and water, looking vaguely out into space. They seem miles apart. He evokes patriarchy, the male power that imposes its law by force. She's endlessly fruitful and sweet but doesn't engage him. He clearly never consults her. Now here they are in one of the oldest known decks, the Marseilles Tarot, first published in the fifteenth century.* This is a totally different Emperor. Relaxed, his posture is nonchalant, his legs are crossed, he's resting against his curved throne, supported by his lady's shield adorned with a golden eagle. He looks adoringly at his Empress, who looks back at him. He's clearly the Empress's faithful knight, awaiting his lady's wishes. "What does a woman want?" asks the old witch in the Arthurian tale of "The Wedding of Sir Gawain and Dame Ragnelle." Not beauty, not love, not children. "We desire most from men / From men both rich and poor /

---

*Use the Camoin-Jodorowsky restored Marseilles Tarot.

To have sovereignty without lies./ For where we have sovereignty, all is ours." Woman wants Sovereignty! And is she queenly! She holds the scepter in her left hand and her shield in the crook of her right elbow. She is the true power to which he defers. Who is he? The self-conscious mind, taking his orders from his queen, the subconscious mind who, basking in the glow of his attention, becomes ever more fruitful and multiplies, as is commanded in Genesis.[10]

What has happened to us that we have forgotten? As illustrated by the Emperor of the Rider-Waite Tarot, the self-conscious mind, causal, rational, and linear, has unmoored itself from the subconscious mind, from the source of playful creativity, and the result is a wilderness of desert and rock. We are no longer allowing ourselves time for jouissance, the eros and ecstasy of creativity and interconnection.

The old teachings tell us that to become fully awake and reach illumined consciousness, our first task is to learn to look at the Empress. To do this, we must deliberately disconnect from the bedazzling and often harsh reality of sun consciousness. Instead, we must turn our eyes to the night. I do not mean this metaphorically. I mean to actually switch our eyes and look inward. We're learning to become like the Marseilles Emperor who knows where creativity originates and, like a good gardener, takes his cues from the playful deity of the garden. Similarly, the pharaohs of Egypt, the biblical patriarchs, and the fairy tale kings ritualistically cross their arms to give precedence to and bless the younger son,* the lesser one, the fool, the moon over the sun. To start practicing this brain switch, perform this simple exercise.

Exercise 24
· · · · · · · · · · ·
The Switch Sign

You're lying on your back in bed, eyes closed, relaxing completely. Watch the rush of images going by. Don't try to identify them. But remain conscious as you are falling asleep.

---

*In Genesis, God prefers the younger son Abel to Cain, the elder. Isaac blesses the younger son Jacob instead of Esau. Jacob blesses Joseph's son Ephraim instead of Manasseh. In many fairy tales, it is the youngest son, often called the fool or simpleton, who gets the kingdom and the princess, instead of his older brothers.

Try instead to catch the exact moment when you fall asleep. You will notice a specific physical sign. This could be a twitch of your shoulders, a lengthening of your spine or fingers or toes. Identify this sign so as to remember it next morning.

· · · · · · · · · · ·

The dizzying array of visuals, sounds, and out of body experiences that flood our consciousness make it difficult to remain conscious. Some of you may find this rush of "visionary scenes that pass before us"[11] confusing or even frightening. Our bodies seem to disintegrate into images; float up into the room; dissolve; re-form as buzzing noises, unfettered shapes, or unidentifiable faces. We are entering into the moonlit landscape. We could say that our mental construct of the world is disintegrating, that we are losing control of a reality we have all agreed upon. Few researchers have asked what this disintegration means. But remember that for something new to emerge, something has to die. The dismantling of forms is necessary for creativity to flow. Creativity is never fixed. Sleep brings us disintegration, renewal, and creativity. It is preceded by the little death of forms. Sadly, many people lose consciousness as they cross the veil between the two worlds, forfeiting their ability to remain conscious at all times.

Can we learn to stay conscious while this is happening? Can we look without fear into death, the void created by this shocking dismantling of the order we believe is keeping us sane? If so, we will see the big bang, revelation, the first appearance of a new creation. By staying conscious as we cross over, we are not only stretching the reaches of our consciousness, but we are also speeding up our own creativity. Creativity is like a little child who becomes more playful when she is paid attention to.

The next step, of course, is remaining conscious while dreaming at night. Do this before lying down to sleep: Choose a small familiar object that you use all the time, such as a ring. Hold it in your hands.

Exercise 25
· · · · · · · · · · ·
Lucid Dreaming

Close your eyes. Breathe out slowly three times, counting from three to one. See the one tall, clear, and bright.

Look at your hands holding the object, feel the object, and decide to bring it into your dream tonight.

Breathe out, and blow a zero out of your mouth, and see it becoming a circle of light before you. In this circle, imagine that you see your hands holding the object, and hear yourself saying: "I will awaken in my dream when I see myself holding this object."

· · · · · · · · · · ·

Being awake while dreaming means that you are consciously watching your creativity at play. It also means that you don't need to wait for morning to respond to the necessity of your images. Imagine how much more rapidly you will improve. The Emperor in you, the conscious self, makes immediate responsive choices to the offerings of the empress. The act of choosing within the dream is a feat that seems impossible for most people. Convention tells us that we have no say in how our dreams unfold, that if you see a river overflowing and you are about to drown, you can't do anything about it. It's how the dream goes, after all. Under such pressure from the dream, most of you will wake up. Don't get me wrong: Waking up is good. But not good enough! What if, instead of waking up, you climb a tree or grab the rungs of a ladder going up to the sky? What if you find the power to calm the river? This is called lucid dreaming.

You can learn to do something immediately, directly in the dream. Why is it important to respond to the necessity of the dream, precisely when it happens? You become present and conscious, like a martial arts master, responding in the moment to whatever challenge presents itself. If you can do this in the dream, think how much more quickly you will respond in everyday life. Conscious choosing is what makes us different from all other species. By using it in both our realities, we practice becoming present and conscious at all times. As long as our self-conscious believes it runs the show, while, in fact, our subconscious is in charge of more than 95 percent of all our activities, we remain split and in denial. And we will continue to be enslaved to our belief systems, emotions, and physical embodiment. The interaction of sun and moon, partnering in free choice and at all times, is the only way to become fully conscious.

The light of the moon will be like the light of the sun; the light of the sun shall be sevenfold, the light of seven days.[12]

Understand this to mean that when your two brains, sun and moon, shine equally, when you are, in effect, bilingual, your inner world will be completely rectified (tikun, correction, will have been made to the seven days of creation, making them shine sevenfold). The dialogue between our two languages will effortlessly flow and enrich our understanding of the Adamic consciousness, making possible the exploration and mastery of olam ne'elam. We are not there yet. Now that we have brought our self-conscious awareness into the dreamtime, let us bring dreaming awareness into daytime self-consciousness.

As I've said before, the moon pales when the sun rises triumphant in the sky, and your self-conscious mind floods all memory of dream states. How is the Emperor to manifest the Empress's wishes if he cannot remember them, or if he cannot consult with her during the daytime? Letting the messages from the subconscious shine through the glare of the self-conscious mind requires practice. What makes it difficult is that when the self-conscious mind is active, the eyes focus, but with the dreaming mind they un-focus. Can these two different states coexist? Here's what you do.

Exercise 26
. . . .
Un-focusing the Eyes

Close your eyes. Breathe out slowly three times, counting from three to one. See the one tall, clear, and bright.

Imagine that you are standing on a dune looking out at the ocean. See how the horizon is curved.

Breathe out. See a sailboat appearing on the left of the horizon. Watch it with focused attention as it sails from left to right on the horizon and disappears.

Breathe out. Again, see a sailboat appear on the left of the horizon. Watch it with focused attention as it sails from left to right on the horizon. When it reaches the center of the horizon, un-focus your eyes to encompass the whole horizon. What happens to the sailboat?

Breathe out. Lift your eyes up to the blue sky.

Breathe out. Bring your eyes down to the horizon and to the sailboat. Now can you see both the unfocused view and the focused sailboat?

Breathe out. Open your eyes.

. . . .

Understanding what the eye movements are may help: Focus brings your eyeballs closer together, un-focusing brings them farther apart in a restful, relaxed position within the eye sockets. By letting your eyes relax in your sockets, you develop your peripheral vision, and allow dreaming to rise to consciousness.

The next time you sit with a friend you haven't seen for a while, try it: focus on your friend, then un-focus, paying attention to the images that float up from your dreaming. Now you are seeing your dreaming with open eyes. The images leap and rise to consciousness. They will inform you about your friend. If red pops up, this will tell you that she's in an intense or angry mood; if a man pops up surrounded by pink, this means that she's feeling enamored about someone. Learning to see your DreamField while focusing is an art of the utmost importance. It begins the process of repair—literally **re-pairing** your two brains, bringing the outer and inner reality closer to a peaceful state of oneness. Let's say you meet a potential business partner. Of course you're going to focus on their appearance, manners, and presentation. But what if your dreaming shows you a man walking away with a bulging suitcase, an image that is making you feel anxious? Which mind are you going to believe, the self-conscious mind that likes the looks and presentation of this man, or the dream mind telling you to be aware that this man might steal all your information?

Here is where most people opt out. The question is always: How can I tell whether this is true imagery coming from my core, or a fantasy I've created out of my own needs and complexes? Fantasy is an interesting phenomenon. As mentioned before,* the self-conscious mind uses and twists the language of the imagination to fit its chosen scenario.

---

*See chapter 3.

Scenarios can arise out of an old complex, a blocked emotional memory that colors your reality (all people wearing black suits are thieves, or men with tans are sure to outshine me); or out of wish fulfillment, such as longing to be loved or admired; or from unexamined belief systems (women aren't as able as men). In other words, you must clear the garbage on the ocean. This is a lengthy process. So what do you do in the meantime?

Here are three approaches: the first, of course, is asking the question. You can do that directly by turning inward, breathing out three times, and asking your question directly of your subconscious, "Is this the partner I need?" Then pay attention to the images that emerge. You can also ask your night dreams.

The second is using Saphire Imagery, the jolt method.

Exercise 27
. . . .
The Angel of Justice

Close your eyes. Breathe out slowly three times, counting from three to one. See the one tall, clear, and bright.

Imagine that you are in your meadow. Look up at the blue sky. Let your eyes wander to the deepest blue in the sky. Rest your eyes on the deepest blue and call on the Angel of Justice to come and answer your question. Call your question out loud in the meadow.

Breathe out. See the sky opening and the Angel of Justice coming down toward you. Watch carefully what the Angel does.

Breathe out. When you have an answer, thank the Angel and watch as the Angel returns to the sky and disappears into the deep blue light.

Breathe out. Open your eyes.
. . . .

The angel of Justice comes down. He's holding a thick stick. He taps me hard on the head. I understand that he's saying: "No!"

Caution: Do not do this exercise if you're not willing to follow the Angel's advice. The Angel is a messenger from your soul. Only ask when you're ready to surrender to your inner truth.
. . . .

The third is verification.

Verification is a practice that exists in time. It is your most trusty tool. No other practice will serve you as well to begin distinguishing between the leap of true imagination and fantasy. While the practice is an ongoing effort, and it will take time before you are convinced that you can trust your images, there is no shortcut to finding out. It is well worth your effort to check whenever you can, whether your inner images are reflecting the truth of what is happening. It should be easy to elicit from your friend whether she's angry or sweet on someone, thus confirming that your images reflected the truth. You can immediately verify. But what about the possible business partner? There's no way to know, except to keep close tabs on what transpires. You will have to wait and watch.

To begin the process of verification, you need your DreamBook. It is in your DreamBook that you write and date these daytime visions of your DreamField. Verification comes when the vision is realized in daily reality. If this happens, go back to your DreamBook, find where you wrote down your vision, or what the voice you heard said. Verification could come today, tomorrow, in three months, or in five years' time. Take a red pen and mark the box yes, or write down exactly what in your vision came true. If you verify often enough, you'll start recognizing the signs of a true vision or voice. In Elijah's experience, the voice has a specific quality. You'll recognize it because it is very simple, quiet, and straightforward, what the Bible calls a "still, small voice."[13] For instance, you hear "turn right." I heard this once on a main thoroughfare in Jerusalem, and I turned right. A moment later a huge explosion rocked the street I'd just left, killing eighty-five people, and injuring many more. Or more happily, you meet someone and the colors in the room brighten up. Since the DreamField speaks in body language, any change in the senses is to be noted. Don't forget to write this down in your DreamBook. Messages can manifest through one or all five of the senses. Your verification will come when that person becomes a close friend.

Your practice is to note and write, without fail, the visions and words that arise in you. When verification has proven true again and again, you will learn to trust those messages from your DreamField. You will begin to trust the creative answers the Empress offers, and you will realize that she always speaks the truth. This intimate knowledge is an inestimable gift that may save your life—as it did mine—or that may save you from costly errors. Trusting that your subconscious is actively participating in your well-being is of immense benefit to you. That it will, as needed, let you know, brings freedom from anxiety. You can build on this assurance and allow your soul to begin guiding you.

Verification also serves to remind you of the thrust of creativity. For instance, planting an oak seed means that, barring unforeseen circumstances, it will grow into an oak tree. Verification is really about proving to yourself that you can trust the seed of creativity—whatever that seed is, good or bad—to unfold as planned. Your DreamField, being the blueprint, is eminently suited to produce for your information all the different moments of the seed's unfolding, right up to its grand finale. That is why so many people appear to *predict* the future. It is already here, enfolded in the seed. As your Understanding (Binah) of what you are seeing unfolds, you are filled with Knowledge (Da'at), just as Adam *knows* Eve, who, as her name tells us, is mother of all living creations. Adam, you might have guessed, is the self-conscious seed of longing hovering over Eve, the subconscious, who was created from his other side (*tsela* means "side" as well as "rib") as he was dreaming. His hovering, his looking, elicits her creativity, and she becomes fruitful and multiplies. Remember that if the seed elicited is bad (fear, rage, resentment, envy, and depression can spawn bad seeds and their attendant ills; creativity doesn't discriminate) it will unfold into badness unless you respond to its necessity. This will correct the trajectory, and the corrected seed will grow into goodness.

Exercise 28
. . . .
Telescoping Tree

Close your eyes. Breathe out slowly three times, counting from three to one. See the one tall, clear, and bright.

Imagine that you have walked deep into the countryside and come upon a tree that impresses and attracts you. Describe it to yourself.

Breathe out. Come close to the tree and put your arms around its trunk. As you hug the tree, put your left ear against the trunk of the tree, listening to the life of the tree.

Breathe out. Enter into the tree, and become one with the tree. You are the trunk, the roots, the branches, and the leaves. Try to feel all the parts of the tree at the same time.

Breathe out. Telescope very fast into yourself: leaves into branches, branches into the trunk, the trunk into the roots, the roots into themselves, and finally, become the original seed in the ground.

Breathe out. All of your consciousness is in the seed. You are the seed in the ground, listening to the murmur of your own life. What is it telling you?

Breathe out. Sense and see the seed very rapidly unfold roots, trunk, branches, and leaves.

Breathe out. You are the full-grown tree, each and every part of you imbued with the message from the seed.

Breathe out. Step out of the tree. Take a look at yourself. How do you look now?

Breathe out. Turn and look at the tree. How does the tree look now?

Breathe out. If you're pleased with what you see, thank your tree, knowing that you can return to it at any time. Walk away in your newfound body, imbued and invigorated by the life message you heard at the core of the seed.

(Breathe out. If the tree is not looking good to you, then go to the little brook nearby, fill your jug with water, and return to water your tree.

Breathe out. Step back to look at your tree now. If needed, continue watering until you're satisfied. You can also water yourself if you don't like the way you look.

Breathe out. Walk away in your newfound body, imbued and invigorated by the life message you heard at the core of the seed.)

Breathe out. Open your eyes

· · · · · · · · · · ·

What does the switch of the Emperor toward the Empress require? Remember what woman wants? Sovereignty. What quality does that require of the Emperor? The biblical text tells us that "God blessed the seventh day and hallowed it, because on it God abstained from all

His work which God created ***to make.***"[14]* God stopped creating. He removed Himself so that we, like Him, could start to make, to hover over the chaos and watch creation emerging. It is this quality of the lover, humble before his lady, that God models for us. Out of selfless love does the lover bow and watch his lady's flowering and responds with lyrical song and psalms of love.

Surrender means a complete switch from emotion to devotion. This is what becoming a Kabbalist means. The Kabbalist makes room to receive (Kabbalah means "receiving") the offerings of a more organic, lively force whose origins lie hidden beyond the subconscious. Would you not want to surrender your own ego and power, knowing that by holding back and watching, you spark the Empress's creativity, and thus serve a greater truth? This is why I have taken a detour to talk to you about verification. You will surrender more easily if you can see again and again that what the Empress shows you is fresher, truer, and more completely consistent with the laws of the universe. You will be healthier, safer, better advised, and more confident if you can trust her creative truth and knowing. Kabbalah says that creation happens at every moment. Thus, at every moment you must be ready to contemplate your inner world and learn from her what your response to life should be.

The dialogue between the two brains quickens the DreamField. As you watch, surrender to what you see, and behave accordingly, it will vibrate at higher and higher rates. When the two brains effortlessly communicate, when sun and moon are at parity, creativity flows like a great river "to water the Garden."[15]

In the next chapter we will see creativity at work.

---

*The Malbim, Ukrainian rabbi (1809–1879) sees "to make" as the object of the verb "created."

5

Signs of Transformation

The Grammar of the Imagination

For in her [wisdom] there is a spirit that is intelligent,
holy, unique, manifold, unpolluted, distinct, invulnerable,
loving the good, dynamic, irresistible, beneficent, humane,
steadfast, sure, free from anxiety, all-powerful, overseeing
all, and penetrating through all spirits.

WISDOM OF SOLOMON 7:22–24

Paul Klee once famously said, "A line is a dot that went for a walk."* In an empty universe, why doesn't the dot stay put? Where does it think it is going? Is it moving for movement's sake? Or is it moving simply because movement is in its nature? Creation means movement. The big bang, the explosive appearance of something out of nothing, expands from the germinal dot to lines. Imagine the dot as the first image. If "image is a living structure,"[1] the explosive movement into millions of lines begins the structure's formation. But where do the lines stop? Is saying to the sea, "This far you may come and no farther"[2] God's prerogative? Or are we also equipped to say to a gen-

---

*Paul Klee (1879–1940) was an artist whose works spanned multiple movements. This quote refers to allowing a new form to appear.

erative movement: stop? The conscious mind can say it and make the movement stop by force. But willpower does not unfold organically, and its resulting effects can only be awkward and troubling. Here's an example of organic unfolding. The meeting of ovum and sperm, our personal big bang, sets the initial dot-cell moving outward in many specific directions, until movement stops at what we have learned to recognize as a fully formed fetus, with its components of bones, toes, fingers, and openings. How does the dot-line-form know when to stop? This is where mystery says, this far and no farther. Ki tov, this is good. Then, once set, like the sea within its boundaries, the form (*yetser*) grows and swells and diminishes, until it dissolves and disappears, allowing for a new form to appear. Tov m'od, this is very good. Can we consciously set those boundaries? No. But our body knows how it's done. The dot-line-form is called yetser in Hebrew, which also means the "imagination." And since imagination (our Empress), is our body language, imagination can show us. We don't have to use will. We only have to look and be led. True imagination, creativity, is wisdom. It has the ingrown wisdom to know where to stop.

Imagination will show us when, like the fetus, our creation has reached its living structure and, like the fetus, is ready to manifest in daily reality. As we have said before, imagination is not fantasy.* You can tell that imagination is true when it moves of its own inner volition, knowing exactly how to unfold and surprising us mightily in the process. Its revelations expose us to an internal balance and a unique beauty that no logical mind could devise.

Who then is the one who, being her own creator, knows the beginning and the end of her own creation? And who then is he, the observer?

She is a raconteur of great force and power. She spins many tales, weaving back and forth different story strands, and he, the listener, wonders when the full picture will emerge. Without her audience she cannot manifest. He is the warp to her weft (the two basic components of weaving). She sings to his moods, his questions, his hopes and dreams.

---

*See chapters 3 and 4.

Then suddenly, pulling together all the strands, she ties a beautiful knot, bows to her marveling audience and—poof!—disappears.

We will not pierce her mystery, but we can learn the grammar of her inventions. Together we will discover the signs that indicate the difference between the fabrications of fantasy spewed up by left brain willfulness and true imagination at work. We will see that she shows her wisdom in ways that you could not begin to fantasize about. True imagination surprises, amazes, enchants, and delivers to us solutions we couldn't have thought up in a million years.

✳

The secret to watching true imagination at work is at first knowing how to remain awake at the borders of sleep. How can you stay awake if you are falling asleep? This is an impossible contradiction. We all know that sleep erases awareness. Yet as we have seen, if you open up to the possibility that duality (either-or) is not the only reality, that paradox (both states exist simultaneously) can also prevail, you may see your whole brain lighting up: the observer in you able to transpierce the night veil, the storyteller in you deft in breaking through the daytime *éblouissement*, its dazzlement.

Practice makes one great. In chapter 3, you learned how to remain awake as you are falling asleep, and how to be awake and actively responding in your night dreams. You also learned to observe the images of the subconscious mind at play during waking awareness. But we need to practice.

Like Zen or Tibetan monks, we sit. But we don't sit on a cushion (though you can do that too, if sitting in a lotus posture is more comfortable for you). Generally, we advise the beginner student to sit on a straight-backed chair, like the pharaohs of old, with their legs and arms uncrossed. The seated position, void of slack, will keep you awake. Then, when you close your eyes, it will be harder to fall asleep. You can imagine that, like the young Tibetan monks in training, you have a lit candle on your head. If you doze even a second, the candle will drip hot wax on your head and wake you up. We won't do that to you. But you get the point: Stay alert as you sink into the dream state, and dream awake.

• • •

There are three techniques, three levels of tapping into the subconscious. They all require rêverie,* a state that is easily entered into by the simple method of breathing out three times slowly, seeing the numbers from three to one.

Visualization asks you to follow a simple prescribed script. It's best used to remind the physical body how to return to homeostasis.

Saphire exercises† are short inductions that create the jolt, dislodging you from the mental and plunging you into the subconscious. They are best used to induce transformation and are your most trusted tool for change and inner growth.

Waking Dream (a paradox, a contradiction in terms) is an exploration of your DreamField. It is the long form of an exercise, but without script or jolt, and without a specific goal. To move through your inner landscape, you can start in a meadow; follow where your dog leads you; or enter into the image of a dream you want to explore.

We will use the long form of the waking dream to inquire into the particularities of true imagination.

Exercise 29
. . . .
A Waking Dream

Close your eyes. Breathe out slowly three times, counting from three to one. See the one tall, clear, and bright.

Imagine that you are in a meadow.

Start by describing to yourself, silently or out loud, what you are seeing.

I am standing in my meadow. The sky is very blue. White birds fly in a V-formation toward the right. I am suddenly feeling quite hopeful.

. . . .

Doing this with a guide is helpful, and even necessary at first. Verbalize what you are seeing. The guide will interact with you by asking

---

*See chapter 3.
†See chapter 3.

you to be more precise and focused about what you see and experience:

> How many birds are there?
>
> **I'm not sure.**
>
> Look again.
>
> **That's strange; I now see only three, but very clearly!**
>
> Are the birds trying to show you something?
>
> **Yes. I see a golden city on a hill in the distance.**
>
> Do you want to go there?
>
> **A man is blocking my way.**
>
> What kind of a man?
>
> **He's very, very tall. I hardly reach up to his ankle.**
>
> How is he dressed?
>
> **All in white.**
>
> What do you feel about him?
>
> **I want him to lift me up . . . he does . . . he shows me the city.**
>
> What kind of a city is it?
>
> **It looks celestial, all golden and shimmering. He tells me I cannot go there now, but he'll put me on the path to reach it.**
>
> What kind of a path is this?
>
> **It's a dirt path, spiraling upward. He tells me it's going to take my whole life to reach the city.**
>
> Ask his name.
>
> **He says his name is Upright.**
>
> So thank Upright for showing you the way.
>
> **He is dissolving now and disappearing.**
>
> Watch until he's completely disappeared. Now feel your feet on the path. Start walking.
>
> Breathe out slowly. Open your eyes, seeing yourself on the path with open eyes.

· · · · · · · · · · ·

The guide's questions are a way of helping you to home in on your images. What are you seeing? What are you feeling? What do you see now? Where are you going, left, right, straight ahead, up, or down? How is the landscape? What are the colors? Describe what is happening. The guide's voice keeps you present in your experience. The questions help you to become more alert, more fiercely awake throughout the dream state. They sharpen your observation skills. Your language improves as you search for the right words to describe what you are seeing and experiencing. In the process, your observing self—the left brain— becomes more refined, more subtle, and more flexible as it plies its trade, words and sentences in describing the creative movements of your imagination—the right brain at work.

What is the dream state? It has all the trappings of our daily world, the six directions, up-down, left-right, forward-back; with colors ranging through all the shades and nuances of the seven rainbow colors; the four elements of Earth, Water, Fire, and Air exist there; every landscape feature from sky, earth, ocean, land, mountain, valley, rock, tree, grass reside there. It knows day and night, wind, rain, sunshine, heat, cold and seasons. It has cabins, barns, houses, buildings, palaces, cities that are furnished like ours. And it is inhabited by animals, aquatic, mammalian, avian, and, of course, human.

But it also has strange hybrid beings with tails or wings, a mix of animal and human, or human and angelic. Angelic beings appear and take central stage. We will return to those later.

Dreaming reveals a world of desires, ranging from the basest to the most sublime; of reactions such as fear and anger, or blocked emotions, sadness, guilt, envy, self-hate; of feelings such as love, compassion, peace, joy, greatly intensified by sudden revelations and transformations.

What it doesn't have is concreteness, the solidity of our daily world. It lacks causality, the linearity of time, the obviousness of materiality. We could be tempted to say that it doesn't actually exist, but that would mean losing out on the dream world's ravishing beauty and its fluidity of movement. Our daily world, while also captivating us by the beauty of its nature and its fauna, constantly confronts us with obstacles, the labor of slogging through time and its related constraints, the heart-break of dealing with other humans and animals, and the daily rounds of repetitive actions we must engage in simply to survive.

What is the dream state about? Freedom.

• • •

The dream state is unhampered by the constraints of time and space. It uses the body as the ground from which to elevate from materiality into movement and energy. Like a stepping-stone, the body's language of physical, emotional, and mental movements draws the bridge between this world and the dream world.* When channeled by practice, the body's desires, reactions, and emotions become the fuel that ignites your journey out of the material body and into the energy body and its world. The dream state is made of chromatic light forms, appearing and disappearing faster than you can blink. Becoming a dreamer means you are learning to hold these light forms steady. You are weaving for yourself a *palace of light*. With practice you'll become *light solid*, a contradiction in terms but true nevertheless. This will enliven the Earth part in you, the homer (matter) of your body, to vibrate to higher frequencies. Your Earth will become the interface between the real world and the light world.

✳

Sit up straight, with your arms and legs uncrossed. Close your eyes. Breathe out slowly three times, counting from three to one, seeing the numbers. See the one tall, clear, and bright. Imagine that you are in a rose garden, caressing a rose petal.

> **I can't see anything.**
> Can you feel something?
> **Some tingling in the fingertips, but I can't see.**
> That's all right. What does the tingling in your fingers tell you?

For most of us it goes without saying that all the senses are involved in the work of the imagination. That is why this noun constructed with the word image (form or yetser in the Hebrew) doesn't make us pause. But for a blind person, the world is constructed through touch, hearing, taste, or scent. A massage therapist doesn't necessarily read the body with her eyes but more commonly through the sensations she receives through her fingertips. These people do not see with their sight

---

*See chapter 1.

sense, but they do *see*. They are able to reconstruct the form using their other senses.

If you're not seeing, but only sensing, just continue sensing and describe how that sensation in-**form**-s you. With practice, every sense can be experienced using another sense, as we are told in Exodus: "And the people *saw* the voices."[3] This is called synesthesia.

One student patiently endured two years of darkness. She felt but she didn't see. Without warning, during an exercise, suddenly revelation came. A world fully formed, baroque to the extreme and very beautiful, appeared to her. We must never push the imagination, but simply look for other ways in. Violence shatters the mirror. But patient perseverance, gentle attentiveness are what she, our faithful storyteller, responds to. Think of fishing, and just wait attentively. If you cannot see, don't despair. Just trust your other senses.

To help you unblock your inner seeing, try this.

Exercise 30
. . . .
A Chair, a Throne

Close your eyes. Breathe out slowly three times, counting from three to one. See the one tall, clear, and bright.

Imagine a chair. Describe it. What shape is it? What material, what color?

Breathe out. Sit on the chair. Is it comfortable? What are you looking at when sitting on the chair?

Breathe out. Now imagine a throne. Describe it. What shape is it? What material, what color?

Breathe out. Sit on the throne. Is it comfortable? What do you see while sitting on the throne?

Breathe out. Open your eyes.
. . . .

A chair is a simple object, easy to visualize. There's no fancy imagination involved. You'll be surprised at how easy it is. The transition from chair to throne is just a breath away, and for most of you, the movement from imitation (the chair) to imagination (the throne) will be effortless.

But for others, inner seeing presents a curious challenge: I can't see, but I can imagine. They are, in fact, seeing, but they are creating a mental block for themselves, stretching a veil across their inner world to protect themselves from what they fear may be too devastating a revelation. Apprehension and fear of what they'll see can dull sensations and dim the colors of the inner world, turning it into a pale imitation of the daily world. Remember that emotional power and its attendant hormonal release are the boost that is needed to light up the inner world. Be patient with yourself, even if you feel that you are only imagining. Don't give up. Let yourself be tricked into the plunge by trying these exercises.

When I say being tricked, I mean just that. We have talked about the need for a jolt to ignite creativity. The jolt sweeps away our habitual reactions—fear, apprehension, sadness, and guilt—that darken our inner landscape, and suddenly we are in the land of pure color. For several months, one conscientious student saw only in black and white. Color is indicative of emotion and feeling. Seeing only in black and white meant: I'm afraid of feeling! Indeed, he stayed very much in his head. One day in class, he fainted. On being revived, he told us he had "suddenly seen in full Technicolor!" In other words, he was tricked into his emotional body and passed out from the shock. This, of course, is quite an extreme reaction, and I've only seen it happen once, so don't worry.

Unexpected and sudden transformations in the images are the sign that true imagination is at work. We are going to examine different ways that image shows transformation. In the following exercise, the transformations mainly occur in the color field. We have seen color transformation as you climb the ladder of night dreams.* In an exercise, color transformation is telling you something important.

Exercise 31
· · · · · · · · · · ·
The Waterfall (Formal)

Close your eyes. Breathe out slowly three times, counting from three to one. See the one tall, clear, and bright.

Imagine that you are walking in the mountains on a warm

---

*See chapter 2.

summer day. You hear the sound of water and follow it. Come to a medium-size waterfall.

Breathe out. Decide to drop your clothes and shoes. Wade through the pool of water at the foot of the waterfall.

Breathe out. Turn your back to the waterfall. Let the water run down your back. Feel its weight, its rhythm, the pinpricks of each water drop opening up the pores of your skin.

Breathe out. Turn to face the waterfall. Don't step in yet. Let the water pour down the front of your body. See the brilliant sheet of water. Feel its weight, its rhythm, the pinpricks of each water drop opening up the pores of your skin.

Breathe out. Step fully under the waterfall. Feel enveloped by the water, feel its weight, its rhythm, the pinpricks of each water drop opening up the pores of your skin.

Breathe out. The waterfall enters your body through your open pores and flows through you, clearing and cleaning your inside body. What do you look like now?

Breathe out. Continue seeing this until your body becomes entirely translucent.

Breathe out. Step away from the waterfall. The sun shines through your body, creating rainbow light. Does any color remain in your body? Where?

Breathe out. Wade back to the embankment. Stretch in the sunlight until you are dry.

Breathe out. See that your old clothes are gone. New clothes are there for you.

Breathe out. Put them on. What do your new clothes look like, in texture, style, and color?

Breathe out. If you're satisfied with your clothes, walk away feeling refreshed and renewed.

· · · · · · · · · · ·

While the exercise is obviously meant as a cleansing, the ease with which the body becomes translucent, the colors that remain in the body, the colors of the clothes all tell us whether transformation has occurred.

My pants are linen, but they are black. I don't like that.
So dip them into the clear waters to wash out the black, then lift them up to the sun to dry.

What color are your pants now?
They're a beautiful vibrant green.
What color is your hair, darker, lighter or the same?
Much blonder and longer.
And the expression on your face?
Serene and happy. I look much younger.

. . . .

The black color of the pants indicates some difficulty in the pelvic region or in the legs. We don't know if the difficulty is physical or emotional. In a sense it doesn't matter. It is the privilege of the dreamer to keep that information private. We don't need to know. What counts is that transformation has occurred, with the color moving from dark to vibrant green. Whatever the dreamer's difficulty, you can be sure that it has been alleviated, because the vibrant green, so fertile and alive, is telling you so.

Here color is not the only sign of transformation. What is the imagination trying to tell you when it shows you that your hair has gotten longer? Hair indicates your level of vital strength, just as it did for the biblical hero Samson. The spontaneous growth of hair is telling you that a transformation toward more vitality has occurred. Did you willfully make this happen? It happened spontaneously. That is what you need to pay attention to. Remember that the body is always seeking to find balance and homeostasis. Wherever there is an unexpected spontaneous movement toward balance and homeostasis, or what the Bible calls ki tov, the good, you can be sure that true imagination has manifested. What has blondness to do with the good? The inside world is not interested in whether you are a white, blond person, or brown with black hair—it is only interested in darkness and light. As you practice looking inward, colors will start vibrating at higher and higher frequencies, and getting clearer and brighter, as we saw in chapter 2 with the ladder of dreaming, In the inside language, as the subconscious field gets attended to, the colors move from dark to light (from black—which is the absence of color—red, orange, yellow, green, indigo, blue, purple, to white—which is all colors combined in the highest vibration).

Are we actually talking of physical vitality? We have left the realm of the physical body to enter the world of the energy body. This energy world is a mirror image of our material world. It shows us a world reversed where instead of working from the bottom up (matter), it works from the top down (energy). We are used to the material world impressing its views and habits on the energy world; here it is the energy world that impresses its images and experiences onto the physical world. Will the impression last? Will you stay serene and happy if you find out that your partner has fallen in love with someone else? If you persist in believing that only the material world is real, you will have a hard time convincing your partner to return. But what if you dream yourself as beautiful, serene, and welcoming? The likelihood is that the partner will respond to your dreaming. Keep these generative images in mind; they are the impetus to your future. Eventually your belief in pain and negativity won't entice you quite as much as your images. Your images will become the driving force behind your actions. You will no longer be enslaved to cause and effect. Will this change your future? We will address manifestation using images, in the next chapter.

What does the expression on the face, showing newfound serenity, happiness, and youthfulness mean? Passing through the veil lands you in an emotional world. Whereas in the material world a stone falling from a building can crush you, in the imaginal world a finger of light will shatter the stone. This dream energy can be used by the man whose legs have been crushed by the falling stone. Through visualizing his healing and his walking, he ends up on the Olympic podium. What makes the dream world move is not cause and effect, but pure raw emotion and feeling, the joy of conquering the inner darkness (the stone that crushes you), and the exhilaration of achieving your goal. Does doing this in the imagination have an effect on the stone falling in the material world? We cannot answer this question yet. But remember that your body *knows*. It will move before even your mind has registered that a stone is falling, and is on its way to crushing you. You will turn aside, unharmed, as the stone crashes into the pavement.

Always note the emotional content of your dreaming: If your expression is serene and happy, if you look younger, you can trust that transformation has occurred. Keep seeing these images of transformation, and your everyday world will begin to conform to them.

• • •

What of growing or shrinking? Let's look at a few responses to the following exercise.

Exercise 32
Breathing with the Tree (Formal)

Close your eyes. Breathe out slowly three times, counting from three to one. See the one tall, clear, and bright.

Imagine that you are walking through a great orchard. There are many different types of trees. Find a tree that really attracts you. Look at it carefully, and describe the tree to yourself.

Breathe out. Walk up to the tree. Sit under the tree, with your back against the tree trunk, and your knees bent. Sink your toes into the rich soil, and feel them becoming long roots. Sink your fingers into the soil, and feel them becoming long roots.

Breathe out slowly. See your breath as a light smoke. With the smoke, breathe out all that tires you, all that obscures you, and all that upsets you. See the light smoke rising up into the canopy of the tree and being absorbed by the leaves of the tree.

See yourself breathing in the oxygen liberated by the leaves of the tree.

See this great ring of breath that links you with your tree.

As you continue breathing with your tree, sense and see the sap rising up the roots through the trunk of the tree and through your spine to the canopy of the tree. See its color.

Continue breathing with your tree until you feel replenished.

Breathe out, lift up your toes and fingers, and step away from your tree. Look at your tree now. What, if anything, has changed? Is the tree taller, smaller, or the same size? Is the shape of the canopy the same or different? Are the leaves the same green, brighter, darker, or a different color?

Breathe out. What do you look like now?

• • • • • • • • • • •

I am very tall, but the tree has shrunk!
How do you feel about the tree shrinking?
I'm afraid I've hurt it.
So go to the little river nearby. Fill your watering can, and bring it back to the tree. Water the tree.

The tree is growing again. Now it's taller than me. That's much better.

. . . .

Here's another response:

The tree is huge, with a much larger canopy, and I'm as tall as the tree! I'm dressed in shimmering white, and the leaves of the tree are shining.

. . . .

Still another:

When I step away from the tree I'm all hunched up and covered in bark and leaves, and the tree is much smaller. It has a hole in its trunk where I was leaning.

How do you feel about being covered in bark?

I like it, but I'm sad that the tree has a hole.

So go to the little river nearby. Fill your watering can, and bring it back to the tree. Water the tree, and water yourself.

The hole in the tree fills up again, and I lose the bark and leaves. The canopy gets larger, and the leaves become shinier. I'm wearing a green gown of the same color, and I too am taller.

. . . .

The exercise has many purposes, the most important being for you to feel nurtured and filled up with oxygen. But for our actual purpose, we note that tall-short is another way the imaginal language communicates.

In the first and third responses, changes in size (tall-short: via the shrunken tree and very tall dreamer) show us that there is a power issue. The first dreamer wants to take all the power for himself. The third dreamer cannot let go of the dependency. But remember that the image is both a diagnosis and a cure. The diagnosis is not fixed. It's already showing the way toward the cure. The dreamer being gently prodded toward a correction by responding to the necessity of the image, the imaginal language readjusts toward the good. The trees get taller and have shinier leaves. The dreamer loves to see his tree get taller, or he gets as tall as his tree and wears more vibrant colors. Having seen and experienced these images is powerful. The dreamers can anchor themselves in the invigorating images they've experienced. The cure is dynamic and builds toward a new future.

As for the second dreamer, the image of him and his tree getting taller together shows us that the meeting has sparked an emotional exhilaration. We see this also in the shimmering colors.

Past and future are not directions in time or space, but into the emotional world of memories and hopes.

Exercise 33
. . . .
Emotional Attractors of Time

Close your eyes. Breathe out slowly three times, counting from three to one. See the one tall, clear, and bright.

Imagine that you are in your meadow. Look around; what attracts you? Go toward what attracts you. In what direction are you going? To your left, to your right, straight ahead?

Breathe out. Push on toward where you're going. What do you find?

I'm going toward the left. I'm entering some woods. The trees get denser as I go deeper into the woods. It's also getting darker. I come to an opening where there is a little old house. I suddenly feel very frightened. I'm sure a ghost lives there; it has the face of my mother.

Has the ghost come out?

Yes, it's a very gray mass of twirling fog. It's moving toward me!

Pull a black bag out of your pocket, and catch the twirling fog in the bag. Pull the drawstring closed, and make a knot. Quickly reverse your steps back to the meadow. Throw the black bag as far as you can to the right.

It explodes. There's something on the ground.

Do you want to go see?

Yes, it's a photo album. I see many pictures of my mother in happy times. It makes me smile.

. . . .

Since nearly 90 percent of humans are right-handed, we are the majority moving into the world using our right hands. This is probably why our emotional world reads right as the future, left as the past. The Italian language calls the left hand *la sinistra,* a reminder that when we are called back into the past, it is generally to deal with unlucky or unfinished business. As we see here, when the abandoned parts of our past are thrown into the future, they *right* themselves.

✳

As we are seeing in example after example, the imagination is consistently faithful to the emotional truth. It shows us what is not right, and then, if we respond to the necessity of the images that are revealed, it will move out of what is not right for us, toward what is good for us, showing that to us, so that we can experience it fully, and never forget it.

Exercise 34
The Desert Turns Green

Close your eyes. Breathe out slowly three times, counting from three to one. See the one tall, clear, and bright.

Imagine that you are alone in a dry, rocky desert, running from a menacing storm forming on the horizon.

Breathe out. Stop running. Lift your right arm up to the sun. Feel it elongating. Feel your hand turning warm, then turning to light. Catch a ray of light, and fashion it into a bow.

Breathe out. Catch another ray of light to make a golden arrow.

Breathe out. When the storm is close, shoot your golden arrow into the eye of the storm.

Breathe out. See what happens to the land when the clouds burst open, and refreshing rains wash the dry earth.

The desert turns green. Wildflowers bloom everywhere. The land is a carpet of rainbow colors. I am no longer afraid. I am amazed by the explosive beauty.

Breathe out. Open your eyes.

Have you seen Kurosawa's magical film, *Dreams*? At one moment the orchard is barren, its branches covered in snow. Then with an emotional intensity totally unexpected and shocking, the trees burst into full bloom, their pink and white blossoms filling our field of vision and our hearts with joyful surprise. So it is with the imagination, the sudden turning over, the creative upset that transforms us and our situation.

So it is also when the imaginal world reveals to us other worldly creatures, as happened to the dreamer-diviner Balaam, when the Lord opened Balaam's eyes. "And he saw the angel of the Lord standing in the way, and his sword drawn in his hand. And he bowed down his head and fell flat on his face."[4] Are angels real? Do they truly exist, or are they just creatures of our imagination? Does the imagination exist independently, as a real world in and of itself? You will have to decide that for yourself.

All you are asked to do at this point is to give credence to this other world and allow it to take precedence over your daily reality. Switching allegiances is what the tarot card of the Hanged Man is showing you: Turn over! Live from your imaginal reality instead of being caught in the sludge of the material world. The tarot is telling you that learning to trust your imagination is part of your journey toward enlightenment.

If colors clarify; if shapes elongate; if landscapes turn green and fecund; if frightful scenes resolve into peacefulness; if beings or the dreamer get lighter, more translucent, and younger; if monsters dissolve, and light beings or angelic ones appear; if emotions turn to expansive feelings, anger, fear, guilt, resentment, sadness effortlessly become peace, joy, love, compassion; and all this happens without forcing—then you can be sure that true imagination is at work for you. You have entered the world of the effortless, the playful, the creative. You have slipped past the cherub holding the revolving fire sword and tricked your way back into your lost Garden of Eden.

Can you then introduce back into your concrete reality your creative discoveries? Will playfulness slip back out of the Garden to lighten the daily drudgery of your existence? Can using the dream images change your everyday reality?

6

Symbol or Metaphor

Day after day uttering speech; night after night expressing
knowledge.

PSALM 19:13

Is it important to understand what your images, night dreams, or visions mean? In the short run, you'll find it's not necessary. You can remain in the dark about their true meaning and still progress, as long as you always respond to the necessity of your images.* The images will take you where your dreaming needs to go. But is that all that counts? Our sages say that "a dream not interpreted is like an unopened letter."[1] Those images are yours; they surface from some deep hidden source within you. What populates your mind's eye has something to do with who you are, and where you are on your journey. These images inform your self-conscious mind. Understanding them is helpful. All this is not in question. What is in question is translating images into words. In the passage from images to words, much can be lost, misinterpreted, or twisted. It is a task rife with danger.

How can talking about your images harm you? Most dream commentators, speaking of dream images, call them symbols. A symbol is something that stands for something else. If you should dream of

---

*See chapter 2.

"a well, a river, a bird, a pot, grapes, a mountain, a reed, an ox, a dog, a lion, a razor, a camel, or a donkey,"[2] you are dreaming of something else. But are you? Does a donkey mean something else? And does that something else mean the same thing for every dreamer? Should you buy a dictionary of symbols to find out what each of those different symbols means? If you do, you'll find out that the meaning of donkey changes from culture to culture. Will the meaning indicated by the dictionary influence you unduly, or lead you astray? Or like the biblical scholar, should you believe that "one who sees a donkey in a dream may anticipate that salvation will come to him"? Understanding may require more care than simply slapping onto your dream or vision a common meaning. Eric Fromm* talks of three different kinds of symbols: the conventional (a flag), the accidental (a personal memory that only has meaning to you), the universal (water is fluid and moving). But does dream language even think to compartmentalize into various types of symbols, or is it a living flow? Where do symbols originate, if, indeed, they exist within the dreaming?

Are there not two issues here, the dream images and their interpretation? We are told that "there is no dream that does not have an interpretation."[3] Does this mean the dreaming does not exist without an interpreter? Who, then, is the you that is dreaming, and the you that interprets? Could it be that it is not the dream that is the problem ("Night after night expressing knowledge"), but the interpretation ("Day after day uttering speech")?

✳

Dreaming is an experience that becomes a story as soon as you tell it to a friend, dictate it into your recording device, or write it down in your DreamBook. We could call this process a reduction: You're reducing the movements, forms, colors, and numbers from the ephemeral quality of a light show to the manifest form of a voice or text. Let's for the moment put aside the passage to manifestation, and let's concentrate on the translation process, the switch from experience to interpretation.

---

*American psychoanalyst (1900–1980), who developed the concept that freedom was a fundamental necessity for humans.

It all starts with an event. To do this, imagine that you are wearing a headset that places you inside 3D virtual reality, or instead just close your eyes and breathe out three times. Let yourself be totally immersed in the following 3D waking dream experience.

> *I'm walking down the street in my bright red shoes. I can clearly hear the sound of my heels on the cobbled street. To my right is a house with a striking yellow door. In the lock is a key. I can smell the climbing jasmine tree. It is very enticing. But to my left is a dark swirling fog that is inexorably pulling me in. It is dark, wet, and cold. It frightens me.*

Your fear jolts you out of your dreaming trance. Your first thought is to dismiss the fear: After all, it's only a dream vision. Two things have happened: You woke up to your everyday reality, and you switched brains. Writing the vision down in your DreamBook helps to exorcize your fear. Remnants of your dream state may still linger, but you're now squarely in your rational mind. You've distanced yourself from your emotions by the act of writing. You're reducing a multifaceted experience to a linear mode. Unless, of course, you are a painter who paints your dreams, as I did for many years, or a poet whose words can still elicit some of those dream variegations.

> *In Nature's temple, living columns rise,*
> *Which oftentimes give tongue to words subdued,*
> *And Man traverses this symbolic wood,*
> *Which looks at him with half familiar eyes.*[4]

CHARLES BAUDELAIRE, "ECHOES"

"Words subdued" are our imperfect ways of translating the experience of the "living columns." The woods, having been named, no longer vibrate with life and are now merely symbolic. But something half-familiar lingers on in the memory of the experience.

Do not confuse the experience (the living columns of trees) with its interpretation (words subdued). **There are no symbols in dreaming.** The shivering of raindrops on your skin, the wet fog, and the scent are not symbols. What turns them into symbols? Your rational mind, trying to reduce a mystery to its condensation. The red shoes are not symbols; they do not represent something other than shoes. You are wearing them, and you can hear the sound of your heels tapping on the cobblestone road. What if, in your daily life, you saw red shoes in a shop window? The color appeals to your senses, you can see yourself walking in the red shoes, filled with vitality, passion, and sex appeal. That sense of liveliness is what makes you buy the shoes. The word "symbol" doesn't apply here, but other words may come to mind: "morphological similarities, dynamic analogies and all sorts of word games"[5] and, as we will see further on, metaphoric clusters of ideas.

How does a dream or vision talk to us? Think of charades. Try to say something using only images. The dream world speaks to us by pulling from its memory bank, the color, form, specific body part that our dreaming tells us is—or needs to become—vital and dynamic in the here and now. What drives the dreaming to have you go on that small but intense journey? Your desire to move toward the radiance and power of that bright yellow. The fact that the yellow is on a door tells you that you have the power to cross a new threshold, so long as you take care of the emotional swirl pulling you back. You do this by responding to the necessity of the dream images. Freeing yourself from the swirling fog opens the path back to the yellow door. Dynamic, creative, and life driven, your dreaming seeks the ki tov, the dynamic living balance of your four bodies (physical, emotional, mental, spirit) within the outer environment. It doesn't rest in any fixed form or meaning. It states with immediacy what or where it is **now,** and where it needs to go. Whereas, by defining the dark swirl as your shadow or id,* you fix the situation in your mind, and it becomes yet another obstacle to the transforming movement of dreaming.

Again, think of the act of dreaming as a magnetic pull, driven by your primitive urge to survive in an optimum state. The dreaming question in your mind is like the yud, the first letter of the tetragrammaton. It is the big bang in your creative field, the magnetic

---

*Id, a concept developed by Sigmund Freud, is the impulsive and unconscious part of the psyche that seeks immediate gratification of basic urges, needs, and desires.

north that will galvanize all the different forces responding to the call of your question. The key and its proper lock move to interpenetrate. The powerful yellow conjoins with the door that needs to be opened. The scent of jasmine, pure, strong, and refreshing reaches out sensation-wise to match your need for renewal. The swirling fog, the dark, the wet, and the cold pull you back toward the emotional black hole you are trying to escape. Paint your dreaming, dance it, sing it, write a poem. It will all become clear without analyses. You *know* the meaning of your dreaming, like Adam *knew* Eve. You *know* that you need to free yourself from the pull of the fog and dance away toward the yellow door. You do not need an interpreter. Your only question is, What is keeping me from my bliss?* **You** are the only one who can answer that. Don't pull away and distance yourself from your feelings. On the contrary, be your feelings. Be *ehyeh asher ehyeh,*[6] I am that I am, the name God identifies Himself with when Moses inquires at the burning bush. It also means I will be what I will be. Be your dreaming, and you will become your dreaming. If not, you lose the momentum and stay stuck in the dark fog, in exile from what your red shoes and the yellow door are promising. We will return to this with the issue of manifestation.

What associations do you have to red shoes? You can cluster them around a central bubble that says: red shoes.

> *Feet, ground, grounding, dynamism, passion, courage, warrior, rebellion, bull, matador, the Sun King, sensuality, sex, joy.*

You can go on and on associating (associations are not logical connections, they come from emotional connections, established within the subconscious), until suddenly a story begins to unfold in your mind. Dream forms come before story. They emerge from an emotional imperative within you that we could call imagination, or the urge to form. You don't yet know what the story will be, but the images rise like good bread and find their own configuration.

---

*Recall Joseph Campbell's quote: "Follow your bliss."

From there to saying this is symbolic is a fine line most people cross at their peril. You cannot arbitrarily assign to a cigar the meaning of penis, or to an apple the meaning of sin. If you affix an assigned meaning to an image, you are stifling its genius. You are interpreting, telling the dreamer or yourself that this (the cigar or the apple) means that (a penis or sin). The difference is so subtle that even now you may not understand the danger of what you're doing. Transposing those dream images into the language of causal analysis (this means that) defeats the purpose and creates false belief systems. And yet how else can we do it? Your words preserve the memory of your images. Without words, your images tend to dissolve and disappear back into the flow of dreaming. The only language that remains true to the mission of your images is one of poetry that retains the layered truths of the image, or else one of literal description. The subconscious is your creative fountain, your imagination, the motor for your images. It is moving, flowing, transforming, and open to many possibilities—and to truly safeguard its qualities, your language must reflect the freedom of your dreaming. If your words fix the dreaming by putting its images into little boxes called symbols, you will unwittingly be muzzling your imagination. By instilling in your mind false belief systems (a cigar is a penis, an apple is sin), you are effectively repressing your creative flow.

Are you someone who comes out of a movie and likes to dissect and analyze what you saw? Or are you someone who likes to let the images resonate within you and prefers not to talk about what you saw? Let us return to the literal meaning of the images. When I wear my red shoes, I am pulled right, but the dark swirl pulls me away to the left. I want to return to the yellow door and the fragrant jasmine tree. Respect what the dream is showing you. Stay with the dream as it is, and live it. Then, when you speak about it, stay close to what you see and sense. Describe. Don't interpret. Or at least keep your interpretation as close to the dream as possible. Joseph, the great dreamer of the Bible, does just that when he opens the dreams of the baker and the cupbearer, who have been thrown into prison by Pharaoh.* He is

---

*See chapter 2.

staying close to the images. The biblical text uses the word "patar," interpret. The sound is similar to "patah," open. The two words are homophones (they sound the same but are written differently), which suggests that their meanings are interrelated and linked, like puns in a dream. This points to a different understanding of the word "interpret" as it is commonly used in English. Don't stray, embroider, or associate. Stay close to the dream!

Do not close up your dream. Do not reduce it. Instead, open it up to its living potential. By staying close to the literal meaning of the dream, you embody the attitude of the Marseilles Tarot Emperor who lovingly and respectfully watches what his mistress, the Empress, does.

You can do the same when opening the dreams or visions of others. Here is the cupbearer's dream:

Behold, there was a grapevine in front of me! On the grapevine were three tendrils. And it was as though it budded. Its blossoms and its clusters ripened into grapes. And Pharaoh's cup was in my hand, and I took the grapes, pressed them into Pharaoh's cup, and I placed the cup on Pharaoh's palm.

Joseph said to him, "This is its opening. The three tendrils are three days. In another three days Pharaoh will lift up your head and restore you to your post."[7]

As you can see, Joseph stays close to the dream, and to the obvious question behind the dream: Will I be reinstated? Behind that question lies the implicit desire to know the timing: When will I be freed? We have spoken of analogy and similarity: Key and yellow are both saying I have the power to open this door. Red shoes say I have the dynamism to resist the dark fog and follow my bliss. Here, beyond the very literal meaning of the dream (the cupbearer's task is to serve Pharaoh his wine cup), there is a grapevine that is taking on a life of its own. It is doing what all grapevines do, budding, blossoming, and producing grapes, but so fast! In the blink of an eye, the grapes are ready to be plucked. Timing has accelerated, and we can't help but be drawn to the only number in the dream: three. Numerals are used to indicate time. Here you would be justified in accusing Joseph of symbol making: Three tendrils mean three days? And yet, what is Joseph doing? He is responding to the unasked question of the dreamer. He is sticking close to the dream: The grapevine blossoms very fast. He could just as well have described three as dynamic, or as a new perspective. Here, instead of symbol making, we have an example of metaphor, the hinting of another meaning beneath the obvious one, a clustering or layering of ideas: three branches, three days. Images speak to us of a present unfolding in the moment, of a future in the making: Indeed, three days later, the cupbearer was reinstated into Pharaoh's good graces.

Here's another dream. Like the dreamer in the following dream, always speak about your dreams, exercises, or waking dreams in the present and in the first person singular.

> I'm standing on dry red earth interspersed with white roots. At my left are two fat, spotted, white, gray, and black snakes, coiled up and hiding their faces. On my right is another snake also coiled up, its face hidden. I'm not too uncomfortable because they are hiding their faces, but snakes are unpredictable. An older man stands to my right. He's a calm, genuinely nice person. He's a tour guide. This man says, "Oh, so they are snakes."

The dreamer didn't understand her images. but she did understand that she should respond to the necessity of the dream:

> I water the dry land. The land turns green. The three snakes slide away in the green grass. The man takes my hand and says, "Don't worry." Where the snakes had been coiled up are now empty patches in the grass.
> I go and stand on one of those empty patches. I feel energy rise up in my body, burning away whatever black energies were in me.

Responding to the necessity of her dream helped the dreamer arrive at a much more comfortable place. Her worry was eliminated, and the black energies in her body were burnt away. Also, the snakes were gone. The man held her hand. The images appeared peaceful and harmonious. She still didn't understand her dream, but having reentered the dream and lived its necessity, she experienced how this cleared away something hidden in her that had been disturbing her for a long time. Did she really need to intellectually understand what her dream meant? No. In fact, finding out what the dream meant before responding to its necessity might be an impediment. Her self-conscious mind could get in the way. Afterward, of course, understanding cannot hurt, as long as the dream opening is always in the service of the dream's flow and search for life, balance, and harmony. Let's give it a try:

Let's stay close to the images and their patterns: a man and a woman, two snakes on the left, one snake on the right, 2 + 1 = 3 snakes, hiding their faces. What does this remind you of? What "dynamic analogies" does it elicit? The story of Adam and Eve presents similar patterns (morphological similarities), except that here there are three snakes, and it isn't Adam and Eve, but the snakes that hide their faces. The theme is nevertheless reminiscent, with an added twist.

Becoming the secondary dreamer of this dream, I open the dream for the original dreamer:

> As the secondary dreamer of this dream, I feel the snakes are a coiled-up power that I associate with my sexual energy. Snakes give me goose bumps all over my skin, like sex does. I am ashamed of some past coupling revealed through the number two. I feel strong sexual energy in my future, the snake to my right, and would like to engage in a new coupling, but shame in the shape of the snake hiding its face is still between me and the man. The dry earth shows me that shame has eaten away at my life force. But the number three (three snakes) is a dynamic number and tells me that I can very quickly change the situation. The calm, wise man is telling me to look on the snakes as a tourist would (he's a tour guide and you're in transit), with detachment. Have no fear; they're only snakes.

After the dream opening, the original dreamer revealed that she had had an extramarital relationship that brought her much shame. She was trying to find a clear path back to her husband.

Nowhere in these dreams have the dream openers even suggested that the dream is symbolic. In fact—they follow the truth of the situation closely. The numbers are not symbolic; instead they carry a compacted meaning. Unpack them, and you'll be able to see them as shortcuts to the meaning the dream is trying to communicate. Two is a duality, or a coupling. Three takes the dreamer out of the two into a new possibility. Three is a new perception, like two eyes focusing on a third point. Three is fast, because if you draw the geometry of three you get a triangle. The triangle, like the prow of a ship, cuts through and adds quickness to its attributes.

If I were to say snakes are a symbol for intestines, or red shoes mean shame, my attention would be drawn away from the true contextual meaning of the images. Insisting that images are symbolic blocks the dream's raison d'être, which is to have a transformative dialogue with you, the self-conscious mind. By responding to the necessity of the dream, you honor the images and allow the subconscious to reconfigure toward life. And indeed, the dreamer came out of this exchange feeling relieved of shame and was able to resume her life with her husband.

Compare your thinking in symbols to a relationship problem. You are angry with your spouse. Instead of calmly mirroring back (describing) to your spouse what you are feeling when they do what offends you, you remain stuck in your reaction. You use an expletive: She's a bitch, or he's an ass. In a way, you've objectified the other. You've stuck your spouse into a little box called bitch or ass. Your spouse, no longer the loving graceful human being you fell in love with, has now morphed into something other, a beast, or an object. See the danger? It will forever corrupt and obscure your primary experience. So many relationships flounder at this juncture! How can one love or even respect another when reducing him or her to a label, a word, a symbol, a little box! The only way to repair (re-pair, bring back together) is to return to the dreaming.

Exercise 35
· · · · · · · · · · ·
Stepping Into Someone Else's Shoes

Close your eyes. Breathe out slowly three times, counting from three to one. See the one tall, clear, and bright.

Visualize that standing, facing you, a few feet away, is someone with whom you are currently having some difficulty.

Breathe out. Imagine yourself stepping out of your body, walking in your DreamBody over to that person, and going to stand in his or her shoes.

Breathe out. From this new vantage point, look back at yourself. How do you see yourself? What do you sense and feel?

Breathe out. What do you say to the "you" standing opposite? Say it, hearing yourself saying it in this person's voice.

Breathe out. Return back to your own body, and look back at the person you just left. What, if anything, has changed?

Breathe out. Open your eyes.
· · · · · · · · · · ·

There is nothing symbolic in loving. Loving requires imagination. To love you must be able to flow into the other, step into their shoes for a moment, or else step into their dreams. Dreaming yourself into another for a moment allows you to live the other's experience with total acceptance. Becoming a secondary dreamer for a moment, you embody the other or their dreaming, and you learn from direct experience who that person is. You're effectively practicing unconditional love.

Your loved ones are not the only ones who risk becoming symbols, with labels such as loser, victim, or bore, affixed to their life force and slowing the flow. You too may be caught in what others think of you, or in your own fixed ideas about yourself. To restore the creative flow, you need to return to your primary language. Dreaming shows us that we are live, multifaceted, dynamic creatures. Let's return to that dynamism by trying to embody different life forms, not only for the aerobics of it, but also for the sheer joy of getting to *know* other life forms.

Exercise 36
. . . .
Becoming the Creatures in the Garden

Close your eyes. Breathe out slowly three times, counting from three to one. See the one tall, clear, and bright.

Imagine that you are resting on a garden bench, watching a lizard resting on a wall.

Breathe out. Jump into the lizard's body, and become the lizard. Look through its eyes, feel through its pores, move as it moves, stretch your long tongue out to catch and eat what it eats. Now rest again, basking in the sun.

Breathe out. Jump out of its body back into yours. Feel the difference.

Breathe out. Jump successfully first into a hen, then into a bee, and into a butterfly.

Breathe out. Jump into the body of a bird and fly off. Experience how it feels to fly and see the world with eyes on either side of your head, and look down on it from above. Fly down to the ground to pick at grains with your beak. Jump out of the bird's body and back into your own.

Breathe out. What has changed for you in your body, your perceptions, your emotions?

Breathe out. Open your eyes.
. . . .

By dreaming another life form for a moment, you are living the full complexity of its existence. "An image is worth a thousand words," says common wisdom. Or as Samuel Johnson puts it, metaphor "gives you two (or more) ideas for one." A cat curled up in an armchair purring is an image compacted with many layers of meaning suggesting a warm home, cuddling up, pleasure, lovemaking, but also thrill, danger, and wildness. A golden chalice shining in a ray of light evokes a white dove, transcendence, heaven, or, just as convincingly, wine, blood, the flaming heart, and love—two seemingly opposite meanings, yet both are connected by living interwoven threads of meaning. How can the losing of self and burning desire coexist? Aren't they contradictory? Yet they do coexist in the same image.

The following story shows you how the sages understood dreaming.

A man had a dream, and he visited twenty-four different dream interpreters residing in Jerusalem. "And that which this one interpreted for me wasn't the same as that which the other interpreted to me. Rather, I received twenty-four different interpretations of the same dream."[8] Not very useful; too much is too much, you'll say. And you're right, to some extent. How can the dreamer orient himself? There are many ways of looking at a dream or a waking vision. All are meaningful, but not necessarily relevant to you today. Pay attention to the one opening that does resonate for you. From one dream image to many different futures, it is your choice to follow the road that attracts you the most. Remember that we are influenced by the interpreter's words. If their words stay close to the dream, if they speak to the ki tov, to the movement toward life in you, if they resonate for you, then listen. Choose your dream interpreters wisely, for "the dream follows the mouth,"[9] say the sages. The words that have entered your ears will influence how you see and feel the dream image, which, in turn, will drive manifestation.

Image, collapsing many meanings into its core, is, by nature, a metaphor, able to transcend duality and to capture the paradoxical nature of life. From the image core, your mind is free to travel down the many different avenues of meaning that are offered to you. This is where you are the master: No dictionary will be able to tell you what most attracts you just now; only you and your subconscious know what resonates.

But this is also where, like most people, you might get lost. You want to be told what to do. You want facts. Facts are scientific and comforting: The chalice is a container, nothing more. If the definition of chalice begins morphing, what can you trust? But quantum physics has begun to dismantle our convictions: Light is not a wave or a particle; it's both. Living in a paradoxical world requires some adjustment. We must let go of certainty, of our need for control. In the inner world, there are no facts, since the image has not yet manifested. And if you, like the scholars, believe that the inner world is a nonreality, it's an easy step to convincing yourselves that images have no meaning. We'll come back to that when we tackle manifestation. The chalice is not a fact, but it is the truth. A truth that shimmers with many meanings, all emotionally powerful, revolving in the mind like the sword of the angel guarding the entry to PRDS, paradise. To enter, you must accept that your images are not one-dimensional, but have revolving meanings, and that you yourself are a many-splendored being, living in emotional worlds populated by multifaceted images. You are a living, walking metaphor. How do you orient yourself? Remember the three tests you must pass to enter PRDS, the garden, and find the treasure.*

P'shat, your story line: Recognize your story line, but don't get caught in it, or you will become a victim of your own story.

Remez, your patterns: Pay attention to them. They will reveal what is really on your mind and what is blocking you.

Drash, your question: What is your most pressing question of the moment? It is your question that will propel you past the angel, into the Garden.

Sod, your treasure: There you will encounter Sod, the secret hidden within your dreaming, that reveals what you must do and where you must go to find your bliss. This is what will set manifestation into motion.

Exercise 37
· · · · · · · · · · ·
Getting Past the Angel Guarding Eden

Close your eyes. Breathe out slowly three times, counting from three to one. See the one tall, clear, and bright.

Reverse quickly through your life story, recognizing its recurring themes.

Breathe out. Go forward, noting all the incidents where repetitive patterns reappear in your story. Note how old you are and in what location they occur.

Breathe out. Go back again through your story, visiting each location and sweeping the recurring patterns to the left.

Breathe out. Return through each cleared location to today.

---

*See chapter 1.

Breathe out. Orient yourself. What direction are you facing?

Breathe out. Turn to face east. Walk toward the rising sun. Watch the revolving lights of the blazing sun.

Breathe out. Come close to the angel guarding the way. Whisper in his ear the one word or sentence that will let you through.

Breathe out. Walk into the Garden, and find your treasure.

Breathe out. Thank the angel as you leave the Garden. Return to your everyday life. Keep the knowledge of your treasure preciously in your heart, to orient yourself toward the future you desire.

Breathe out. Open your eyes.

· · · · · · · · · · ·

The man who received twenty-four interpretations to his dream reported that all twenty-four interpretations came true. How is that possible, all twenty-four? And if images aren't real, how can they manifest results in our reality? This is the next question we need to address.

PART II

Taming the Leviathan

Interactions with the Subconscious

*We can't solve problems by using the same kind of thinking
we used when we created them.*

EINSTEIN

My mother always said I was dreaming my life away. She was right. I was not so impressed with the way the *real* world was muddling along. Yes, progress was unfolding at a dizzying rate; yes, we were benefiting from giant technological leaps forward. We had running water, anesthetics, antibiotics, planes, computers, and cell phones. But what is progress, if so many around me were still battling to find a sense of direction and meaning in their lives, still floundering in relationship problems, their health issues, even basic survival? In fact, the issues piling up today appear far more intractable and threatening than they ever were. Setting out to prove to myself (if not to my mother) that dreaming affects outcomes in reality, through my continuing dialogue with the subconscious, I learned to address the problems confronting my society, family, friends, students, and myself. I have outlined for you the methodology to plunge into your subconscious and find the creative answers that can enhance or radically change your life. Now you must put those lessons into practice and face your very own Leviathan, the great beast that thrashes to and fro within you, manifesting your untamed emotions and memories that need to be acknowledged and weeded out. The chapters that follow are ways for you to deal with your beast while developing different aspects of your life, using dreaming. How do you manifest your heart's desires, the abundance, the joy, and the fulfillment you dream of? How do you clear intractable complexes or ancestral, repetitive patterns? How do you return to your inner source, and rediscovering the playful creative child within you? How do you heal your relationships and return to the radiance of first love? When time poverty seems to be a daily and ever more exhausting problem, how do you become the master of time? When your body loses hope, when it gets ill, can you speak to it, will it hear you? If you remember that the language of the subconscious is image, then a whole new vista of possibilities opens up for you. Knowing how your dreaming can directly affect your everyday life, wouldn't you like to explore its possibilities?

Our world is one vast organism or ecosystem. Call it a giant DreamField. These chapters will teach you to use your subconscious in a practical way and will help you to situate yourself where you belong, within its beneficent flow.

7

Playing with Manifestation

Dreams pass into the reality of action. From the actions stems the dream again; and this interdependence produces the highest form of living.

ANÄIS NIN

What is reality? Should you consider your dream images as actual worlds that exist in an etheric *other* reality? Or as pure fantasy—what some scientists have called "garbage of the brain"? "The images of the dream . . . are figuratively true, but literally false."[1] Are your dream images literally false because they do not exist in the real world? Your self-conscious mind will agree with that statement. But will your subconscious mind? While you are dreaming, your images are completely real to you; you don't question their validity. This dichotomy is worth observing.

Once Zhuang Zhou* dreamt he was a butterfly. Upon awakening he didn't know if he was Zhuang Zhou who had dreamt he was a butterfly or a butterfly dreaming that he was Zhuang Zhou.

---

*Zhuang Zhou (369–301 BCE), influential Chinese philosopher, credited with writing the Zhuangzi, one of the foundational texts of Taoism. He lived during a flourishing period for Chinese philosophy, the time of the Hundred Schools of Thought. He has continued to influence philosophers to this day, notably Martin Buber and Martin Heidegger.

Which world is real? In ancient Vedic literature, what we call the real world is seen as maya, an illusion so powerful it can make us believe in its absolute reality. "The wise behold with their mind, in their heart, the sun, made manifest by the illusion of the Asura."[2] The Veda is suggesting that we can see through the illusion (the Asuras are nature deities) to reach the true reality, called here the sun. This is how the Zohar puts it:

> To read the writ of the Torah literally is akin to telling someone that they are a magnificent cloak, as if the person is nothing more than what they wear. Certainly, a body exists behind the cloak, and certainly a soul behind the body . . . and within that soul yet another, and another.[3]

Understand the writ of the Torah (the five books of Moses) as the story line, the everyday reality. The Zohar is basically pointing us in the same direction: Beyond the illusion of the cloak is the body, and beyond the body, the soul, and yet more soul. The word "reality" loses its meaning, since the *real* reality is at the opposite spectrum from appearances. Let's remember that Kabbalah defines four worlds, Emanation, Creation, Formation and Manifestation, all real in their own different ways.

To review:

> Emanation, Atsilut, is the big bang, the dot of the letter yud in God's name, from which all creation emanates. Call it desire.
> Creation, Bri'ah, is the expanding dot, the matrix of space-time. Call it imagination.
> Formation, Yetsirah, is the ephemeral trying on of forms. Call it dreaming.
> Manifestation, Asiyah, is the manifest compound of the other three worlds. Call it reality.

Saying that only this reality is *real* blocks a far deeper truth that is best expressed by Einstein's famous formula, $E = mc^2$. How does the movement from matter to energy, or from energy to matter happen?

Between Zhuang Zhou and the butterfly there must be some distinction!
This is called the transformation of things.

Dream images are part of Yetsirah, the world where transformation is occurring. Are your dream images *figuratively* true? Only in the fugitive appearance of the image! A table is a table in the dream but might suddenly transform into a cloud. The cloud then becomes "figuratively true" as long as it stays a cloud. Certainly, at this level, your images are not yet about manifesting, but about trying on possible formations.

When do they become manifest? The world we live in (Asiyah), that we call real, is a consensual world. We all agree that a table is a table. We cling for dear life to this definition of table as real. If the table were to begin to morph, we would be seriously thrown off balance. We forget that life offers us many examples of transformation in the manifest world (water becomes vapor, becomes a cloud, becomes rain, turns to ice, returns to water). The passage back to dissolving forms is seen as dangerous for our sanity. And yet both the Vedas and the Zohar are suggesting that the dissolving of forms leads us back to truth, a reality far beyond what we call reality.

Maybe the word "real" is the problem. If we eliminate it, we are free to consider the power of our inner images to propel us forward. Does that imply that visualizing a table means you can make it materialize? Will the table turn up in your dining room, either by a sleight of hand or by a series of events that culminate in the table of your dream manifesting at your doorstep? Some of you would call this magical thinking. Yet does anything get done in this world unless you have already dreamed it?

✳

While "classically, the image is always defined by reference to the real," the Hebrews perceived it otherwise. They saw the dream as "God revealing Himself to men by images and figures," the dot of the yud* descending like a tail of fire into the worlds of structure and form to

---

*Yud is the tenth letter of the Hebrew alphabet. It is also the first letter of the tetragrammaton, YHWH (Yahweh). It can be seen as a dot in the void, a big bang, and the tail is the movement creating time-space.

finally manifest a world objective to the eye and touch. If the world's destiny is birthed through God's imagination, our own destiny must also be inherent in our imagination, made in the image of God's imagination. Like God's, our imagination must be able to carry the phantasmagorical images or scenarios of our dreams or visions into objective reality. How do we know that? The Book of Genesis shows us the Creator creating the world in six days, then resting on the seventh:

On it God abstained from all His work, which God created to make.[4]

One way to understand this cryptic phraseology is to say: God stopped creating so that "to make" (la'asot in the Hebrew) or manifest could now happen. Or another interpretation: His creation, man, could, in turn, learn to make, to manifest. Creation *ex nihilo* (*bara Elohim,* God created) is God's province, but man can learn to make, to use the existing created forms to procreate, to replicate, to compose. God removing Himself allows man to play with forms, and to assemble and sew together the garment of the objective illusion that is our world. A dream interpreter is called a PTR, *poter,* whereas a tailor is called a TPR, *tafar,** with the same letters forming a different configuration, suggesting that assembling and sewing together different forms is the work of a dreamer.

In the Garden of Eden, the passage from dreaming to making is instantaneous. Adam speaks the names of the animals, and they appear. By eating of the forbidden fruit, Eve *makes* a new world and becomes the mother of all living (which is the meaning of her name, Havah, in Hebrew), but she loses the instantaneous ability to manifest that Adam enjoyed. "In pain shall you give birth."[5] She transmitted to us the freedom *to make* but forfeited for us the instantaneity that we can only recover by returning to the Garden. How do we do that?

Let's sit a moment with the old belief system that dreaming is unreal. The moment you say the dream world is unreal, you dismiss its extraordinary creative power. What is dreaming? Whether by night or day, it is your creative ability to la'asot,[6] your ability to make yourself and the world around you. Your dreaming is a fact in motion, since

---

*The P, *pei* in Hebrew, can be pronounced "pe" or "fe."

you are creating yourself at every moment. You are your dreaming. Your body, your emotions, and your thoughts are all rising out of the creative output that is you constantly making yourself. "By breaking with the objectivity which fascinates waking consciousness, and by reinstating the human subject in its radical freedom, the dream discloses paradoxically the movement of freedom toward the world, the point of origin from which freedom makes itself world."[7]

So let us agree that all four worlds are real. From energy to matter and from matter to energy, don't block the movement with false belief systems, for it will definitely curtail your ability to manifest. Keep the fluidity going by respecting the offerings of your imagination and allowing the dreaming to play, and to try on different forms and combinations. "All the breaks you need in life wait within your imagination. Imagination is the workshop of your mind, capable of turning mind energy into accomplishment and wealth."[8] If so, why do some images materialize while others don't? Exactly as a worker in his workshop will try, and reject, and try something different until he finds the right combination, so too in the space of the imagination. A certainty, a knowing that this is it will arise in you when you reach the right combination. And the excitement will push you onward to accomplish and manifest.

What happens if even then, doubts arise? Qualms about your ability to bring your ideas to fruition, worries about taking a risk, trepidation about what others may say, and procrastination are all ways of diminishing the value of your dreaming. Your lack of self-confidence will block your creativity and paralyze your efforts to bring your dreaming to fruition. Worse, since "all thought has a tendency to clothe itself in its physical equivalent,"[9] you will manifest your worst doubts, fears, and worries. And when they come true, you'll feel justified in saying, I knew this couldn't work or I knew this was going to happen! Yes, you did! Because you chose to stay with your negative images and not to rectify or clean out your fears, doubts, and worries. Think of them as nonrecyclable waste. They will not biodegrade by themselves. You, the self-conscious one, will have to decide to change something. You will have to open up your subconscious like you do a computer program and consciously clear the glitches. You are far more powerful than you realize. At each moment, you are seeing your images becoming reality, only those images may be the negative ones that make your worst fears come true. Time to let those go, so that you can manifest your true creativity.

Exercise 38
Getting Rid of Fears, Doubts, and Worries

Close your eyes. Breathe out slowly three times, counting from three to one. See the one tall, clear, and bright.

Sit at an open window. Have on your lap a box of many-colored balloons. Choose a balloon that has the color of your fears.

Breathe out. Blow your fears into the balloon and knot the tail of the balloon.

Breathe out. Choose a balloon that has the color of your doubts. Blow your doubts into the balloon and knot its tail.

Breathe out. Do the same for anxiety.

Breathe out. Now you have three balloons whose colors you don't like. Let them float out of your window.

Breathe out. Grab three rays of light and using them as darts pop the balloons. See the deflated balloons being carried away to the left by the wind and disappearing.

Breathe out. Now choose balloon colors you like for success, abundance and joy and whatever else makes you happy. Blow up your balloons and let them go.

Breathe out. Watch all your balloons rising up into the sky, colorful and lively.

Breathe out. Open your eyes, seeing this with open eyes. Breathe out. Open your eyes, seeing this new image with open eyes.

You may be one of those lucky souls whose self-confidence is strong even in the face of failure. But for most of us, self-confidence is dependent on what we can manifest, which is a vicious circle, as you can only manifest what you believe in. If you believe in your own doubts, you will manifest failure. If you see yourself charging forward, confident of success, you will open the way toward a good manifestation. People equate your worth with what you manifest. Therefore, it's up to you to convince yourself of your own worth. Put yourself in the shoes of your defense lawyer making the case for you. If you do not know your own worth, how can others see it, or if they do see it, how can they convince you of it?

Exercise 39
. . . .
The Value of Worth

Close your eyes. Breathe out slowly three times, counting from three to one. See the one tall, clear, and bright.

Ask yourself, who decides your worth? Is it you, your parents, your siblings, society, peers, your inner self, God?

Breathe out. Imagine yourself as a newborn baby and look into its eyes. What is its worth?

Breathe out. Open your eyes, knowing your true worth with open eyes.

. . . .

You have swept away your fears, doubts, and worries. You have seen your true worth. Now you must prove your worth to yourself and to others by transforming "mind energy into accomplishment and wealth."[10] Only in persevering with, and experiencing strongly, the dream images that have struck you can they materialize. The choice of images to pursue is not a logical calculation, but an emotional knowing. You may find that your images speak of an outcome against all odds: Trust that they are what you must pursue. This work of perseverance is called *kavanah*, intention. Your perseverance and dedication to your dream images, your burning desire to see them come to fruition in the objective world, are what will make those images manifest. You may be floating those images in your subconscious for years, waiting for the right time to bring them to fruition. Your images are like seeds in the ground. With the right amount of water, the right amount of sunshine and trust, they will grow and blossom.

Exercise 40
. . . .
Bull's-Eye

Close your eyes. Breathe out slowly three times, counting from three to one. See the one tall, clear, and bright.

Imagine that you are in a large field. Across the field is a large target, black on white. The center is a large black dot.

Breathe out. Know and see perfectly what it is that you want to accomplish. Know that the goal is the bull's-eye.

Breathe out. You are holding a bow and arrow. A master archer is your guide as you prepare to release your arrow.

Breathe out. Close your dream eyes, and see your arrow flying straight into the bull's-eye.

Breathe out. Open your eyes, and shoot, knowing you cannot fail.

Breathe out. See your arrow shooting straight into the bull's-eye.

Breathe out. Open your eyes.

· · · · · · · · · · ·

There are many loops and distractions away from the main path. If you have lost sight of your goal, don't waste time on regrets or guilt; they are an indulgence you can't afford.

Exercise 41
· · · · · · · · · · ·
Goodbye, Regrets and Guilt

Close your eyes. Breathe out slowly three times, counting from three to one. See the one tall, clear, and bright.

You are standing in your meadow. Look up at the sun.

Breathe out. Stretch up your hands and arms. Sense and see your arms become longer and longer and your hands turn to light.

Breathe out. Put your hands of light into your body, and take out all regrets and guilt.

Breathe out. Lift your hands, filled with regrets and guilt, up to the sky; see your arms elongate; and soon see your hands disappear into the blue sky.

Breathe out. When you no longer feel the weight of your regrets and guilt in your hands, bring them down.

Breathe out. Look at your empty hands; what are you feeling? Breathe in the blue light from the sky; see it filling the vacated spaces easily.

Breathe out. Open your eyes.

· · · · · · · · · · ·

Since you live in time, setting a schedule is essential to the realization of your goal. Schedules might have to depend on outside circumstances, but the most successful deadlines are those that are set by your dreaming.

Exercise 42

. . . .

Deadline

Close your eyes. Breathe out slowly three times, counting from three to one. See the one tall, clear, and bright.

Visualize your goal. Knowing that "a goal is a dream with a deadline"[11] catch a ray of light and draw a circle of light in the upper right-hand corner of the sky.

Breathe out. Catch another ray of light, and see it becoming a golden pen.

Breathe out. Write in gold letters above the circle: date at which my goal will manifest. Specify your goal.

Breathe out. Look into the circle, and see the date appear. Ask for day, month, year. Trust your own eyes.

Breathe out. Open your eyes, seeing the date with open eyes.

. . . .

Write the date on a piece of paper, and pin it up where you can see it every day. Keep walking toward your goal. Stay focused, one-pointed. Follow your burning desire. Let nothing distract you.

Exercise 43

. . . .

Little Devils

Close your eyes. Breathe out slowly three times, counting from three to one. See the one tall, clear, and bright.

Walk toward the bull's-eye, seeing your arrow firmly planted in its center.

Breathe out. As you cross the field, on either side of you is a little devil trying to distract you from reaching your goal.

Breathe out. What is happening? How do you get to your goal? Do you get to your goal?

Breathe out. Open your eyes.

. . . .

The Talmud tells us that "nothing is made known in this world but what is made known in advance by means of a dream or a proclamation."[12] Your subconscious knows. It exists in a Now comprising the past, the present, and the future. How is that possible? Imagine an ocean without boundaries called the imagination. Aquatic forms or sequences of forms pop up and disappear. Below the surface is the kernel of all-knowing called your soul. It knows and reveals to you, through the pop-ups that appear at the surface of the ocean, all your potentialities. It *knows,* to give you an example, how many children you are destined to have. You are free to choose to surrender to your *knowing,* or to turn away. If you refuse to have the number of children your soul has signed up for, it is your prerogative, but it may be to your detriment. You will be taking a diverting path away from the truth, and your birthing pains will be that much greater. You are free to choose your *knowing* or to refuse it.

You cannot manifest what your imagination hasn't already seen. You cannot paint like Gauguin, because your dreaming doesn't see like him. You won't be a millionaire if your soul has decided otherwise. The self-help book *The Secret* by Rhonda Byrne has sold you a lie. Outside forces may make you think you want to be a millionaire, and you can visualize, for instance, a check written to you for a million dollars. But you cannot manifest it if your dreaming hasn't made it known to you beforehand; it is impossible. It's as if you decided to be a football player, but your body is puny and undersized. Your dreaming is your energy form. Your body is the manifestation of that energy form. Why you would be puny, and not made to be a millionaire, is the secret of genetics, your ancestral history, and your soul. There is much more to be said about that, but we will discuss it in chapter 9 when we talk about ancestry.

You can be sure of one thing: What your dreaming has shown you, you can be or do. You can and will manifest your dreaming so long as you surrender to it, put all your emotional energy behind your images, and do not block the flow of your imagination. We'll discuss blockages in the next chapter.

Kabbalah says that each one of us is born with a mission. Think of your mission as your angel. The angel never gets distracted. It has only one leg, and it flies like an arrow to its goal. Which means once you've found your angel, don't let yourself get distracted. By accomplishing your mission, you are helping the *tikun olam*, the repair of the world. To give you a personal example, when I was twenty-nine, I had a vision: I saw a school for dreamers. I could see the buildings and the departments. Like the academies of the bnei ha-nevi'im, the schools of the Sons of the Prophets that flourished in biblical times, my school was about teaching dreaming and its powerful uses to modern communities. I saw a number of different departments dedicated to using dreaming for healing, for trauma, for mothers-to-be, for companies, for coaching actors, for prayer and spiritual development. Forty years later the school I dreamed of exists in the objective world. I called it The School of Images® (SOI). Located in NYC, it has branches in the Americas, Asia, Australia, Europe, and Russia, and it has specialized departments, just as my vision had shown me. Writing books was also part of my vision, and as you can see, that's what I'm doing whenever my teaching schedule allows. So the dreams come true. I use those words to emphasize again that dreaming, far from being unreal, is the most powerful reality advocate you have.

✳

Wandering through Berakhot a and b, the folio of the Talmud dedicated to the art of dreaming, one comes across this strange statement: "Three types of dreams are destined to be fulfilled. These are: a dream one sees in the morning, just before he wakes up; a dream that his friend dreamt about him; and a dream that is interpreted within a dream. And some say: a dream that was repeated is likewise destined to be fulfilled." What do these types of dreams all have in common? The dreamtime seems insistent on saying one thing: Pay attention! It does so by different means: by forcing us to remember—by bringing the dream close to waking consciousness; giving us goose bumps when another dreamer tells us what we haven't been able to hear; jolting us, by revealing the meaning of the dream within the dreamtime; and repeating the same message, in case we didn't get it. A repetitive dream can be good or bad. You can be stuck in a blocked pattern or like Joseph, who had two similar dreams* ". . . his brothers were jealous of him, but his father kept the

---

*See chapter 2.

matter in mind."[13] Keep the matter in mind, either to rectify the dream if it is portentous, or to make it manifest if it is fortuitous. You have four ways of making a fortuitous dream manifest:

Bringing what the dream wants into clear consciousness;
Listening, not resisting or blocking what resonates as truth when others dream about you, or open your dreams;
Opening your own dreams;
Rehearsing the good images in your mind.

If you wish to make manifest your goal, you must do the work that God stepped away from. Now it's your turn. But making, la'asot, doesn't necessarily require effort. The sweat of your brow may be required in the objective world to finish the work of making, and to concretely bring brick and mortar together. But in Genesis, mention of making appears before matter. Making is about making it come true. That means, for you, returning into the dreaming. You can't believe that simply holding an image of your goal in mind can bring about the desired outcome? You can't believe that we can manifest from mental energy something concrete in the objective world? Breathe out and pause. It all happens in the pause, the rest on the seventh day, the moment of letting go and letting the image fly to its destination. Sai Baba, the Indian guru, comes to mind as being known to materialize *vibhuti* (sacred ash) out of thin air. While some accused him of sleight of hand, it was never proven. Was he a magician? Or was he truly able to materialize vibhuti as well as fruit, candy, flowers, and even jewelry? If so, he appears to be an exception, for like Adam he was able to transform energy into matter instantaneously.

Yet you too participate in "the transformation of things," as Zhuang Zhou, the Chinese sage, put it, pretty much instantly. You give a dollar and get a coffee. You make a phone call and acquire a new client. Reality's boundaries with the dream world are porous, and "the transformation of things" can happen fast. Manifesting a table may mean that you follow the inner movement, the still small voice of the inside, as I did one morning in SoHo, followed by my infuriated husband. Being an Aries, fiery, he was ready, he declared, to divorce me if we didn't get a dining room table today. "Where are you going?" I didn't know, but I was going to have a coffee, and then . . . I was going down this street, and then . . . I was going into this thrift shop, and then . . . I was going up the stairs with my husband pulling at my coattails. At the top of the stairs, pushed into a corner, amidst piles of old clothing, was a magnificent art deco table, priced ridiculously low. My husband signed the check, eyebrows raised, in silence. The truth is I didn't want to be divorced, so I had a burning desire and a pointed question. Also I love art deco. Magical thinking? No, simply the power of dreaming to magnetize what you are looking for. After writing this paragraph last night, I left my desk to go to a Broadway show. At the ticket booth, the clerk couldn't find our tickets. The show was fully booked. I could have emoted, made a dreadful scene, and left disappointed. Instead, "I imagine us seated in the orchestra," and breathe out. Pause. At that moment, a man rushed to the counter: "My wife is sick; can I return these tickets?" Here was instantaneous manifestation, in case I was ever in doubt.

How does one define what just happened? The word that comes to mind is synchronicity. As defined by the *Oxford Dictionary,* synchronicity is "the simultaneous occurrence of events which appear significantly related but have no discernible causal connection." This doesn't explain anything, unless you have a *quantum mind.* "No discernible causal connection" but forms and timing fitting into each other perfectly is exactly how dreaming occurs. I'm sure you too have experienced in your life synchronous events that astonished you and that you couldn't explain logically, but they made you happy! What if you were to be proactive, to *make* this happen? Return to your dreaming, visualize your goal, and hold your image calmly and happily in mind. The key is to have calmed your emotions by switching to feeling. Don't panic or get angry (that's emotions); just visualize your end goal and feel happy (that's a feeling) as you hold it present in your mind. Trust the power of your imagination to form the outer world. Then "let go and let God!" And you will see your inner images magnetize an outer reality that fits perfectly, like a piece in a puzzle. Remember when this happens to make a note in your DreamBook, in the box called verification.*

*See chapter 4.

Here is an exercise to help you surrender to your dreaming. Have a simple goal in mind. You're looking for the perfect gift for a friend but have no idea what to give her, or where to find it. Her birthday is tomorrow, and it's a big one, so you have an urgent need to find just the right thing. This exercise is best done in a city.

Exercise 44
. . . .
The Walk

Decide to take a walk, keeping your goal in the back of your mind.

There is no fixed itinerary.

When you come to a crossing, if the lights are green for pedestrians, cross.

If not, turn and cross in the other direction.

Continue walking, letting the lights dictate where you are going.

If something attracts you as you walk down the streets, stop and look. Go into shops.

Anything that attracts you, go for it.

But remain relaxed and easy. There is no effort here, only play.

Continue your walk until you have found the perfect gift, or continue walking for half an hour.

. . . .

Don't forget to write in your DreamBook what happened. If nothing happened, at the very least, it's a fun way to spend half an hour, and by taking a different route from your usual, you will feel refreshed by the new sights. If you haven't found what you were looking for, something else may have caught your attention. Learning to get two worlds to fit together like mirror images takes a little practice. Repeat the exercise whenever you can. You might not get any results for a while, until suddenly synchronicity happens for you, not necessarily on the walk, but at a theater booth.

The playful, happy attitude is key. What helps to enhance your happiness is light. You need the light of the sun to grow strong and healthy; you need it to become powerful. The sun's energy is like gas in your tank. You can use it well or for dire purposes. As you know, with manifestation, there can be no in-between states: You are either a pessimist manifesting a sad world or an optimist manifesting a glad world. Either way you will be manifesting. What helps to orient manifestation is your solar plexus, the sun in your body. This is a great network or ring of nerves, concentrated below the rib cage, in the pit of the stomach. While you cannot control the vagaries of the weather that determine how much sun you'll get, you can control your solar plexus. Your personal sun shines or hides itself, depending not on clouds, but on your emotions. Observe your solar plexus now. Is it contracted or expanded? Some people have a chronically contracted solar plexus. The solar plexus closes up when you're frightened or shines out when you're happy. While you may not have consciously noticed it in others, you can be sure that those who are successful have a radiant solar plexus.

In a bad situation, your solar plexus can either be so tight it lets no light out or so open it leaks out all its energy. A great shock, like an accident or terrible news, will jolt your solar plexus wide open. Many people have described this phenomenon where the DreamBody escapes and floats up out of the physical body. This is a natural survival mechanism. The first thing to do for people in shock is to close the solar plexus: Put your hands, a pillow, or a folded coat over the solar plexus. This will bring the person in shock back into his or her body. People who stay too long out of body can get sick or even die. If your solar plexus is chronically tight, that too can make you sick and incapable of manifesting properly: Push it open by expanding your stomach. This must be done again and again until the body loses its bad habit of constricting. You will know it is done when you have no more pain in the solar plexus. The solar plexus opens and closes rhythmically. But it will contract arrhythmically as soon as you are in danger; apprehensive about an important interview, an exam you are about to take, speaking in public, or impressing new clients; or experiencing a host of other public tests you must face. To use your solar plexus to manifest, to shine light upon those you wish to impress favorably, or to attract to you the clients you need, here is the exercise to do.

Exercise 45

. . . .

The Solar Plexus (Formal)

Close your eyes. Breathe out slowly three times, counting from three to one. See the one tall, clear, and bright.

Imagine that you're standing in your meadow. Look up at the blue sky, and see where the sun is. If the sun is to your left, watch as the sun travels across the sky until it reaches noontime and the sun is right above you.

Breathe out. Elongate your arms toward the sun. Feel your hands getting warm, turning to light.

Breathe out. Catch the sun in your two hands, and bring it down. Put it in your solar plexus. See it igniting the sun in your body, then quickly put the sun back in the sky.

Breathe out. See the sun ignited in your solar plexus, radiating out in all directions. See it as a great wheel of light. See how others are attracted to your light and warmth and start walking toward you from all directions.

Breathe out. Open your eyes.

. . . .

Practice this three times, the day before a stressful experience, then early next morning. If the stressful experience happens in the evening, do it two more times that day. Make sure that the third time is just before the stressful event is scheduled to happen. As you go into the interview or onstage, throw the light on your audience. To manifest clients, do the exercise formally, every day in the morning for twenty-one days starting from the new moon, or from one period to the next.

✱

Imagery is the language of the inside. Images drive your health or illness. Images drive your feelings or emotions. Images drive your freedom or blocked belief systems. Once you understand the power of your images to make or break you, you will be able to change your life for the good. You will be able to manifest what you dream. Your dreaming is as concrete as the chair I sit in. Use it well. It is your power of embodiment and manifestation.

8

Dreamfields and Complexes

And the living creatures ran to and fro like flashes of lightning.

EZEKIEL 1:14

What are you made of? Are you flesh and only that? Or are you only energy? The Kabbalah says: "Every moment we are being emanated, willed into existence across the simultaneous stages of unfolding known as the Four Worlds."[1] The universe is unfolding simultaneously in four levels: inception, creation, form, manifestation. Think of it as four transparent diagrams, one above the other. This means that we are, at every moment, simultaneously experiencing within ourselves the bursting-forth spirit of the big bang (conception), the fiery energy of the unfolding (embryo, fetus), the boundary forming "until here shall you go and no further,"[2] and the fascia and skin wrapping of the finished product, manifesting a formed human being. We are all at once spiriting-energizing-forming-fleshing and constantly in the process of exchanging information between these four worlds within us. We move incessantly between energy and flesh, vitality and death, movement and pause. Yet our belief system fixes us squarely at the level of manifestation, and we ignore, at our peril, the other three realities that inhabit us. If we could access them, could these other three levels help us to deal with manifestation, or to heal problems we experience in our flesh?

Many modern thinkers stay caught in the hamor, the material level the sages call the donkey level,* believing in all its physical limitations, pains and slow deterioration. For most of us breaking away from the belief in pain to experience other realities is nearly impossible. Our flesh hurts, our emotions confound, our thoughts torment us, and we cannot rise to spirit, for the heavy blanket of clouds that obscure it.

We have discussed how to climb the ladder of dreaming that takes us from the nightmare/repetitive/busy manifestations of our daily lives to light and to sublime oneness. But now we must deepen our understanding. While the work may appear linear—all we need to do is go up the ladder of dreams—it is certainly not just vertical. It does not consist of floating out of our bodies into an etheric alternate reality while ignoring the fire and fury of everyday existence. We are not meant to detach ourselves from the nightmare/repetitive/busy manifestations of our daily lives, but instead to heal them. In fact, these knots or nodules of blocked energy are the obstacle course we must learn to confront. Without an obstacle to pit ourselves against, there is no reason for us to grow. As God says in Genesis: "It is not good for man to be alone. I will make him a helper k'negdo, against him."[3] Most of our blocks and repetitive patterns appear in relationship to another or to the world. Why do these blocks, patterns, and pains recur again and again, to the point where we are sick of them? As we know, "habit is stronger than reason." For most of us, only when we are driven to unbearable pain do we finally decide to tackle our bad habits. Maybe that is our inner cue: the scale tips, and we either die or learn a new behavior.

Reality has different facets, layers, and directions. We must run and return, run and return, again and again, between light and hamor (matter), like the living creatures of Ezekiel's vision, exploring the many directions and layers of our dreamfields. Since our dreamfields are four-dimensional, and maybe even five-dimensional, we must learn to navigate their complexity. If stuck energy blocks our way, it is the occasion to clear it by using any kind of transforming action that might work,

---

*See chapter 3.

such as imaginally plunging in, encircling, climbing above, sweeping to the left, destroying, melting, or burning the obstacle. Our life is about clearing what blocks our exploration. Those blocks are the impulse for us to weave an ever-larger network of experiences that flows and stretches out in the six directions of space and time. By consciously facing and dissolving our blockages, we enlarge our experiences, and turn our DreamField into pure consciousness.

Our DreamField is the basis of our existence. We emerge out of that DreamField, not the other way around. Our DreamField is the constantly changing, ever creating network on which our bodies, as we know them, shape themselves and manifest. That we believe in the fixed manifestation, instead of concentrating on the ever-evolving creation that we are, is where we get caught. We are not made of flesh, but of a matrix of moving imagery. Movement is the signature quality of our incarnation, starting with the first cell that unfolds into two, then four, then eight cells, then thousands clustering around a fluid-filled vacuum called a blastocyst. Mysteriously, the fluid-filled vacuum contains the blueprint or DNA patterning (the image) from which all our unfolding originates. Yet instead of reveling in the unfolding, we try to fix our manifestation into an idealized form. We strive to hold our form back from its inevitable auto-destruction. In the process, we block the wild adventure that can send us exploring forward and backward in time, left and right in space, up into spirit and down into matter, pushing our frontiers beyond our wildest imaginings and enjoying discoveries we never dreamed of. By engaging the wild adventure, we will find that we are also strengthening and solidifying the central point of light that is our root or soul.

✳

What is a DreamField but the great matrix called Garden of Eden, the endlessly creative unfolding power? When "HaShem God took Adam and placed him in the Garden of Eden, to work it and to guard it,"[4] the Garden and Adam were one, encompassing the whole universe. As a descendant of Adam, you inherit the Garden to work it and to guard it. But have you really worked it or guarded it? How large is your garden, how vast your DreamField? The answer is that it is not as vast as Adam haRishon's, the first male/female but it is as vast as your consciousness can grasp. Can you make it larger? Can you strengthen its creative muscle? What blocks it from spreading, like a great golden web to the outer edges of the universe?

The word "Eden" in Hebrew means delight. When we feel delight, like Adam haRishon, we are infinitely expanded. Delight for a moment returns us to being who we really are, the Adam of the Garden working it and guarding it. Delight clothes us in infinite radiance that spreads and expands, washing away all ills, blocks, and habits. "Happy is the share of one who attains this garment of which we have spoken, in which the righteous are clothed in the Garden of Eden!" says the Zohar.[5]

But when Adam and Eve are expelled from the Garden, their DreamField contracts. They lose their radiance, as they separate from Divine source, and feel their nakedness for the first time. Their expansiveness is reduced to animal skins God gives them to cover themselves. The serpent, royally erect, loses its legs and is condemned to crawl on its belly. Fear and shame constrict their DreamField, and the consequences are what we all suffer: enmity, pain, effort, and illness. We are all today fallen Adams and Eves, but we are also potentially radiant Adams and Eves, it is our choice. However, instead of seeking to repair our DreamField, we more often blame the consequences on God and rebel by building our own towers of Babel.[6] Giving birth, the creative sign of a healthy DreamField, became even more difficult.

> A woman making bricks was not allowed to be released in the hour of childbirth, but brought forth while she was making bricks.[7]

The midrash imagines the baby falling into the clay and becoming encased in a brick, the mother's creativity smothered and fixated.[8] Instead of the unquenchable creative flow embodied in Eve-Havah's name, mother of all living, here the mother's heart becomes heavier and heavier as she continues her task of turning fluidity into hardness.

What are the first signs of a DreamField problem? A blockage of energy, illustrated by repetitive gestures, repetitive dreams, and mental blocks. We generally call these repetitive behaviors bad habits, but in modern psychological terms they are called symptoms. Symptoms appear in all four bodies, physical, emotional, mental, and spiritual,* examples of which abound. You will easily recognize physical or emotional symptoms. Mental symptoms are harder to see, as we don't question our fixed ideas. I mentioned in the preface that I had inherited my mother's attitude toward everything Jewish. I wasn't actively anti-Semitic, I just was an anti-Semite. I had never questioned that intellectual position. It would require a k'negdo (confronted with an obstacle) event for me to realize I had a blockage. If the definition of health is being fluid and open, then I definitely wasn't healthy. As for spirit, our fourth body, the greatest blockage is accidie, another word for apathy and indifference toward the mystery, or hubris, excessive self-confidence and pride.

Take a moment to observe repetitive patterns in your life.

Exercise 46
. . . .
Repetitive Movements

Close your eyes. Breathe out slowly three times, counting from three to one. See the one tall, clear, and bright.

Into a mirror ask to be shown a pattern that repeats in one of your four bodies. What image are you shown? What body is affected?

Breathe out. Ask yourself what you need to do to respond to the necessity of your image. And do it until resolution of the image. What are you feeling?

Breathe out. Open your eyes, seeing the new image with open eyes.

. . . .

While we can identify the level at which the symptom manifests, all four bodies are involved, because in the final analysis they are one. To

*I don't mention the fifth body, yehidah, God consciousness, since, by definition, there are no blockages at that level. See chapter 2.

give you an example, here is the story of an older man who was plagued by feelings of inferiority. "My mother had eight pugs and she loved them better than she loved me!" While he had reached the peak of his profession, for which he was much envied, he couldn't enjoy the fruits of his success. His original wounding was emotional, but his mental and spirit bodies were deeply affected, and he died of prostate cancer, quite a metaphor for a blocked creative flow. Carl Jung calls this "core pattern of emotions, memories, perceptions and wishes" a complex. The man had an inferiority complex.

Exercise 47
. . . .
Symptom Clearing

Close your eyes. Breathe out slowly three times, counting from three to one. See the one tall, clear, and bright.

Look at a habitual symptom. What part of your physical body is involved?

Breathe out. What emotion is involved? See and feel the movement of this emotion in your physical body.

Breathe out. What is your fixed idea about this?

Breathe out. What memory is attached to this symptom?

Breathe out. Return to before you experienced this symptom. What do you experience and discover?

Breathe out. See, feel, and know how to repair and restore your four bodies to their original truth.

Breathe out. Open your eyes.

. . . .

In this exercise we returned to a time before the symptom came into existence. Feeling oneself free of the memory and symptom associated may be enough to relieve you of their presence.

Why do we have memories imprinted in particular parts of our bodies? Memory starts with sensory information: It smells, tastes, sounds like . . . If it is accompanied by an emotion such as, anger, fear, disgust, or horror, the sensory impact is exacerbated. Emotions have specific constrictive pathways in our bodies. The more you indulge in an emotion, the deeper you dig the pathway's groove. Anger and fear are primary emotions. If they cannot express themselves, they are pulled back into the body and become stagnant energies, blockages. Anger becomes irritation initially, but when it is more entrenched, it becomes frustration, sadness, boredom, confusion, depression, and self-hate. Fear becomes anxiety, guilt, resentment, and shame. Jealousy and envy belong to both primary emotions. **All emotions are constrictive.**

Exercise 48
. . . .
The Pathways of Emotion

Close your eyes. Breathe out slowly three times, counting from three to one. See the one tall, clear, and bright.

Start with a primary emotion, anger or fear. Relive your latest or most intense memory of experiencing that emotion. Observe the movement in your body.

Breathe out. What color is your emotion?

Breathe out. Sweep the emotion out of your body to the left.
. . . .

Does it rise up from the lower belly all the way up to your face and arms? (Anger.) Does it constrict your solar plexus, causing you to double over? (Fear.)

Exercise 49
. . . .
Switching from Emotions to Feeling

Breathe out. Feel the exact opposite sensation. Where is it in your body? What color is it? How does it move?

Breathe out. Give it a name.

Breathe out. Open your eyes.
. . . .

Do these two exercises together. I've separated them so that you can clearly see the difference. We could have simply swept the emotion to the left and called it quits. But bad habits cannot simply be erased: They must be replaced. This is what you're doing by switching from emotion to feeling.

How does the opposite sensation move? If you've done the switch properly, your body expands like concentric circles in water after you've tossed in a pebble. **All feelings are expansive:** love, peace, harmony, compassion, delight, creativity, joy, exultation, and awe, these concentric circles of energy that I'm calling feeling will wash away your emotional pathway, enlarging your DreamField and restoring you to your true creative self.

Repetitive emotions spawn repetitive bad behavior. You can try dealing with your bad anger habit by changing your behavioral patterns. But emotion is quick to rise and takes you unaware. By then it's too late. Wouldn't it be better to go right to the source? What pushes your button when repetitive emotions are triggered is a sensation, a word, an expression that triggers a memory. The seed of the bad habit, symptom or complex, is still there encapsulated in a memory from which you haven't been able to distance yourself. This memory is not in the past; it exists today, now, in your DreamField, and it is blocking the creative "running to and fro." The following dream illustrates this dynamic: "I'm trying to go up this village street, but a great white cow is blocking the way, and I can't get through." The dreamer is consistently blocked by unresolved emotions toward a withholding and, in his case, incestuous mother, the great white cow.

To retrieve a memory, go to the location in your body where the emotion is felt. The body is like a book, and it stores memories in your cells. I remember once passing my hands above a young woman's body to clear her energy field. "You are six, and you have a rabbit in your womb!" The reaction was immediate. She burst into uncontrollable sobs: "My daddy killed my rabbit when I was six!"

Traumatic memory is imprinted by a shock. The therapeutic community has long believed that telling the story releases the sufferer. But I believe, from years of dealing with sufferers, that unless the attention is drawn away from the story toward a new sensation or image, retelling the story will only imprint the memory deeper. EMDR*

---

*Eye movement desensitization and reprocessing. If you are recounting a distressful event, your eyes will automatically look downward. Following the therapist's finger, the sufferer's eyes shift into an upward movement. The theory is that the event cannot stay implanted as a painful memory in the brain if the eyes move in a positive upward manner.

and tapping therapy* claim to use such shifting successfully. For my part, the most organic and powerful way to clear traumatic memory is to correct the images in the subconscious, by going back to those images, smells, and physical sensations that are imprinted in the cells. The work is to transform the experience. Once the sufferer experiences the revelation of a new image, that image effectively replaces the old images. How does one respond to the necessity of the white cow? Here are some answers I've gotten from my students: I can climb over, dig a tunnel under, fly over, cut the cow in two. The important thing is to be able to get past the blockage and see what is beyond. What is beyond is an unobstructed view of the DreamField and its myriad possibilities, which had been blocked by the white cow.

We are made of dream images, and those dream images can affect our four bodies. The emotional shock of the father killing this young woman's pet rabbit affected her mental and physical bodies. She developed an autoimmune disease and was no longer able to conceive. But after our work, she was able to think of having a baby in a whole new way. She adopted a beautiful little girl.

Like Oedipus, whose name means "swollen ankles," we can't simply walk away from our complexes. The Greeks were pessimists and believed in fate: Oedipus was fated to live and die by his complex. In psychology we call this the Oedipal complex, the desire to kill one's father and marry one's mother (the opposite for girls). This is a developmental childhood stage that all of us must successfully navigate. But have we done so?

Exercise 50
. . . .
The Four Stages of Development

Close your eyes. Breathe out slowly three times, counting from three to one. See the one tall, clear, and bright.

See, feel, and have an image that encapsulates your experience of gestation in the womb;

---

*Tapping along acupressure meridians to release stress while recounting emotionally distressful memories.

Breathe out. See, feel, and have an image that encapsulates your experience of birthing;

Breathe out. See, feel, and have an image that encapsulates your experience of bonding;

Breathe out. See, feel, and have an image that encapsulates your experience of socializing.

Breathe out. See how these four great moments repeat themselves on a different octave every seven years.

Breathe out. Go through each seven-year period recognizing the sameness and difference of these four moments in your life.

Breathe out. Respond to the necessity of each image: gestation, birthing, bonding, socializing.

Breathe out. What are you feeling now?

Breathe out. Open your eyes.

. . . .

To transform our complexes, we have no better guide than fairy tales. Unlike the Greek myths, fairy tales end with happily ever after. Evolved over centuries of storytelling in weaving rooms or village squares, these communal dreams give us the hope and trust that dreaming can overcome bad habits, symptoms, and complexes. Do we live happily ever after? Obviously not! So what does this classical ending really mean?

All fairy tales start with a poisonous seed. Like the Greek myth of the oracle that fixes Oedipus's fate (he cannot escape killing his father and marrying his mother), the fairy tale always begins timelessly, once upon a time, any time, all-time, or frozen in time. The king who will only marry a lady more beautiful than his dead wife (Donkeyskin); the mother who wants to keep her daughter all to herself (Rapunzel); the father who boasts that his daughter can spin gold (Rumpelstiltskin); the would-be parents who'll accept any kind of a child, even one as small as a thumb, so long as they can get a child (Tom Thumb); the grandmother who vicariously lives through her granddaughter by sending her the red cap of sexuality, thus putting her on the road to temptation and danger (Red Riding Hood); these are all poisonous seeds, closed networks. How can telling stories, not factual stories, but communal dreams like fairy tales, help to move lives out of stuck places into creative fulfillment?

Are fairy tales about distraction, stepping away from our embodiment, being free for a moment from our sameness, our habits, and our blocks? That sounds like paradise. But distraction is like any drug, drink, sex, or even food, it is a false paradise. Since we are the creative power behind our DreamField, we cannot step away for long from our embodiment without loosening our ties to life. Yet many people will do anything to escape from their bonds. The price they pay is not being present in their sensations and in their bodies, and therefore not being able to deal with the necessity of their situation. This can sometimes lead to death. We need to be firmly rooted in our bodies in the here and now to be able to deal with the poisonous seed we are confronted with.

I'm not saying there are not many good reasons to escape: accident, trauma, unbearable pain, untenable life situation, or addiction, for example. The DreamBody escaping its physical bonds and floating above the body is an instantaneous natural phenomenon of survival in the face of a shocking situation. It rushes out through the suddenly wide-open solar plexus or up through the top of the head. After 9/11 in New York City, people were all floating above their bodies, like Macy's Parade balloons, an eerie sight for those of us who can *see*. But you can't stay out of your body for too long. This is one of the problems of PTSD.* Like soldiers returning from war zones, New Yorkers urgently needed to get back into their bodies and become grounded again.

Exercise 51
. . . .
Grounding

Close your eyes. Breathe out slowly three times, counting from three to one. See the one tall, clear, and bright.

Imagine that you are floating in the sky like a balloon and can't find your way back to Earth.

Breathe out. Imagine that you grow roots out of the soles of your feet, and send them growing down to Earth.

---

*Post-traumatic stress disorder.

Breathe out. See the roots entering and planting themselves solidly in the earth.

Breathe out. Feel that your solidly planted roots are pulling you back down to Earth.

Breathe out. Feel the soles of your feet resting on the earth. Feel your weight as you stand on the earth.

Breathe out. Start walking, feeling that this Earth is your anchor.

Breathe out. Open your eyes, feeling this with open eyes.

・・・・・・・・・・・

But then what if the DreamBody can't or won't reintegrate its physical boundaries? What if the life situation is so untenable that floating out of the body is the only way to survive? To live half in, and half out, is often the heroic stance adopted by children to survive difficult family situations. Is Cinderella an escapee? Through playing the good girl, the martyr in the face of unrelenting abuse from those who should love her, she is in fact disembodying herself from her true instincts. She's playing the angel to their devils. She looks like a flesh and blood girl, but her name, meaning cinder or ashes, tells us that she's not in her body. Like the mourners of old, covered in sackcloth and ashes, she's mourning herself, her true instincts, and her emotions. She has accepted the fact that to survive, she must hide who she really is. And what better way than to dissociate? What brings her back into her body is a jolt, the proclamation of a ball, a great and possible new future with love attached. Hope has put her right back into her body. Now she must have a gown and shoes, and a carriage with horses and footmen. Her instincts of pleasure and comfort and beauty are rushing back to her. She is coming alive again.

But the clock strikes midnight, and the bell-like sound reawakens all her bad habits that come rushing back on cue. At midnight, Cinderella returns to be a miserable girl again, covered in ashes and sackcloth. The habit of despair, doubt, and hopelessness destroys the hope exactly on time. Habits work in rhythms and don't appear all the time, only at certain fixed times or when certain triggers have been released.

We were madly in love, talking marriage and children. For six months, we were never out of each other's sight. He made plans to leave his restrictive job and lifestyle. He loved the new horizons I was opening up for him. Then he went abroad where he met up with all his old cronies. I don't know what happened, but he returned a different man. He said he no longer loved me and that the relationship was over. He returned to his narrow, restricted form of living.

The midnight stroke had tolled, and for him so far there has been no jolt out of his old blockage, his belief in his own inadequacies and failure. Luckily for Cinderella, her blockage, her habit of dissociating, becomes the way to her cure. When she dissociates at the stroke of midnight (which we know was inevitable, since bad habits, which are twisted instincts, are programmed like breathing or sleep to a certain time pattern), she loses her shoe, her grounding. Luckily for her, the prince finds the shoe and tries to fit the shoe to its owner's foot. The prince is the sign for her to take up the challenge, put on her shoes, and start walking on this Earth. "I am embodied, therefore I experience that I am."[9]

Who is the prince? Sometimes the prince is someone the universe sends to us as a gift, to help us overcome our bad habit. This could be a therapist, a mentor, or a friend. Sometimes the prince is someone our dreaming sends us to help us overcome our blockage. We may need both, for there is nothing harder than to clear bad habits.

> We were slaves of Pharaoh in Egypt, but the Lord brought us out with a mighty hand.[10]

It takes the mighty hand of the Lord to lead us out of Egypt! Egypt, Mitsrayim in Hebrew, means "the narrow land." If the mighty hand for Cinderella is the prince, no pun intended, again we ask who is the prince? Let's conceptualize the story of Cinderella as a dream where each person in the dream is a part of the dreamer. The father, the active dynamic part of the self, is dead. The dreamer is battling with a dependency issue, her overwhelming desire to be loved by the mother. The mother is a bad mother to her, but good in a dynamic dreaming way, as by her opposition to Cinderella's collapsed state, she is pushing Cinderella to grow up. The sisters are projections of her rebellious self, mirror images, opposites of the good girl complex. Now can you see who the prince is? Her dynamic self (father, prince) is resurfacing from the dead, and is urging her to come down to Earth, to ground herself, to stand in her own two shoes. And what beautiful shoes they are!

Exercise 52
. . . .
Listening to the Body

Close your eyes. Breathe out slowly three times, counting from three to one. See the one tall, clear, and bright.

Feel and sense that it is only by knowing how to hear our body, and how to speak to it, that we unblock its blocked parts and are present to ourselves.

Breathe out. Know that it is this presence to ourselves that lets us be present to the world, and present to others.

Breathe out. Open your eyes, feeling this with open eyes.
. . . .

Remember that fairy tales are communal dreams. Understanding that you are each and every part of the dream will help you to understand the message of the fairy tale (identifying the poisoned seed in your DreamField), and to embody its ultimate transformation. Imagine that like the queen in "Snow White," you make a wish that reflects your vanity rather than your truth. "How I wish I had a daughter that had skin as white as snow, lips as red as blood, and hair as black as ebony." But as the daughter grows up, and you're confronted with her youth and beauty, the red alarm button that triggers your complex lights up. You die to your old self, the good mother, and you become the wicked stepmother. (The Grimm brothers called her stepmother because they were afraid that people would be turned off by the idea of a bad mother.) Before the mirror, in love with your own reflection you are in a wasteland of envy, and refusal to see the truth, until the mirror's voice, your inner voice, jolts you into the beginning movements of transformation. "Snow White is more beautiful!" Who is Snow White?

Exercise 53
. . . .
Snow White

Close your eyes. Breathe out slowly three times, counting from three to one. See the one tall, clear, and bright.

Be the wicked stepmother, looking into the magic mirror on the wall. Ask the mirror: Who is the fairest of us all?

Breathe out. Hear the words: "Snow White is fairer." See her.

Breathe out. Enter the mirror and become Snow White. Pay attention to the difference in feeling between the stepmother and Snow White. Who do you prefer to be?

Breathe out. Come out of the mirror, and look into it; what do you see now?

Breathe out. Open your eyes.

. . . .

Looking out at you from your inner mirror is your soul. She is embodied in your heart, which the queen tries to kill, by sending the hunter after her in the forest, with orders to bring her heart back. The ravages of the vanity complex—having to be seen as the most beautiful, or die— are apparent, when the queen desires to eat the heart. Meanwhile the dreaming is at work in the hidden depths of the earth: the seven dwarfs (your trusty inner allies) are digging for the treasures (the forces for ki tov, good) hidden in the queen's own interior land. But the complex is so insistent that it manages to trick even the soul. Snow White takes a bite of the poisoned apple (poisoned seed) and falls into a comatose sleep. What wakes her up? The prince, the active principle, attracted to the beauty of the soul. At the wedding of soul and active principle (choice), the queen is given red-hot shoes that burn the complex to smithereens. And from that moment on, they lived happily ever after.

In other words, it is possible to get rid of a complex. And when a complex is dissolved, it doesn't return. For a moment, filled with happiness and delight, you can again expand throughout your DreamField. You can run to and fro like a flash of lightning, enlarging your consciousness, and stretching your possibilities ever further. Until life forces you to face and conquer another complex, and another, as did Herakles (Hercules in Latin), who faced twelve tasks before he was freed and became a shining star in the firmament of his own matrix, his DreamField.

To be rid of a complex, it is good to take on the different roles that appear in the fairy tale, or in your own life story. See your life story and its repetitive patterns as a dream, in which all the protagonists are parts of yourself. Your mother, your father, your partner, your spouse, children, boss, colleagues, are all mirror images of yourself. It is good to step into their shoes for a moment.*

Exercise 54
· · · · · · · · · · ·
Switching Roles

Close your eyes. Breathe out slowly three times, counting from three to one. See the one tall, clear, and bright.
　　See, feel, and live being
　　A scullery maid and a queen;
　　A child and a parent;
　　A human being and an animal;
　　A wicked witch and a good mother;
　　A dwarf and a prince.
　　Breathe out. What has changed for you?
　　Breathe out. Open your eyes.
· · · · · · · · · · ·

Playing at different roles frees you from being stuck in the one role assigned to you by your complex.

Exercise 55
· · · · · · · · · · ·
Shape-Shifting

Close your eyes. Breathe out slowly three times, counting from three to one. See the one tall, clear, and bright.
　　See, feel, and live being a mouse, and turning into a horse.
　　Breathe out. Be a pumpkin, and turn into a carriage.
　　Breathe out. Be a lizard, and turn into a footman.
　　Breathe out. Be a scullery maid, and turn into a princess.

---

*See chapter 6, exercise 35.

Breathe out. At the stroke of midnight, see, feel, and live returning to your original state. What do you feel? What changes for
you? What, if anything, do you decide to do?

Breathe out. Open your eyes.

· · · · · · · · · · ·

Shape-shifting will help loosen your attachment to the role you're
playing. It will also make you aware of the motivations behind other
people's role-playing. In "Hansel and Gretel," you can better comprehend
the roles the mother plays, if you see each transformation as a role. The
bad mother who refuses Hansel and Gretel food is in fact the good
mother, trying to wean them from her breast. But she is still ambivalent
about letting go of her infants, and allowing them to grow, so she
reverts back to her old role of nurturer. As her behavior is no longer
appropriate for their age, she is now called witch. She plies the children
with milk and sweets, in the process metaphorically eating them alive
(not allowing them space to grow), until Gretel, sick of the dependency
(she's behaving like the active principle here) she had been complicit in,
shoves the witch into the oven. The transformation happens through
burning. The complex goes up in flames, and the mother-witch becomes
the good duck who helps them across the river. She is now treating them
appropriately for their age development. They are young adolescents,
able to use their own aptitudes and riches as signified by the treasures
they find in the witch's house. They live happily ever after because none
of them are holding onto their old roles. They are accepting to change,
to grow up, and to embody new roles.

Having allowed yourself to shape-shift with your closest and
dearest, like Gretel, it is time to attack the complex. Remember that
you can clear it by sweeping to the left, dissolving, destroying, melting,
burning, or any other form of transforming action.

Exercise 56
· · · · · · · · · · ·
Boulders

Close your eyes. Breathe out slowly three times, counting from three
to one. See the one tall, clear, and bright.

Imagine the obstacles in your life (symptoms, bad habits, and complexes) as large boulders in the ocean. Watch as the work of wind and water slowly dissolves the boulders, until all that is left is a polished stone washed up by the waves.

Breathe out. Pick up the stone, and hold it in the palm of your hand. What do you do with it?

Breathe out. Open your eyes.

· · · · · · · · · · ·

There are, of course many imaginative ways of clearing symptoms, bad habits, and complexes. Fairy tale endings will give you ideas. You can choose what best suits you. But remember, it is always good to have internal allies, as did Snow White with the seven dwarfs. You can call on your helpers, guardian angels, animal allies, and ancestors.

Exercise 57
· · · · · · · · · · ·
The Golden Key

Close your eyes. Breathe out slowly three times, counting from three to one. See the one tall, clear, and bright.

Imagine that you are given a golden key to liberate the light princess and the lost princess.

Breathe out. See them acting to bring out the best in you.

Breathe out. Open your eyes.

· · · · · · · · · · ·

✳

"O brother, I have an internal wound!" says King Shahryar in *One Thousand and One Nights*. Betrayed by a woman, his subconscious compelled him to use women, only to kill them in the morning. Better to dispose of them before they had time to betray him. What cures him? A female voice, with a thousand and one ways of weaving the matrix into new configurations.

Exercise 58
· · · · · · · · · · ·
Interweaving

Close your eyes. Breathe out slowly three times, counting from three to one. See the one tall, clear, and bright.

Listen to the silence of the forest. Hear all the different sounds that are constructing this silence. Feel and know how they are weaving together, but recognize how they are both threatening and enlivening.

Breathe out. Look at the play of shadow and light between the trunks of the trees and the branches, and let yourself be filled by the visions and imagery coming from them.

Breathe out. Smell the different fragrances, and taste the berries and fruits of the forest.

Breathe out. Hear a female voice whispering through the forest; what is she saying?

Breathe out. Open your eyes.

. . . .

Listen to your dreaming voice, the "still small voice"[11] that seduces you back into the mystery! She is called the Empress, Eve, Scheherazade, the mother of all living. If all goes well, if you have allowed yourself to be "re-enchanted"[12] as Bruno Bettelheim calls it, a new vision of your DreamField will have filled your wondering senses. Together you will birth a child of light, as did Scheherazade and King Shahryar, and you will live happily ever after, at least vis-à-vis the complex that had previously enslaved you. It will no longer ever trouble you. That is the promise of "they lived happily ever after."

9

Ancestral Patterns

Everything that does not rise into consciousness comes back as fate.

CARL JUNG

Who are we? Where do we come from? Where do we go? Most of us would say that we come from the void, and we're returning to the void. But somehow that doesn't quite cut it. We look like our parents, or the maternal great-uncle, or the grandmother on our father's side. Why do we look the way we do? In our bones, coloring, and musculature, are we continuing our ancestors' bodies? If our bodies are created by the DreamField, is it the parents' dreamfields that somehow merge in a big bang, a yud moment,* to bring forth a new creation, unique but also encapsulating information provided by the ancestral pool? We could say that following the injunction to be fruitful and multiply,[1] the many entangled dreamfields of our ancestors bring the past forward in what Stanley Keleman called "the long body." Just imagine the ancestral pool from which bubbles burst forth, float freely for a moment, explode, and disappear back into the ancestral pool, only to be replaced by more bubbles. While our incarnations may be mere blips on the surface of the family DreamField, they are crucial, since

---

*The first letter of God's name.

through our earthly incarnation we are free to use the information given to either damage or correct the ancestral pool in any way we see fit. But will we be able to identify and exercise our choices?

The DreamField is a matrix of experiencing. It catches holographic images within its net that affect and transform every part of the net. The DreamField acts like our proverbial hundredth monkey. According to the story, a monkey discovers how to wash a sweet potato. Soon all the other monkeys are washing their sweet potatoes. When a critical mass is reached (a hundred monkeys), the learned behavior jumps across space, and suddenly on other islands, whole groups of monkeys who have never witnessed any of their kind washing sweet potatoes are now washing their own sweet potatoes. While the hundredth monkey theory has been debunked, something similar, but much faster, in fact instantaneous, happens, without apparent contact, within a family DreamField. A member of the family, while living at the antipodes, out of contact with other family members, will resonate to the same blueprint as the rest of the family. Quantum dreaming? Across space there are many examples of people picking up on the death of one of their family members, or on a traumatic family event. Think of radio waves. You turn on the radio and tune it to your favorite channel, and immediately across huge swaths of land, you can hear as if you were there. It is your emotional or mental predilections that determine the channel you listen to, and in the dreamtime, it is the same. Subconscious cues, perhaps programmed into the blood that you share with other family members, attune you to hidden family patterns. We could call this telepathy, as the messages travel through space. Do those messages also travel forward and backward through time?

I sat with my teacher Colette on a beautiful fall day. I'd traveled from New York to Jerusalem to be with her two days prior. Some sudden urge had provoked my visit. The Second Intifada* was raging, and my son didn't want me to go. But I knew I had to go. If I was going, he decided he would go too. "She is my grandmother!" he insisted. Her simple message to me that morning was reminiscent of my son's proclamation: "Don't

---

*Palestinian uprising against Israel, 2000–2005.

forget your ancestors!" I wondered whether she was referring to my birth family or to hers. The portrait of a great-grandmother from centuries ago hung above Colette's bed. As always, her dark, mysterious eyes followed me around the room. A great-grandfather stood beneath an image of the Shekhinah* and surveyed us with severity, his long white beard shining above the darkness of his djellaba.† Suddenly Colette pointed her finger at me and shouted: "Go!" I was shocked and ran out of her house in great confusion. That is when she chose to die. I didn't know it yet, but in that instant, she had become my ancestor.

Ancestors are in our dreamfields. Their ways and secrets become ours. When I got home, still in a trance from her passing, I pulled out a book from my library, opened it, and read. I cannot reproduce the exact text, as I've never been able to find it again. It said: When the master says "Go!" to the disciple, it means 'Take up the torch. Now is your time. Go and teach!' The family message was passing through time, and my work was to facilitate its continuation. I could damage the work, pass it on as it was given me, or "ameliorate" it, as we are meant to ameliorate the dream.‡ In the first years after her death, I would look down at my hands and see hers. Her goodness was with me; so were her few flaws. Would I be able to honor her by freeing myself, by becoming me, not her? Would I be able to embody the work and make it my own, with my own goodness and my own flaws? What parts of her would I keep? What parts would I reject or discard? Did I have a choice?

After the Flood, when God destroyed all of humanity except Noah and his family and a male/female pair of each of the animal species, Noah planted a vine in the new world and got drunk. As he lay naked in his tent, his son Ham (the name means "hot") entered the tent, saw his father's nakedness, and did him damage.§ Ham later reported the matter derisively to his two brothers who, justifiably disgusted at his lack of

---

*The feminine divine presence, dwelling within us and among us in the world of manifestation.

†Long, loose unisex robe worn in North Africa.

‡See chapter 2.

§The Talmud asks, did he simply gloat at his father's fallen state? Did he use him sexually? Did he castrate him? In one way or another, his impulsive behavior damaged the family DreamField.

respect, entered the tent backward and covered their father's nakedness. Noah, on awakening, realized what had happened, and he cursed not Ham, but Ham's fourth son, Canaan! The reasoning, commentators tell us, is that, because of the damage done to him, Noah would no longer be able to father a fourth son. But four also means, in dream language, something stable, something fixed. "A slave of slaves shall he be."[2] The implication was that Canaan and his descendants would be slaves to the raw, uncontrolled sexuality exhibited by their progenitor Ham, that sexuality unbridled would be their cursed pattern and complex. "For I the Lord thy God am a jealous God, visiting the sins of the fathers upon the children onto the third and fourth generation."[3]

Does God really visit the sins of the fathers on their sons? Is this true? Is it fair?

✳

Bodies are open books for those of you who know how to read their shapes. They are also open books if you practice dreaming. Through turning your eyes inward, you plunge into the experiential memory imprinted into your body cells. You see the inner shape of these experiences, which combines both the event and your response to it. Generally it is the intensity of an event that seeds a memory. Delight and happiness or horror and pain create events that vibrate at a very high speed in the body. It is a rare image that surfaces without some form of emotional potency. This is fine if the experience resolves, and the body returns to harmony at the same or at a higher rhythm. If it doesn't, the rhythmic harmony of the ecosystem begins to degrade.

I was on a kibbutz in the Negev during the Yom Kippur War. We weren't too far from the border, and we could hear the cannon roaring in the desert. My neighbor went off to war, as did most of the men, and he returned on a furlough three weeks later. He hadn't taken his boots off the whole time. I cut them off his feet. Being in the front line commandos, he had horror stories to tell, but he was very calm. That night he had a dream.

I am standing knee-high in a muddy swamp. Suddenly a monstrous form rises out of the mud and towers over me. I catch a bamboo reed and plunge it into the creature's eye. It collapses and disappears into the swamp.

As you can see, this man was healthy. Faced with a Goliath, he acted as a young David did; he responded to the necessity of the image. We can surmise that his energy body returned to harmony, but at a higher octave than before. I hadn't met Colette yet, but I knew what it meant. His images showed him tending toward integration. I knew he was safe from what we today would call PTSD, post-traumatic stress disorder. Remember, unless you are prepared to tackle your images, shock of their immediacy can hasten fragmentation. This man found in himself the courage to deal with his horror images. Transforming fear into courage, emotion into feeling, will propel us up the ladder of vibrations toward the light. He went back to the Sinai in a new pair of boots, clear-eyed and confident and, I am glad to say, returned unscathed. A corrected DreamField, we will see, can keep our four bodies safe, even in the midst of chaos and war.

What if this were you and you hadn't faced your fear, turning it into courage? That failure then becomes an intense negative memory. Guilt, shame, and self-hate are the three devils that torment you and act as barriers in the creative flow of your DreamField. If you don't do something about it, the fragmentation, the lack of reintegration into the dream flow, becomes a poisoned seed, existing timelessly, once upon a time, any time, all time, or frozen in time. The devils take on forms and colors that are disturbing and dark and populate your DreamField.

Everything that does not rise into consciousness comes back as destiny.[4]*

The better translation for this word might be "fate" (we will reserve the word "destiny" for the future you choose for yourself). You are fated

---

*Carl Jung, Swiss psychiatrist and psychoanalyst, 1875–1961. A close collaborator of Sigmund Freud, he later split from his mentor and founded analytical psychology.

to perpetuate the guilt, shame, or self-hate; fated to be blinded to the pattern, like Oedipus's family was: King Laius giving orders to kill the baby son who might one day supplant him, Oedipus killing the father who had rejected him and marrying his mother, his sons killing each other in a vain effort to get his throne. While the story line says that Oedipus blinds himself when he finds out he married his mother, the pattern level shows that he and all his family line were always blind to these subconscious urges, and their fates were sealed. "Once upon a time" does not transform into "happily ever after." Instead, endless strife, jealous rage, and vengeful destruction, in the form of the three Erinyes or Furies, pursue Oedipus and his family. His sons and his daughter Antigone all die tragically. What are we to understand here? The Greeks, like the Hebrews, are clearly saying: The sins of the fathers are visited upon the children."[5] We could surmise that because of the holographic nature of dreamfields, the informational organization of every member of that family will be affected by Oedipus's complex. The resonance of rejection of the son by the father, murder, and incest, with its attendant devilish images, will infiltrate the dreamfields of children, of children of siblings, and cousins near and far removed. All members of the family will be affected by the blockage. Should we believe the Greeks and the Hebrews?

In *Totem and Taboo*, Sigmund Freud sketched out the idea of a collective soul to explain how one person's unconscious material could be transmitted to another person's unconscious. Carl Jung, developing the idea of a collective unconscious, opened the door to many different and evolving theories on the subconscious dynamics of the family. But it was French psychologists, studying family lineages in depth, in what they referred to as transgenerational analysis, who really opened up the field. More specifically, Anne Ancelin Schutzenberger, founder of the method psychogenealogy, studied the families of her patients, going back four generations. She then had them draw up a family tree in a diagram she called a genosociogram. What was she looking for? All the major events of our ancestors' lives: births, marriages, deaths, illnesses, accidents, scandals, separations, traumatic events, family secrets—but more importantly, any events or behaviors of one sort or another that repeated for generations. She convincingly demonstrated that in the "long body" many patterns repeat.

Exercise 59
. . . .
Name Patterns

Close your eyes. Breathe out slowly three times, counting from three to one. See the one tall, clear, and bright.

Look at your close and extended family, and search for name patterns. Does someone in your family have the same name as an uncle, aunt, or grandparent?

Breathe out. What do you recognize, if anything, between the ancestor or family member's fate and the one who received his or her name?

Breathe out. What images or memories come up?

Breathe out. Open your eyes, seeing the new image with open eyes.

. . . .

Here's an example of entangled name and fate. A man named Elan goes to Israel to defend the new country and is killed in Hebron. In commemoration, his sister gives her son the same name. Many years later the son goes to Israel, catches a bug that goes undetected, and dies of it. Interestingly, he never wanted to go to Israel, because he always said Israel would kill him, like it did his uncle. He was right.

Exercise 60
. . . .
Family Placement

Close your eyes. Breathe out slowly three times, counting from three to one. See the one tall, clear, and bright.

Look at your placement in the family. Are you the first child, the second, the third, and so on?

Breathe out. Are there any patterns that you can identify between yourself and another member of your family having the same placement?

Breathe out. If yes, see if you can identify similar emotional or behavioral patterns.

Breathe out. Open your eyes.

. . . .

In Bali children are called by their placement: one, two, three, or Ketut: four. After Ketut, there are no more family names. "Why?" I asked my chauffeur. "As a method of contraception," he told me. I wasn't sure if he was joking. If not, it's pretty astute. It reveals how numbers exert a quasi-magical spell on us. Tell a child who is having a tantrum that you'll count from ten to one, and that by one, he has to be in bed. Lengthen the suspense by adding half numbers, two, three-quarters of two, one half of two, a quarter of two . . . one! By one, the child is in bed! Here's an example of placement pattern: A man is the first child, but his young mother doesn't relate to him. When the second child arrives, also a boy, the mother, by then more mature, falls in love with her second baby. Later in life, her first son marries and has a son. All goes well. But when a second son is born, the father becomes crazed with anger and jealousy, telling his wife he doesn't want the child, he wants her all to himself. It's a clear case of abandonment and sibling rivalry transposed to his wife and second son. The story continues with his first son, who, having internalized the father's pattern, pursues his campaign of jealousy and rage against the younger brother, or second son.

Exercise 61
. . . .
Family Dates

Close your eyes. Breathe out slowly three times, counting from three to one. See the one tall, clear, and bright.

Identify recurring dates in the family: births, deaths, accidents, illnesses, financial or professional successes, or disasters.

Breathe out. What memories, and what images are associated with those dates?

Breathe out. Open your eyes.
. . . .

As I pointed out in my book *DreamBirth,* conception is more likely to occur on family dates. With births, the entanglement of two family dreamfields combines possible dates that are recurring in both families. Let's say a maternal grandfather is born on July 10 and a paternal sister is born July 6. These dates become entangled, so that the probability of conceiving around these dates is higher. Illnesses also tend to follow dates.

In a family where all the women develop breast cancer at the same age, the probability that they will all die at the same age is greater. If a family member has committed suicide, other family members with depression are more prone to follow in their footsteps, especially on the egregious date. If the father's company went bankrupt when he was fifty-two, the son and his company are vulnerable during his fifty-second year. Check dates. This is the reason you don't want to schedule a surgery, a wedding, or a crucially important meeting on a difficult family date.

What about family secrets? Do they also act as bell-like symptoms, patterns that will have their way whether you're aware of them or not? The proverbial skeleton in the closet and the ghost in an ancestor's past exist in the subconscious.

Exercise 62
. . . .
Repairing the Ancestral Garden

Close your eyes. Breathe out slowly three times, counting from three to one. See the one tall, clear, and bright.

Ask your guardian angel and helpers to accompany you.

Breathe out. Imagine entering the ancestral garden. What does it look like? Does it need to be tended?

Breathe out. Call on an ancestor who has a grievance or unfinished business to reveal themselves. Trust what the dreaming shows you. Ask how you can help.

Breathe out. With the help of your guardian angel and helpers, find a way to help your ancestor to repair what they need to have repaired.

Breathe out. When the repair has been done, tell your ancestor they are free, and send them to where souls live in peace and harmony.

Breathe out. Now restore the garden, by weeding, pruning and gardening until the garden blooms.

Breathe out. Open your eyes, seeing the restored garden with open eyes.

. . . .

However hidden they are, family secrets will resurface one day, like flotsam. They will either be completely revealed, or else their patterns will. Here is a case documented by Anne Ancelin Schutzenberger. A man came to see her because he found himself in an untenable situation. He loved his wife, but he had a mistress and couldn't understand why. After investigation, it turned out that his father had a similar extramarital situation, as had his grandfather. The pattern had originated with the grandfather but continued to play out in the grandson's life.

While Ancelin Schutzenberger perfectly identified pattern formation, she did not identify what should, by this point in the book be obvious: Pattern formation is the way dream language comes together and speaks to us. In the dreaming, as we saw in chapters 1 and 2, forms, colors, numbers, and dates aggregate because of affinity, similarity, or complementarities. We are not dealing here with cause and effect, but with dream and affect. We are all dreamers affected by the patterns of cycles that are those also of nature, and of the planets. Our life's movements—call them instincts—are in rhythmic patterns. We breathe in rhythm. We eat, sleep, make love, and move in rhythm. Our dreaming or "mythic imagery is the body speaking to itself about itself."[6] As all of nature does, the subconscious speaks in patterns, as **Remez,** the second level of DreamOpening, proves.

The third level, **Drash,** questioning, speaks to the longing of all bodies to find internal stability,* ki tov, within their own personal DreamField, and within the larger dreamfields of family, nature, and the universe. How do we cure repetitive damaging patterns in the family lineage? By recognizing that they are repetitive dreams. And as with all repetitive dreams, we respond to their necessity.

We will then see the old pattern dissolving, and **Sod,** the treasure, or fourth level of DreamOpening, will appear in restorative images that will facilitate a revived flow in the family DreamField, and a restored harmony within the larger dreamfields of nature and the universe.

Is it possible? Yes, and the change is instantaneous. Only you

---

*What in medicine is called homeostasis.

cannot do it by simply bringing the patterns to consciousness, as Jung and the psychogenealogists seemed to suggest. The tikun, or correction of the images, is essential. As the shape shifts in your DreamField from dark, nightmarish images to bright, healthy images, so also do your four bodies shift back to health. To help us return to a unified field, if I might borrow a term from modern physics, or to help us to surrender (Kabbalah means "surrender"), as mystics would call it, to our personal and family ki tov, let us first do a memory clearing exercise.

Exercise 63
. . . .
The Cylindrical Mirror (Formal)

Close your eyes. Breathe out slowly three times, counting from three to one. See the one tall, clear, and bright.

Imagine that you stand before a tall, cylindrical mirror.

Breathe out. As the cylindrical mirror starts turning, see difficult memories you want to be rid of escaping as smoke from every pore, and every fold of your body.

Breathe out. You don't need to know what those memories are. See the smoke floating off to the left.

Breathe out. Make sure to let go of the memories hidden between the folds of your toes and fingers, behind your ears, and between your legs.

Breathe out. Continue watching as long as the cylindrical mirror is turning. When it stops, you know you have let go of the memories you can let go of today.

Breathe out. Look at yourself in the mirror. How do you look now?

Breathe out. Open your eyes, seeing the new image with open eyes.

. . . .

At the end of the exercise, you should be seeing yourself in the mirror looking much perkier and brighter. This is an exercise you can continue doing as a formal practice for twenty-one days, or between two menstrual cycles. But while clearing general memories is a good thing, particularly entrenched patterns need more specific exercises.

There are two types of memories, memory linked to emotion, and memory linked to feeling.* It is the first kind of memory that creates blockage. When anger and fear, our primary emotions of fight or flight, have run their course, exhausting their raison d'être, all is well. (For anger: You killed the tiger that was ready to pounce. For fear: You ran back to your hut and closed the door just in time.) But when they cannot or are not allowed to run their course ("Do not hit your sister" or "Boys don't cry"), the emotions turn inward and become secondary emotions, energies blocked in holding patterns. The stronger the emotion, the deeper the holding pattern. Because these holding patterns are difficult to endure (either emotionally or physically), people seek relief by resorting to what looks like instinctual behavior—but only mimics instinct while disrupting the natural rhythm. They eat when they aren't hungry, which can lead to all sorts of abdominal disorders. They oversleep, or have insomnia, with all the cascade of consequences attached to a disrupted sleep pattern. They engage in sexual perversions, or movement to excess. Their fear turned to anxiety can disrupt the instinctual rhythm of breathing, resulting in abnormal breathing patterns, asthma, desire to smoke, and need for stimulants. Secondary instinctual behaviors with all their attendant ills are part of the complex pattern that you may find perpetuating down through generation after generation, creating "an intense field of many levels of energies, in constant process," tending in this case toward fragmentation. Once the complex pattern has settled in, with its disruptive rhythms and abnormal neurological pathways, it is difficult to revert back to normal pathways. The nervous system has become habituated.

Behavior management strategies won't cut it in the long run,† because the images that govern how the body functions are embedded deep in the DreamField. Symptoms, complexes, and patterns all start with an event that imprints itself into the DreamField. Whether we are dealing with our own events, or with family history, the process of correction is the same: We need to return to the source.

---

*See exercises 47–49.

†Unless they're based on feeling or on higher divine guidance, as in AA (Alcoholics Anonymous).

Exercise 64
· · · · · · · · · · ·
The Family Tapestry

Close your eyes. Breathe out slowly three times, counting from three to one. See the one tall, clear, and bright.

Imagine that you take the whole day, starting at dawn to weave your family's story into a tapestry.

Breathe out. At nightfall take a look at your tapestry. Pay attention to the parts in the tapestry that you don't like, to colors and stories that stand out in a disagreeable way.

Breathe out. Start undoing your tapestry color by color. Take the night to do it.

Breathe out. At dawn your tapestry is undone.

Now breathe out twice. Start weaving a new tapestry of the family story, keeping what you like, and leaving what you don't like. You can use different colors if you wish.

Breathe out. See your finished family tapestry. Are you satisfied? Continue until you are perfectly satisfied.

Breathe out. Open your eyes, seeing the new tapestry with open eyes.

· · · · · · · · · · ·

Memory is not all-inclusive. Think of it, as we've already said, as so many pop-ups, or bubbles, in the flow of a great river. Memories frame moments and flows, giving them boundary forms and images you can relate to. Subterranean memories and flows, of which you are not aware, also exist. By discarding unpleasant memories, you are making room for new memories to float up to the surface of your consciousness. All those hard feelings that plagued you about your mother are gone. Now you're remembering only the fun times with her. Of course, the clearing work is not so easy to do when time has eroded many of the memories blocking your familial DreamField through multiple generations. Your only way of catching the tail of those memories is by observing repetitive painful patterns in yourself and maybe in other members of the family. Asking questions of family members may help. But there is a faster way: asking your subconscious. You can always verify afterward with older members of the family whether what has arisen for you from the ancestral DreamField is true.

First identify the nagging pattern you've observed in yourself and other members of the family that you wish to clear. Then do this exercise. This is the main exercise for clearing an ancestral pattern.*

Exercise 65
. . . .
Clearing Ancestral Trauma

Close your eyes. Breathe out slowly three times, counting from three to one. See the one tall, clear, and bright.

Recognize a recurring pattern in your life. Observe whether this is also a familial pattern.

Breathe out. Return back through your life, noting the pattern as it occurs. Do this fast. Do not linger.

Breathe out. Go to the very first time in your life that you observe this pattern. How old are you? Where are you? Who else is there? What is the event?

Breathe out. Cut the cord between you and the other person(s).

. . . .

Breathe out. Return into your mother's womb. Return backward through the gestational development, watching to see whether you experience the same emotions that are consistent with this pattern. Note the gestational ages when you feel it most strongly.

Breathe out. Go back to the time of conception. What feelings do you experience?

Breathe out. Go back to before incarnation. Look down at your two parents, and ask what attracted you to them.

Breathe out. Ask what is your mission in life. Make sure to clearly recognize your mission before moving on.

. . . .

Breathe out. Turn 180 degrees. Looking at the familial dream-fields of your father and your mother; ask which one needs to be addressed to clear this recurring pattern you are working on. See the DreamField that needs to be addressed lighting up.

Breathe out. Ask to be taken directly to the very first event that triggered this pattern, and its repetition down the family line. This

---

*You will do best if you can listen to the taped recording of this exercise, as it is quite long. See Learn More at the end of this book.

event could have happened many generations ago. **Trust your dreaming, and the images you are being shown.** Describe exactly what is happening, and who it is happening to. Describe everything you are shown about the event.

. . . .

Breathe out three times counting from three to one. Roll back this person's life to show you what was happening before this traumatic event occurred.

Breathe out. Roll this person's life forward. How has the event impacted this person's life? What has this person's life been like since the damaging event?

Breathe out. Come to the person's time of death. What are this person's feelings and thoughts at the time of passing?

Breathe out three times counting from three to one. You, today, go stand next to your ancestor as they experience the traumatic event. Tell your ancestor you are going to cut the cord that has held their soul, and all the souls of the family lineage, in bondage to this memory.

Breathe out. Call on the great force of transformation that you can visualize as the archangel Michael. See the blue sky opening, Michael descending, dressed in his sapphire blue robe, holding the sapphire blue sword of fire.

Breathe out. Ask his permission to borrow the sword.

Breathe out. Using Michael's sword, cut the cord connecting this ancestor to the traumatic event. See what happens to the perpetrator(s) or to the scene.

Breathe out. If the perpetrator(s) is/are still there, continue cutting invisible cords until the perpetrator(s) has/have gone or dissolved.

Breathe out. Tell your ancestor that their soul is now free and can go where souls live. Watch as the soul leaves.

. . . .

Breathe out three times, counting from three to one. There is a bucket of water at your feet. Plunge the tip of the sword into the water. See the sapphire blue fire charging the water. Now you have firewater.

Breathe out. Return the sword to archangel Michael, thanking him. Ask for his blessing.

Breathe out. Feel his hand on your head. See and feel the sapphire blue fire passing through every cell in your body, clearing and cleansing it of this old pattern. The fire will stop running through your body when it is done.

Breathe out. See your cells returning to their natural healthy alignment.

Breathe out. Look into the eyes of the archangel and hear his blessing.

Breathe out. Watch as he returns into his heavenly abode.

· · · · · · · · · · ·

Breathe out three times, counting from three to one. See the line of your ancestors all the way down to your children and their children, cousins, nephews and nieces, and their children.

Breathe out. Take the firewater, and throw it down the line. Watch what happens to the lineage.

Breathe out. There is one drop left in the bucket. Pick it up on the tip of your index finger, and place it on your body where the body wants it.

Breathe out. Open your eyes, knowing the repair is done and the pattern cleared out for you, for all your ancestry and for your living and future family members.

· · · · · · · · · · ·

How do you know if what you've seen is a historical fact involving one of your ancestors? You can make inquiries, or you may never know. It's not that important. What is important is that those images were logged in your subconscious, have surfaced at your inquiry, and were transformed. It's done! So simple. And it will remain done unless you perversely call back your bad habits. Habits are what you must watch for. Imagine the following scenario: You've stopped smoking, and your cravings are gone; then a smoking buddy taunts you with a cigarette, and out of some perverse challenge to yourself, you take the cigarette. That's when the old habit can reassert itself. Any temptation? The best way to get rid of habits is to sweep them out of your subconscious and replace them with a feeling.

Exercise 66
· · · · · · · · · · ·
The Golden Broom

Close your eyes. Breathe out slowly three times, counting from three to one. See the one tall, clear, and bright.

Imagine that you have a little golden broom.

Breathe out. Sweep the temptation out of your body to the left.

Breathe out. Return to the feeling of peaceful body you had when not smoking (or drinking or eating or whatever your bad habit is). See where the feeling is located in your body. See its color. Give it a name.

Breathe out. Open your eyes, hearing the name and seeing the color with open eyes.

· · · · · · · · · · ·

You have cleared an ancestral pattern, and you're basking in the newfound freedom. But it's not enough to rest on your laurels. Ask to be shown other ancestral patterns that block your access to greater consciousness. You can do it by asking your night dreams,* or simply your daytime consciousness.† Ancestral patterns abound in family dreamfields, but you want to peel them off slowly, for, as the Talmud tells us, if you peel an onion to its core at night, by morning you're dead. In other words, you wouldn't want to lose your identity all at once. Peel off one layer first, then rebuild slowly, before moving on to the next layer.

Take your time. Observe yourself. Ask yourself if your qualities are inherited. While the good fairy godmothers shower us with good qualities, there is also a bad fairy godmother who curses us with a bad quality or two passed on by our ancestors. Can we choose what we want to discard, and what we want to keep?

Exercise 67
· · · · · · · · · · ·
Choosing Ancestral Gifts

Close your eyes. Breathe out slowly three times, counting from three to one. See the one tall, clear, and bright.

---

*See exercise 12: Asking a Question of your Dream.

†Let it be a question you keep at the back of your mind. See chapter 10 for more information.

You are standing on a vast empty plain. You know you are the last in a long line of ancestors snaking out behind you, but you don't turn around to look.

Breathe out. Hear a rumble starting way back and growing louder as it comes closer, and feel a ripple of movement like a wave coming toward you.

Breathe out. Something is put into your hand from behind.

Breathe out. Look at what you have in your hand. Do you accept the gift or reject it?

Breathe out. If you don't want the gift, then put whatever it is to your left. If you do accept the gift, put it to your right.

Breathe out. Hear the rumble, and feel the ripple again. Look at what is put in your hand. Put it to your left or to your right, as you choose.

Breathe out. Hear the rumble, and the ripple one more time. Look at what is put in your hand. Put it to your left or to your right, as you choose.

Breathe out. If you have something on your left, burn it, dig a hole in the ground, and bury the ashes.

Breathe out. Gather what you have chosen to keep, and walk off to the right, holding the gift(s) given you by your ancestors (if you have chosen to discard all gifts, that's fine too).

Breathe out. Open your eyes, seeing the gift(s) with open eyes.

· · · · · · · · · · ·

Ancestors are alive and well in your subconscious field. They are your inheritance and represent a huge untapped potential for you. After pruning the field for bad qualities, you can think of your ancestors as an advisory board whose many aptitudes you can employ at will, since they exist in your personal and family dreamfields. Know that you can always ask them questions and make use of their knowledge and aptitudes. Ask for their help, and let the subconscious speak.

Exercise 68
· · · · · · · · · · ·
The Ancestral Tree

Close your eyes. Breathe out slowly three times, counting from three to one. See the one tall, clear, and bright.

See your ancestral tree. See that the roots are strong and healthy, and deeply rooted in your ancestral field.

Breathe out. See the trunk tall and straight; the foliage is abundant and very green.

Breathe out. See that cameo faces of your ancestors are hanging from the branches.

Breathe out. Walk around the tree. Find the ancestor you like the best, and ask for advice.

Breathe out. Find the one who is wise and knows best. Listen to them.

Breathe out. Find the one you dislike most, hear what they have to say that is most distasteful to you.

Breathe out. Thank your ancestors for their advices.

Breathe out. Open your eyes.

. . . .

Knowing how to correct the familial DreamField brings up a big question: Am I my brother's keeper? If anything that happens to you affects the familial DreamField, then anything that happens to another member of the family affects you. We are mirror images of each other. By correcting the ancestral patterns, are you changing the granduncle, the grandmother, the great-grandfather? We will never know, since they are long gone. But we know from experience in this lifetime that we can never change another. Our only responsibility is to respond to the necessity of the obstructive images that appear in our DreamField. In so doing, we are changing the DreamField configuration, and therefore anyone connected to it must, of necessity, even if only subconsciously, sense the change and adapt. Your granduncle, your grandmother, your great-grandfather or simply your twice-removed cousin will have to adapt to the new shift. Thus, by changing your DreamField patterns, you are creating the conditions that will shift the family DreamField. As your consciousness grows, you will realize that your small shifts and corrections will affect larger dreamfields that are communal, national, or even universal. Our small acts of courage and love for our neighbors have huge implications in the larger matrix, the collective unconscious of the world, and the universe.

Think of your heart as the physical manifestation of the yud, the pumping wonder to this extraordinary adventure of coming to life and manifesting through your familial DreamField. The first yud, the big bang of your conception, starts your creative adventure and continues expanding toward its own destiny, opening to its many potential avenues of expression. Where are the roots to this first yud? They go back generations to the first man and woman. But who sets off the big bang? Who lights the first yud?

Exercise 69
. . . .
The First Candle

Close your eyes. Breathe out slowly three times, counting from three to one. See the one tall, clear, and bright.

Imagine that your life force is the flame of a candle that has been lit from generation to generation until it has lit your own life force.

Breathe out. If you have children, see that you have extended your flame to light their life forces.

Breathe out. Go back through all the flames that lit your ancestors' life forces to the very first flame. Who lit that first one?

Breathe out. Return through all the flames to yours; what has changed in your life force?

Breathe out. Open your eyes.
. . . .

This yud, this creative dot in the middle of the void, first becomes lines, then forms, then heart and body, then all your ancestors' bodies until your own and will continue to manifest through your body, dreaming new bodies, new forms, and new outcomes.

As Blake puts it: "The Eternal Body of Man is the Imagination, God Himself, the Divine Body . . . we are its members."[7]

✳

After Colette's death, I took a trip across the south of France, wanting to visit the ancestral localities she had talked to me about. I visited Carcassonne, Narbonne, and Lunel, finding no trace of the important Jewish communities that had flourished there in the Middle Ages. But a surprise awaited me inside a little village bookstore. I found a book about the Jews of the twelfth century in Provence. When I opened it, in the middle of the page, the first word that caught my eye was my mother's family name, du Cailar! Was this the same du Cailar family? Were they Jewish? After much research, and the corroboration of my cousin Jacques du Cailar, it turned out that, "lost in the fogs of time," as my cousin put it, the du Cailars were Jewish. Their ancestral seat, Le Cailar, was a kilometer away from Posquières,* where Isaac the Blind had his yeshiva.† The du Cailars not only owned the land on which the yeshiva operated, but they were Isaac the Blind's students. After eight hundred years, my anti-Semite mother's daughter had returned to her ancestral practices. Was Colette's family allied to ours by blood? I don't know, but the alliance forged by families dreaming together is clearly alive and well eight centuries later, a testament to her dying wish: "Remember your ancestors!"

---

*Now called Vauvert.

†Jewish school focused on the study of Talmud, Torah, and halacha.

10

The Inner Child
From Duality to Singularity

Rabbi El'azar opened, "Lift your eyes on high and see: Who created these? (Isaiah 40:26) Lift your eyes on high. To which site? The site toward which all eyes gaze. Which is that? Opening of the eyes."

ZOHAR 5:26 OR PETACH EINAYI

Where do we come from? Why do we come into this world? And why to the particular ancestry we seem so arbitrarily assigned to, and for whose sins we must pay, unless we learn to clear our lineage?* Does our incarnation depend only on the chromosomal mix of the "long body"? What about our quirks, and unique qualities, our smiles, our funny looks? Do they necessarily come from a grandmother or great-grandfather, or is there something unique that makes us who we are, a combination of DNA and soul? Does our soul consciousness have a choice as to where it will incarnate? Or does its unique energy configuration draw it irresistibly toward another nucleus whose patterns feel familiar? Form locks into form, embryo to maternal womb, one striving against the other, k'negdo,† to stimulate change and transformation. We

---

*See chapter 9.

†Gen 2:18. Eve was created as *ezer k'negdo* to Adam, meaning, "a help to stand against Adam."

are born with animal instincts, but of all animals on this Earth, we are the most vulnerable. We come into this world naked, unprotected. Our high-pitched wails—an annoyance that can't be ignored—are the only defense we have against the world. We are the proverbial Fool, the zero card of the tarot's Major Arcana. Fairy tales like to call us simpleton. In Egyptian myth, in Greek drama, in the Hebrew Bible, in Christian hagiography, this concentrated mass of energy consciousness, this first-born child, is an intrusion to be pursued and destroyed. The threat of death hangs over the innocent.

Powerful males, the gods Seth or Saturn, pharaohs of the stiff neck, Kings Laius, Herod, or simply the family tyrants attacking a newborn? That they should feel threatened by an infant in arms seems ridiculous until we look on these stories as recurring dreams. Think of how many newborn visions, inspirations, ideas we have squashed because our logical mind (our inner tyrant) rejected them as unpractical, while, sub rosa, the subconscious voice continues urging us, as the song says, to come out into the moonlight and "Tiptoe through the Tulips."*

Think of these stories as dreams in which each protagonist is a part of yourself. Who is the powerful adult male in you, destroying your innocence? You will claim you're a victim, and that may well be true. You were once a newborn, clean and pure, smelling of milk and sweetness. Someone purposely or inadvertently hurt you, and you lost your innocence, as we all do in the process of growing up. Your subconscious, having endured many traumas, has hardened you against dangers, and in defense, the victim has become the tyrant. Today you are an adult, responsible for who you are. Your victimhood (you may hate me for saying this) is a choice. Your tyranny, the one you inflict on yourself and others, is a choice. They go hand in hand, a dual obstacle to your freedom: You are the victim, tyrannizing your entourage with your victimhood. You are the tyrant whose hidden victimhood you try to hide, even from yourself. Do not turn away now, for you already have your dreaming tools to clear traumas. If you don't clear them, traumas will pile up with advancing age, and you will become a disheartened,

*Song written in 1929 for the movie *Gold Diggers of Broadway,* made into a novelty hit by Tiny Tim in 1968.

angry bully or pitiful victim (mirror image roles). But do you really want to go from tyrannizing your environment to being an innocent? Naivete is not an enviable quality. But what about a reclaimed innocence, one that you strove for and chose with open eyes?

> Assuredly I say to you, unless you are converted, and become as little children, you will by no means, enter the kingdom of heaven.[1]

Mythically these endangered children, Horus, Isaac, Moses, and, yes, Jesus of Galilee, whose real birth date is not Christmas (Sorry!), are all traditionally born in the springtime, when nature emerges from her long winter, and what was gestated in the darkness of the earth suddenly bursts forth. Oh, revelation! Horus is a miracle child, whose father, Osiris, was cut in fourteen parts by Seth (the god of time and linearity) and scattered to the four corners of Egypt. His mother, Isis, found and re-membered Osiris, but his penis was missing, having been swallowed by a fish (a metaphor for loss of the creative ebullience of the subconscious). Thoth, the god who invented hieroglyphs,* re-**form**-ed the penis out of gold, and Isis conceived and gave birth to a golden child, whose right eye shone like the sun and whose left eye glowed like the moon. Isaac was born of barren parents, who at ninety and one hundred, were told by God that they would conceive. Isaac is the child of Sarah's amazement, conceived from her laughter that brought forth her menses. At her age that such a thing should happen! What joy! And his name means "laughter." Moses, whose very existence had been forfeited by Pharaoh, is born with a face so radiant that the room is filled with the light of the sun and the moon combined. Floating on the Nile in a basket of reeds, who else but Pharaoh's daughter (read: his merciful side) rescues and adopts Moses, bringing him up in the very house of the tyrant. Jesus is born in a manger and escapes to Egypt when his life, like that of all male infants born in Bethlehem, is threatened by King Herod.

Does this mean that a jolt, a shock, or danger to our survival can bring about the marriage of the two brains, the sun and the moon?

---

*A character or sacred pictograph of the ancient Egyptian writing system.

This is not the first time we have encountered sun and moon, Emperor and Empress conjoined. The eye of consciousness inseminates the subconscious moon. She conceives, bringing forth a never before seen revelation that lights up our inner screen, metaphorically a child of light. In the Hebrew calendar Shavuot,* the holiday when the wheat reaches its full flowering, called Pentecost in the Christian tradition, is also the day of revelation. We wait all night for the skies to open up and to reveal . . . a child of light of our own making ("On the seventh day God created the world to make."). On this day it is said Moses climbed Mount Horeb, the mountain of desolation (Hareb means "to lay waste." Hereb is the Bible's word for "sword"). Old forms must be destroyed to give way to the new—new laws, new stories, the Torah. Thereafter on this day, the Hebrews brought the *bikkurim,* the first fruit from their orchards, to the temple. While the outer temple doesn't exist anymore, your inner temple does. On this night when you "lift your eyes on high and see . . ." or, turning your eyes inward, to the "site toward which all eyes gaze," what are the unblemished first fruits, the first revelations, you bring to your inner temple? "May it be the divine will that I not leave this house empty."[2] The Zohar,† the foundational work of Jewish mysticism, calls this conception of the new, "opening of the eyes."

Does enlightenment go through a conversion back to innocence, a rediscovery of the pathways to these newborn creations in your subconscious? Pushing away the tyrants of doubt, despair, and disillusion, you will see light emerging from dullness into a kaleidoscope of rainbow colors, and then crystallizing into brilliant white light.

✳

How do we start the journey back to the momentous singularity of pure innocence that is hidden within each one of us? For many people in the Western world, Christmas is a moment set apart, a time of peace illustrated by a radiant newborn in a manger. The scene is called the

---

*On the sixth day of the Hebrew lunar month of Sivan (generally sometime between May and June).

†Published in Spain in the thirteenth century by Moses de Leon, it is a commentary on the mystical aspects of the Torah.

adoration for a reason. Wherever there is a newborn anywhere in the world, eyes are irresistibly attracted, people bend to smile and bask in its aura. The attraction of the new, the untainted, is beguiling. I am reminded of this amazing photograph of a father, color tattooed from neck to waist, holding his naked newborn in his arms, innocence in the arms of sophistication! But something else is also happening in the scene of the manger. Why are all these people there, the mother, the father, the beasts (cow or bull, donkey), the shepherds and their flock of sheep, the three wise men? And above them all shines a great luminous star. Are they a haphazard gathering of people, or are they trying to point us toward something?

Is the truth simply hidden in plain sight? Such a familiar and well-loved scene, yet no one asks what it all means. Let's go step-by-step, exploring why each of these figures has made it into the Christmas iconography. Like all dreams, the nativity scene is a map pointing us in the ki tov, the good direction. For the dream so obviously to have all eyes turned toward the child of light suggests a teaching: that each of these protagonists were not always so aligned. The necessity of the dream, and of Christmas, is precisely to realign them to the light. We can all attest to the fact that in our own lives, our relationships need tikun, correction. Are the parents, the beasts, the sheep, the three kings the very forces that contributed to destroying our innocence in the first place? Let us look at each of these figures in their negative aspects:

The father and the mother, who have wittingly or unwittingly, hurt, humiliated, or betrayed us;

Our inner beasts, our emotions (anger, fear, sadness, anxiety, jealousy, envy, guilt, resentment) that, untamed, have led us to behave like animals;

Our sheep, our bad habits that have strayed away from the integrated movement of the flock (instincts that no longer function for our well-being; we'll call them secondary instincts), so that we no longer follow the will of the inner shepherd who guards our health and well-being;

Our wise men, the body, the heart, and the mind (Balthazar, black as earth, is our body; Melchior, our gold, is our heart; Gaspar, who carries myrrh, is our mind) we have pitted against each other, neglecting one to the enhancement of the other;

The star that shines above this scene is our intuition (that manifests in visions, dreams, or in a "still small voice") that we haven't attended to or listened to, that alone can guide us through this chaos back home to a reconquered innocence, for "unless we are converted and become as little children," we cannot bring the kingdom of heaven down into our lives, and happiness will elude us.

Let's start this journey where it began, with our three kings, the body, the heart, and the mind. We start with Balthazar, the body, and with your five senses. It is through the five senses that you reconstruct the world in your brain. Opening of the eyes, like the term imagery, is an inclusive term that embraces all five senses, "whether we see with our eyes or with our ears or with any of our other senses that kick in when we are without the use of either,"* since the image has the unique ability to elicit all senses. In the story of Isis searching for her husband, it is the five senses that tell her where to find him. The five senses are called little children. They are innocents, who sense just what they sense; they don't lie. But it is through the five senses that our hurts are registered: hurtful sights; hurtful words; hurtful smells, tastes, or touch. You can well understand that someone who has been touched violently or inappropriately sets up a subconscious barrier that blocks their skin from a normal interaction with the world. The same occurs with each of the senses. An accumulation of these hurts will separate us from our joy and innocence. Let us begin by clearing the entryways.

The eyes are our greatest accumulator of traumatic images—as I can well attest, since my eyes, after my husband died, could not bear strong light. It took the gentle hands of a healer on my eyes for the hurtful image—his face at death—to resurface and be cleared. After I made peace with the image, my difficulty with strong light instantly vanished.

---

*Gershon Winkler, "Eye-eye sir!" Facebook post, March 22, 2019.

Exercise 70

Eye Opening

Close your eyes. Breathe out slowly three times, counting from three to one. See the one tall, clear, and bright.

Sense and see the sphincter muscle around your left eye opening up. See your eye as a great globe filled with waters.

Breathe out. Look at the waters of the eye, and see if they are clear. If not, breathe out. Imagine the many little channels of water that feed the eye, pouring clear waters from the atmosphere into the globe of your eye. See the dirty waters being pushed out and the globe of the eye filling up with clear clean waters until the waters of the eye are completely clear.

Breathe out. Now look at the other eye; see if its waters are clear. If not, breathe out. Do what you did for the other eye, seeing the waters pouring in, washing the eye clean, until the waters of the eye are completely clear.

Breathe out. Sense and see the sphincter muscles closing comfortably around the globes of your eyes.

Breathe out. What is the first image you see with your clean eyes?

Breathe out. Open your eyes, seeing the new image with open eyes.

The ears accumulate many hurtful sounds and words. Here's the case of a young girl who always sat at her mother's right side at the dining room table. She recounts how her mother's strident and angry voice felt like an arrow piercing her ear. She had constant pain and trouble with her left ear. Doctors couldn't find any physical cause for her pain and dismissed her problem as emotional. It took some cleaning and healing through exercises such as the following one, but finally the pain disappeared and hasn't reappeared. In her case, it was the ears that opened.

Exercise 71

Ear Opening

Close your eyes. Breathe out slowly three times, counting from three to one. See the one tall, clear, and bright.

Imagine that you're lying on a beach on a sunny day. You're listening to the waves. Feel your ears growing and becoming very large nautilus shells.

Breathe out. Step out of your physical body in your DreamBody, and enter your left ear, holding a broom. Go into the deepest part of the shell.

Breathe out. Retrace your steps, sweeping out in a spiraling movement. Sweep out everything that is blocking your ear.

Breathe out. Go to the right ear. Do the same thing. Go into the deepest part of the shell.

Breathe out. Retrace your steps, sweeping out in a spiraling movement. Sweep out everything that is blocking your ear.

Breathe out. Reenter your body. See your ears returning to their normal size. Listen now with your two ears; what is the first sound you hear?

Breathe out. Open your ears, hearing that first sound with open eyes.

. . . .

As you know, smells can be powerful triggers to traumatic memories. A specific smell will conjure up a full-blown episode from your past. Dissolving smells at their roots is the best way to go. But here is a more generalized exercise that will begin the clearing. Also remember that many illnesses announce themselves with a strange smell that comes from the body and lingers. This exercise will help. You can also practice it when you have an upper respiratory difficulty.

Exercise 72
. . . .
Nose Opening

Close your eyes. Breathe out slowly three times, counting from three to one. See the one tall, clear, and bright.

Imagine standing in your meadow on a clear bright day. Where is the sun? If it's to the left, watch it as it travels across the sky until it's above you, or to your right.

Breathe out. Imagine that you hold a small spiraling brush, such as one used to clean bottles. Lift it to the sun, dip it into the sun, and quickly take it out. See it filled with light.

Breathe out. Twirl it up your left nostril, then all the way out again, clearing and dissolving the smells and the shapes of the molecules that are connected to those smells.

Breathe out. Lift your brush to the sun, dip it into the sun to clear it and to fill it with light again.

Breathe out. Bring it down to your right nostril. Twirl it up your nostril, then all the way out again, clearing and dissolving the smells and the shapes of the molecules that are connected to those smells.

Breathe out. Lift your brush to the sun, dip it into the sun to clear it and to fill it with light again.

Breathe out. Breathe in; what is the first smell that comes to your nostrils?

Breathe out. Open your eyes, smelling that first smell.

. . . .

Taste is connected to smell. If you cannot smell, you won't taste either. The expression, "it leaves a bad taste in the mouth" is true. Energy has a taste. Some situations and some people will actually elicit a bad taste in the mouth. Do not judge the other; just recognize what it does to you, clear it, and step away from the situation, or the person.

Exercise 73
. . . .
Tongue Opening

Close your eyes. Breathe out slowly three times, counting from three to one. See the one tall, clear, and bright.

Imagine that you open your mouth wide and your tongue unrolls like a red carpet all the way down to the ground and stretches out on the green grass.

Breathe out. Take a transparent vacuum and vacuum your tongue starting from the tip and going all the way up into your throat. Make sure you stay longer in those areas that need more vacuuming.

Breathe out. Roll up your tongue.

Breathe out. Empty your vacuum cleaner into a hole that you dig in the ground to your left.

Breathe out. What is the first taste on your tongue?

Breathe out. Open your eyes, tasting your first taste with open eyes.

. . . .

Finally, the skin is your largest sense organ, and, because of its large surface, very receptive to all that is happening around you. I have known people with intractable pain on large swaths of their skin. It is often connected to a traumatic incident that affected that particular area. Here's a general exercise to clear traumatic incidents imprinted on your skin, based on an old Santeria ritual.

Exercise 74
. . . .
Skin Opening

Close your eyes. Breathe out slowly three times, counting from three to one. See the one tall, clear, and bright.

Imagine that you have a newly laid egg. Start rolling it systematically all over your skin. Don't miss any part of your skin. You can imagine your arm growing to accommodate rolling the egg over and down your back. Don't forget the soles of your feet, and the palms of your hands, and your skull.

Breathe out. Break the egg into a full glass of water.

Breathe out. Pour the water and egg mixture into a hole that you dig in the ground to your left.

Breathe out. Sense and see your skin. What does it feel and look like now? What is your first experience now of the world around you?

Breathe out. Open your eyes, sensing your first experience with open eyes.

. . . .

You can repeat these exercises on a formal basis,* especially if you have a physical problem with any one of your senses. When clearing your sensations, you are opening the pathways of light that can now all conjoin within you, and form the guiding star. If you pay attention, this light will guide you by speaking to you in images or sounds, smells and tastes, or darkening or lightening of the skin. These intuitive messages, when attended to, begin focusing your two other kings, heart and mind, toward the inner world.

✳

---

*See Introduction.

There are two children in us, the child of light we have lost sight of and the suffering, traumatized child that still lives in us, soiled and tainted by hurts, betrayals, humiliations, and violence. This suffering child longs to be reunited with his twin, because he re-members it is his true nature to be illuminated with joy. The Sun card in the Marseilles Tarot deck shows us the wounded child finally reaching his twin who awaits him, arm outstretched, to bring him into the temenos, the sacred space marked by a low encircling wall. The wounded one has come over troubled waters and still boasts the tail of an imp, a leftover from his beastly days at the Devil's feet.* The receiving twin stands on "the white earth of the new world" and has three dots in a triangle on her left side, marking her "active consciousness."[3] Their hands crisscross to touch neck and heart; big toes meet, indicating that the twins' minds, hearts, and bodies are working in unison. The sun at its zenith shows them standing without shadow, showered with tongues of fire like the apostles at Pentecost, reunited at last.

> Happy is he who still loves something he loved in the nursery: he has not been broken in two by time; he is not two men, but one, and he has saved not only his soul but his life.[4]

But for most of us we are still "two men." The journey is yet to begin. The victim child in us is still crouching in the past, his frozen form acting as a tyrannical draw away from the healthy flow of imagery. We need an "opening" of the way, a coaxing of the frozen form toward the freedom of movement. The suffering child must be enticed back into play.

Exercise 75
· · · · · · · · · · ·
Rescuing the Suffering Child

Close your eyes. Breathe out slowly three times, counting from three to one. See the one tall, clear, and bright.

Look into yourself. Where is your suffering child? What are they doing? What do they need?

---

*See the Devil Card.

Breathe out. What do you feel, seeing your suffering child? What can you do to help your suffering child? Do they need to be taken care of, or do they need to come away from the place where you found them?

Breathe out. Do for your suffering child what you can for them today.

Breathe out. Open your eyes.

· · · · · · · · · · ·

Remember that while the little child in you may still be caught in the traumas of the past, this doesn't mean that the past exists. While we may be living with calcified images of the past that still have the power to exude miasmas of despair, it is helpful to realize that they are only repetitive dreams. Their presence may appear unyielding and unchanging to you, but let's go back to the idea of Mount Horeb,* the need to destroy the fixed, the repetitive "idolatrous" forms. The work is to return them back to their origins, thereby to chaos, and back to the creative ebullience of the bikkurim, the first fruits of the subconscious. This means letting go of the old familiar pains, the old habit of being a victim. The simplicity of it is astounding: By dissolving the old images and trusting to the creative, you are repairing your life.

Exercise 76
· · · · · · · · · · ·
Healing the Wounded Self

Close your eyes. Breathe out slowly three times, counting from three to one. See the one tall, clear, and bright.

Look into your body. Ask where you are hurting. Go look at the location of your hurt.

Breathe out. What memories arise out of this place of wounding? See the images. How old are you in those memories? Who is there with you? What is happening?

Breathe out. Go and stand next to the younger you, and say to them, "From now on, I will take care of you." Now let that younger

---

*Mount Horeb or Mount Sinai are either the same mountain (or adjacent mountains) on which Moses received the Ten Commandments and the Hebrew Bible. Horeb means "desolation," "dryness," or "glow/heat."

you express their emotions to the person or persons who have harmed them in whatever way is appropriate for their age. Having a tantrum, hitting, and kicking are fine, as long as those old emotions come out of their body.

Breathe out. Cut the negative cord between the younger you and whoever is disturbing them. Use a knife, sword, scissors, whatever works for you. Watch what happens to the disturbing other. You can continue cutting cords and even invisible cords until this other has disappeared.

Breathe out. Take the younger you out to a meadow, and tell them that they are free to play, pick flowers, climb trees, swim, throw pebbles, and grow up.

Breathe out. Play with them, and watch as this younger you grows up.

Breathe out. When the other you has grown to your size, embrace them. Look deep into their eyes. Hold them close and closer until something happens.

Breathe out. Open your eyes.

· · · · · · · · · · ·

In most cases, the two of you will merge. If you don't, continue to love that other you until you do. Don't force it; just love the other one. You can do the embracing part of the exercise every evening for a minute until the merging happens. In some traditions, this is called a soul retrieval. It is a retrieval of energies blocked in an old pattern. When the prodigal son (or daughter) returns home, a great feast of new images bubbles up. "And a river went out of Eden to water the garden."

Not only do sensory or emotional blocks obstruct the river of the imagination, belief systems are just as obdurate. One of the ways our belief systems act against our freedom and creativity is that we are very attached to the stories we tell ourselves.

Exercise 77
· · · · · · · · · ·
Stories We Tell Ourselves

Close your eyes. Breathe out slowly three times, counting from three to one. See the one tall, clear, and bright.

Ask yourself if you believe one or all of the following statements:

Life is unfair; you didn't get what you deserve; you were rejected; another person got more than you did; you were abused.

Breathe out. Looking into a mirror, sense and see how this story you believe is reflected in your body.

Breathe out. See and recognize how the world reflects back to you the stories you project.

Breathe out. Lift your index finger to the sun. Bring it down, and in the mirror, correct on your body what needs to be corrected. What are you feeling now? How has the story changed?

Breathe out. Open your eyes, seeing your corrected body with open eyes.

. . . .

There is a difference between complaining and accepting. Try saying the following, with no drama, no embellishment attached. State the fact simply: I was not loved; I was rejected; I was compared unfavorably with my sibling; I was abused.

Exercise 78
. . . .
Acceptance

Close your eyes. Breathe out slowly three times, counting from three to one. See the one tall, clear, and bright.

See yourself in a sandy desert. Write your complaint in the sand.

Breathe out. Accept it completely as the truth of what you feel.

Breathe out. Call out your complaint loudly in the desert.

Breathe out. See what comes back to you from the desert.

Breathe out. What has happened to the writing on the sand?

Breathe out. Open your eyes.

. . . .

Your story does not vanish suddenly, but you may notice that your mood lightens. As you continue to work on your inner cleaning, the story shifts imperceptibly, until one day it is gone. You now have more inner space for *new* memories to emerge. It is as if, like the toppling of an old building, the DreamField's real estate has cleared and new vistas opened up. The "opening of eyes" is continuing to happen. Suddenly you're remembering fun times you had with your mom that you had completely obliterated. Remember that this is a work in progress. As my teacher Colette used to say, "What has been done in time must be undone with time."

Exercise 79
. . . .
The Devastated City

Close your eyes. Breathe out slowly three times, counting from three to one. See the one tall, clear, and bright.

Take your child's hand, and cross a devastated city.

Breathe out. Listen to your child's question. What do you answer?

Breathe out. Keep listening and answering.

Breathe out. Come out of the devastated city, and walk away into green fields. What does your child say now?

Breathe out. Open your eyes.
. . . .

If you are still full of painful emotions, doing the next exercise whenever you need it will help.

Exercise 80
. . . .
Ocean of Tears

Close your eyes. Breathe out slowly three times, counting from three to one. See the one tall, clear, and bright.

Imagine that you are crying all the tears in your body. See them pouring out of your eyes and gathering in a pool at your feet.

Breathe out. Continue to cry. See the pool become a lake, and then an ocean.

Breathe out. Dive into the ocean, and swim downward toward the center of the ocean. Find the treasure that's waiting for you there.

Breathe out. Swim off to the other shore. Come out of the ocean carrying your treasure.

Breathe out. Put the treasure down. Dry yourself in the sunlight.

Breathe out. Pick up your treasure; what do you have?

Breathe out. Look over your left shoulder; what has happened to the ocean?

Breathe out. Walk away, taking your treasure with you.
Breathe out. Open your eyes.

. . . .

Having cleared the physical, emotional and mental bodies as best we can today, let us see if we can forge a working collaboration between the three kings.

Exercise 81
. . . .
The Three Wise Kings

Close your eyes. Breathe out slowly three times, counting from three to one. See the one tall, clear, and bright.

See, feel, and know what has kept your three kings from collaborating? Which king sees himself as superior? Which king sees himself as undervalued and victimized?

Breathe out. Find a way to make peace between the three kings.

Breathe out. See, feel, and know what gift your wise king, the body, is giving you.

Breathe out. What gift does the wise king of your heart give you?

Breathe out. What does the wise king of your mind give you?

Breathe out. See how the three wise kings can collaborate to guide you to the next revelation on your path.

Breathe out. Know that step-by-step each revelation on your path grows your inner light and reveals more and more of the child of light that is uniquely you.

Breathe out. Open your eyes, seeing with open eyes the next image on your path.

. . . .

✳

The return journey to reclaim our innocence is not easy. We must deal with the shepherds and their flock. One stray animal, one instinct gone awry, compromises the whole flock. We must also deal with the beasts that have strayed into the manger. They appear tamed, but one movement askew and the bull might lose its temper, the cow might stop producing milk, and the donkey might refuse to budge. We'll get back to the flock—our instincts—and the beasts—our emotions. Meanwhile the greatest obstacle to the journey—while also its major protagonists— turns out to be our two stewards, the mother and the father to the light being we are longing and searching for. They are the two pillars to the inner sanctum. Entering or exiting is impossible without passing between those two.

Exercise 82
. . . .
Honoring Your Parent

Close your eyes. Breathe out slowly three times, counting from three to one. See the one tall, clear, and bright.

Imagine that you stand opposite your parent. Pay attention to what you feel in your body. Pay attention to any constriction, darkness, or difficulty.

Breathe out. Having localized the pain, put your hand there and vocalize it, sounding out the constriction, darkness, or difficulty, until it has left your body.

Breathe out. Breathe in the blue radiant light from the sky to fill the newly cleared areas with blue light.

Breathe out. Looking at your parent now, accept the truth of who your parent is. What changes then?

Breathe out. Thank your parent for giving you life. Bow in honor and gratitude.

(If you cannot do this, understand that your parents are only the parents of your physical body.

Breathe out. See who the parents of your emotional body, mental body, spirit body are. Honor them and bow to them.)

Breathe out. Open your eyes.
. . . .

Are we compelled to love our parents? No. The fourth commandment doesn't mention love, it asks us to honor them and recognize their primordial necessity. For those of you who've studied the Hekhalot literature,* the texts describe an aspirant's quest to enter the palace gates, only to be confronted by two guards, mother and father, to the

---

*Palace texts from the early CE relate to visions of ascents into heavenly palaces.

passageway. Their duality is the first test. Playing one against the other will not work. The aspirant will be beaten back, twisted into unnatural shapes and frozen in his incapacity to go beyond the guards. Being entirely dependent for his survival on his parents, a child is the aspirant who cannot transcend his guards/parents and must find unnatural ways to adapt.

Exercise 83
· · · · · · · · · · ·
Heroic Measures

Close your eyes. Breathe out slowly three times, counting from three to one. See the one tall, clear, and bright.

See, feel, and know what heroic measures you took to protect yourself in a dysfunctional family or environment.

Breathe out. Recognize how those heroic measures no longer serve you well.

Breathe out. What better way do you choose today to protect yourself?

Breathe out. Open your eyes.
· · · · · · · · · · ·

Understand that to tame the two great powers standing in your way, you must first remove their negative image inside yourself. When those violent, angry images inside you are gone, you will find that the threatening guardians have disappeared, and lo and behold! Here are your parents, manageable human beings with character flaws, and qualities you can admire. Nothing has been said, but your parents will have subliminally picked up that your shape has changed, and they will have no choice but to subconsciously change their own inner shape. Remember how the basketball hoop inevitably attracts a basketball? If your solar plexus is collapsed inwardly, some round object, such as a ball, a fist, or a head, will come to fill the cavity. If you straighten up and fill out your solar plexus, the ball, the fist, the head will not seek you out. It cannot be otherwise in the DreamField, where inner shapes fit into each other like pieces of a puzzle. Change your inner shape, and the guardians will have no choice but to change theirs.

Exercise 84
. . . .
Taking Your Parents Out of Your Body

Breathe out slowly three times, counting from three to one. See the one as tall, clear, and bright.

Turn your eyes inward, and looking into your whole body, find what part your mother resides in.

Breathe out. What part does your father reside in?

Breathe out. How do you feel with your parents within? See the reason for them to be in this specific body part.

Breathe out. Slowly remove your parent out of you. If you don't succeed immediately, try removing them with your two hands. Breathe out. If this doesn't succeed, do it with a knife.

Breathe out. Place your parent to your right or to your left, as you see fit.

Breathe out. Pour cool spring water over the areas that your parents have just vacated. Ask every cell in your body to return to its natural healthy alignment.

Breathe out, and open your eyes, feeling free and whole.

. . . .

Maintaining this new posture means you're also going to have to change the habitual emotional pathways that have traditionally accompanied the negative images of your two guardians/parents. Let's say that for years, you've been frightened or angry. Anger and fear are primary emotions, your fight-or-flight response. But since you haven't been able to express them (the guardians/parents have made it impossible), your energies have been repressed and are banging around inside your body like wild beasts in a cage. These trapped energies, we'll call them **secondary emotions,** always manifest through a contraction. Their pathways are deeply imprinted in your physical body. Map them out by observing their pathways in your body next time you feel frustration. Do the same for sadness, depression, anxiety, shame, guilt, resentment, jealousy, doubt, and other emotions. If you turn your eyes into your body you'll also see that they sport unpleasant colors such as bloody reds, khaki greens, or other mixed or glaring colors. These colors should remind you of the nefesh* level on

---

*See chapter 2.

the dream ladder, for indeed your trapped emotions are a reason you have nightmarish, repetitive, or busy dreams.

Exercise 85
. . . .
Emotions and Feelings

Breathe out slowly three times, counting from three to one. See the one as tall, clear, and bright.

Turn your eyes inward, and sense your body from head to toe. In what part of your body does your frustration reside? How does it move?

Breathe out. Having localized it, put your hands to this body part, and conjure up the sound of your frustration. Vocalize it, and let it out.

Breathe out. Now sense the opposite sensation in your body. What color is it? How does it move? What name do you give it?

Breathe out. Open your eyes, feeling this with open eyes.
. . . .

You have just mapped out an entirely new sensation and given it a name. What you are now experiencing is a **feeling.** Love, joy, serenity, compassion, peace, courage, and trust are all feelings. Their pathways are expansive, and like expanding rings on a pond when a stone has been thrown in, they wash away other more jagged pathways. **A feeling will instantly clear out all emotions. You cannot be angry when you feel love.** There is no place in your body for the two to coexist. **Whereas emotions are reactions, a feeling is a response.** Check yourself and see if the constrictive pathway hasn't indeed become an expansive clear movement. The colors too will change to clear or bright colors, echoing the colors of ruah* (the clear dream) and neshamah† (the great dream) on the ladder of dreaming. The clear dream shows the transforming way toward the ki tov, which is a feeling, and the great dream shows its attainment.

---

*See chapter 2.
†Id.

204 TAMING THE LEVIATHAN

Exercise 86

· · · · · · · · · · ·

Renewed Energy

Breathe out slowly three times, counting from three to one. See the one as tall, clear, and bright.

Turn your eyes inward and sense your body from head to toe. In what part of your renewed body does your vital energy reside? In what part does your joy reside? In what part does your love reside?

Breathe out. Sense them, and keep them preciously within you.

Breathe out. Open your eyes, feeling your renewed energy with open eyes.

· · · · · · · · · · ·

Who are the sheep? They are your instincts. When the shepherd is in control of his flock, all his sheep move in tandem. Your shepherd is your timekeeper. He makes sure that you breathe at a peaceful rhythm, that you eat when your body is hungry, and that you move, rest, sleep, or wake according to deep inner rhythms only your inner shepherd knows and orchestrates. He is the keeper of your instincts. Your instincts are disrupted when you are angry or frightened. If the fight-or-flight response has protected you, the energies swing back into their natural groove. But what happens when your fight-or-flight has been repressed, and you're feeling so frustrated or anxious that you can no longer bear the physical constriction of your secondary emotions? Your energy swings back to the instincts but doesn't settle back into its groove. Instead, it disrupts your natural timetable. You find yourself eating when you're not hungry, or smoking a cigarette to alleviate your anxiety. All addictions follow this aberrant pathway. One of your sheep has gone astray, disrupting the rest of the flock, and it's difficult to get the flock back in sync. We call these stray instincts bad habits or **secondary instincts.** Choose one bad habit, and do this exercise for twenty-one days, or between menses.

Exercise 87
· · · · · · · · · · ·
Stop One Minute

Breathe out slowly three times, counting from three to one. See the one as tall, clear, and bright.

You are about to stray from your natural instincts by eating a cake. Before eating it, stop one minute.

When the minute is up, what do you feel like doing?

Breathe out. Open your eyes.

· · · · · · · · · · ·

After one minute, you may not even want to eat the cake. Even if you do go ahead and eat the cake, your body will feel calmer. Gathering back all our stray sheep can only be done in time. Don't try to repair all your secondary instincts at the same time. Repair one instinct a month.

Exercise 88
· · · · · · · · · ·
Shepherd Gathers His Flock

Breathe out slowly three times, counting from three to one. See the one as tall, clear, and bright.

Imagine that you are the shepherd whose sheep have strayed. Stretch your arms out wide, and gather all your sheep to you. What do you feel? What has changed for you? What feeling do you identify in yourself now?

Breathe out. Open your eyes, feeling this with open eyes.

· · · · · · · · · · ·

✳

Dream stories have much in common. In the story of Abraham and Sarah, three angels (later in the story of the child of light, Jesus of Galilee, they become the three kings) come as messengers to say that Sarah will conceive. Something very astonishing happens at the moment when, shocked by their message, Sarah laughs: The three angels become one. "The lord said unto Abraham, Wherefore did Sarah laugh? . . . Is anything too hard for the Lord?"[5] Conceiving our own child of light is now possible, whether as a vision of light, a great dream, our own joy, our innocence. "If therefore thine eye be single, thy whole body shall be full of light."[6]

Exercise 89

· · · · · · · · · · ·

Bikkurim, the Premises or First Fruit

Breathe out slowly three times, counting from three to one. See the one as tall, clear, and bright.

Hear the first bird singing at dawn;

Hear the first peek of a green shoot above the earth;

Hear the first blossom opening;

Hear the first wind blowing;

Hear the first sound of water;

Hear the first star;

Hear the still small voice, what does it say?

Breathe out. Open your eyes.

· · · · · · · · · · ·

The guards have dropped their weapons. The subconscious beckons us back through the doorway. Beyond is a hidden marvel that, like a bubbling brook, waters our garden and constantly renews us. Creation is happening here. Now is pure joy; it is your innocence reclaimed.

Exercise 90

· · · · · · · · · · ·

Joy, the Hidden Marvel

Breathe out slowly three times, counting from three to one. See the one as tall, clear, and bright.

Feel and sense joy as the promise of life. Know how this eternal joy is only of the moment.

Breathe out. Feel and know how this instant of joy is the marvel of life that is bringing us above ourselves.

Breathe out. Feel and know how discovering the hidden marvel of the instant of joy is the reason for all forms of quests.

Breathe out. See and know the magnificence that is in you. Keep in mind only images of health, strength, success, kindness, joy, and love.

Breathe out. Open your eyes.

· · · · · · · · · · ·

✳

You cannot love another unless you love yourself. But now that you have merged again with your inner child, you are ready to turn outward to attract another. You're now ready to finally meet your mirror image, "bone of your bones and flesh of your flesh,"[7] your k'negdo, the one against whom you must measure yourself and grow, the helpmate and soul partner you are destined to travel with through this lifetime. You may still be searching or already be in a relationship. The journey toward the other never stops. It will always trigger more yearning and seeking and forming. It will require reinventing yourself again and again.

11

Misery and Splendor
Restoring Relationships

One touches the other, even air cannot come between them.

JOB 41:8

We live in relationship. Even if we're hermits on the top of a mountain we cannot help but relate to the blade of grass, the brook, the sun, and the stars. By simply focusing on a tree, an animal, another person, or even on an object, we create the twosome that is a fundamental law of our universe. In this world of duality, we are always looking for—or fighting against—that other part of the equation, whether it's hot versus cold, hard versus soft, or male versus female. Just as heaven reaches for Earth, and our right hand for our left, so are we looking for—or fearing—the perfect fit that will make us whole. Duality is the signature of our universe, which is why Bereshit (Genesis) starts with the second letter of the alphabet. To make sure we fully understand this fundamental law, we are told that Adam, an androgynous male/female creature, is made in the image of God. This suggests that God's divine oneness is androgynous, a radical concept in biblical thought. The difference between God and man is that God may have *shnei panim*, two faces, but is never other than one, whereas for our world to be set in motion, a splitting in two is necessary. God severs Adam—a drastic cut, and essential granting of freedom—which we constantly strive to repair. Do we live it as a wound, an insult, or a challenge? God sets Eve k'negdo, against Adam, that she may test herself against his form.[1] Set loose, she explores other options, lets herself be tempted by the many undulating forms the serpent offers, and tastes of a fruit forbidden in its unripe configuration. She entices Adam, and pain ensues, because, as Joseph Gikatilla, a Spanish Kabbalist from the thirteenth century tells us, in the couple's passionate haste to partake, they didn't wait for the moment when their mirror images had ripened to fit exactly into each other, into the complete form they were always meant to be.[2] We are in a world of doing, where our actions, our handiwork, make our reality. If, as Kabbalists tell us, the perfect union is the one where two forms, face-to-face, re-create the primordial androgyny, there is work to be done to bring them to once again face each other.

Can we trust that all form has its corresponding fit? By definition, an incomplete form cannot emanate from the divinity. In a perfect creation, male and female are joined together, like hand and glove. Thus the oral tradition tells us that at the birth of each of the sons of Jacob, a twin sister was born, whom they later married. Does this suggest that couples are predestined to be together? "An echo of the Voice comes from Mount Horeb and proclaims: The daughter of this one is destined for this one, even beyond the seas."[3] If so, how do twin souls find each other in this world of separateness?* I remember reading about an old American Indian tradition where grandparents at the birth of a grandson incubate a dream, asking to be shown who the boy's soul mate is; then they weave and embroider her wedding dress. All this is done in secret, and when the grandson grows to adulthood, the grandparents watch whether he gravitates to his destined partner. If he does, they ceremoniously present the wedding dress to the girl's family. In both American Indian and Jewish traditions, man is not alone; man's original state is as part of a couple and must seek to return to this state of union.

Gikatilla describes three kinds of marriage, that of the *tzadik*

---

*See the Introduction. Male and female must be read as archetypal tensions, not as types of people. Couples of all sexual orientations have those same dichotomies.

(righteous), that of the *benoni* (average), that of the *ra* (bad). The tzadik will never sample other forms. Like an arrow to the bull's-eye, he finds and recognizes his soul mate and marries her. The ra will never meet his soul mate, because he is too far removed from the righteous path. The benoni, like Adam,* will sample different forms, and taste the fruit before it's ripe. It is the benoni we will concern ourselves with, as it is rare today for young people not to sample. They are not alone in their confusion. We are told that King David himself was a benoni. He had "a hard inclination," which made him hasty. He succumbed to the "transient gratification of his immediate desires"[4] and took other partners. Yet the soul destined for him since the six days of creation was Batsheva. When he finally merited finding her again, she was married to another man. In his haste, he took her before she was free of her marriage. David's impatience brought pain, like Adam's, and like our own, when we enter into relationships at the wrong time, or one that doesn't fit us. When our souls are not in alignment with their inner truth, it is our bodies that hurt. David lost his firstborn and his throne. If only, we are told, he had waited until the time was ripe, he would have become like God, eternal through love.

This begs the question: Is the single most important goal of our lifetime to find and fit the two parts of our dual soul together again? By striving to live harmoniously with our other half, are we repairing the world? Kabbalists call this "making the Name," or giving form to the divinity. We can all agree that love, when it comes our way, is a divine ecstasy, and for a moment, re-creates paradise on Earth. Is it not a pursuit worthy of all our attention? But already from experience, we know the pains and hardships of relationship. We have agonized over our love affairs and obsessed about them endlessly, to no avail. The striving for love cannot follow the pathways of logic, but must, of necessity, plunge the depths of the subconscious.

✳

---

*Adam has a first wife called Lilith. When she leaves him after a quarrel as to who has power, he takes Eve as wife. She offers him the forbidden fruit, which commentators say is unripe when they both eat it.

Whether or not we believe in the concept of souls and soul mates, we all understand from experience that a perfect alignment is difficult to find, and just as difficult to sustain. Like tightrope dancers, either we strive to maintain a precarious balance or we are playing blindman's buff, to identify and catch the right partner, or elusive other. It is relationship that causes us most angst and questioning. Our yearning to be whole never ceases. This word "longing," interestingly, comes from the idea of elongation. Our longing stretches us out toward an unknown, toward something that looks desirable, or something that's not yet there. "Lekh lekha," Go, says God to Abraham, but where to? To an unknown that we hope will complete us. And when we encounter it, our feelings of respect, gratitude, and love, or our reactions—fear, repulsion, and desire to possess or to destroy—will show us who we really are. For lekh lekha also means "go to yourself." And a relationship, from the get-go, reveals us to ourselves. Are you truly wanting to find your soul mate? Or if you already have a partner, are you getting out of your own way to allow for that ineffable time-stopping moment when the two of you become as two mirrors reflecting each other? You may think so, but deeper imperatives could be blocking the way. So many have come to me crying with longing, raging against fate, or their partner, not aware of the part they played in blocking the realization of their hopes. Your first task is to come to the full awareness that you create your own life.* You are responsible for freeing your subconscious programs that block you from attracting your soul mate, or from saying with joyful recognition, "This at last is bone of my bones and flesh of my flesh."⁵

What does relating mean? How do we reinvest the world and ourselves with respectful, grateful, and loving relating?

There is an ancient story from the Bible that gives us a clue. It is the story of the people of the Tower of Babel. Once upon a time, the text tells us, "the whole earth was of one language and of common purpose." But as soon as the people decided to "make a name for themselves, lest they be dispersed across the whole Earth."⁶ In effect, as soon as naming entered the picture, the men and women who were building

---

*See chapter 7.

the tower began to babble.* What is this mysterious common language? The emphasis on naming as the cause of our ancestors' misfortune— these dispersed people were descended from Shem, which translates to "name"—suggests that this language was radically different from the ones we now use. Before Babel, these people were "of common purpose." What can this common purpose be? What do we all long for? Happiness, of course, along with love, goodness, and peace. Can our one language be the lingua franca of the heart?

How do we return to feeling? What is blocking our way? We seem to seesaw very easily from desire to emotion, from thwarted instincts to reactivity. We live in a world where instant gratification is expected, where the common purpose is largely disregarded. Being caught in the loop of our own self-interests, our desire "to make a name for ourselves," how can we detach ourselves enough to contemplate another possibility? How can we take a leap out of this general impoverishment into the world of feeling?

Love happens when we least expect it, in an instant. We take a turn in the road and are caught breathless before a wondrous sight. We meet a stranger, our heart stops, and it is done; we are in love. A smile, a child's face, beauty, a poem, music, or great art can do that to us. Without that jolt we cannot plunge into the mysterious world of feeling, where we are made whole. But can we wait for the unexpected? We are in such dire need. Is there a way to throw ourselves haphazardly into wholeness? What common forgotten language must we rediscover to help us with the plunge? You have guessed it: There is no love without imagination. How can we love others if we cannot leap out of ourselves toward them, to hold them, metaphorically, in our arms, to include them, encompass them, to merge with them and become one? "Love thy neighbor as thyself."[7] This jolt out of our petty selves is served not by our rational minds but by our imagination.

As we know, imagination is devalued, put down as so much fantasy and daydreaming. If we go with the premise that we must be true to the facts, that we must unravel every conflicting statement of "he said, she said" in their war of attrition, we once again ignore the common language. What reality are we talking about? We have two brains: our

---

*Babel means "confusion has come."

sun, the verbal, causal, logical, and linear—and our moon, the imaginal, dreamy, creative, spontaneous, leaping, playful, and surprising. The accumulation of data and the gaining of true knowledge and *knowing* of another are two different realities, yet we pit one against the other. They cannot exist apart without ill consequences, as is so abundantly clear. Separating the heartfelt embodied experience of inner reality from the verifiable step-by-step appraisal of outer reality will not help us resolve the miseries and difficulties of relationship. Can we at least agree to respect both realities, as a first step toward creating a "common purpose?"

The Jewish philosopher Martin Buber coined these dual modes of being as I-It and I-Thou:

> I-It is lived in monologue where the It becomes "a passive object of knowledge" from which the I is "realistically alienated."
> I-Thou, on the contrary, is "the companionship of creation, whenever we come near one another, because we are bound up in relation to the same center."[8]

Can this describe our struggles? Two forms of relating that paradoxically place us in both camps, as observers and as participants. Accepting that both have a role to play, how can we tease out the difficulties of relating? Imagine yourself sitting at the kitchen table, angrily accusing your partner, pounding insults and words at him or her. It's hard to give up the angry pleasure of naming the other! This reminds me of a scene I witnessed between my teacher and her husband. I was sitting in the garden with them one afternoon, when something he said provoked her anger. She started off on a tirade of grievances that seemed to have no end. He hid behind his newspaper, and I shrank into my corner, appalled. Suddenly she stopped, kissed his hand, and said coquettishly: "Mais je vous aime, chéri."* He came out from behind his newspaper, kissed her hand, and with a big smile replied: "Moi aussi, chérie!"† I never forgot that instant switch from I-It to I-Thou.

---

*But I love you, darling!
†Me too, darling!

Exercise 91
. . . .
I-It and I-Thou

Breathe out slowly three times, counting from three to one. See the one as tall, clear, and bright.

In front of someone you are having difficulties with, say: I-It. What is It? What allows you to say that?

Breathe out. Say: I-Thou. What is Thou? What allows you to say that?

Breathe out. Open your eyes.

. . . .

Ahavah, love in the sacred Hebrew language, uses A, the sound of the heart, three times. If you breathe out three times slowly, counting backward to the one with your eyes closed, reversing from this world into the inner world, then imagine a circle. Watch what appears in the circle. You have begun your journey back to ahavah, the experiencing. You will see something that was hidden to you, some magical beautiful aspect of the other you are contemplating, and beyond what you are able to see. You will be touched by a feeling of the other's mystery and power. Imagine if we all practiced turning inward, if we all unabashedly allowed ourselves this luxury before embarking on tough peace negotiations with our estranged partners. Love shines like a gem, and by its warmth, attracts more warmth, goodness, harmony, and peace. It is all done not by naming what you dislike, but by going back into your room, closing the door, and letting your imagination stretch out and envelop the other. While we are perfect creatures, perfectly whole, and perfectly wise as to what is best for us, our stories, emotions, and grudges also have a strong hold on us. That it might take some effort to give them up is undeniable. God goes back and forth ten times before finally manifesting His complete form, the one He loves, Adam, His image. Abraham goes through ten tests before finally offering his complete love and surrender to God, thus completing the form and making himself in the image. It may take as many tests for you to reach your ultimate desire. The numeral 10 looks like a man peering into his round mirror at himself transposed.

Exercise 92

· · · · · · · · · · ·

Yearnings

Breathe out slowly three times, counting from three to one. See the
one as tall, clear, and bright.

Go through your different yearnings from the most banal to
the most sublime, as if through concentric circles, until you come to
your ultimate yearning. How do you see it in the round mirror of
the zero?

Breathe out. Open your eyes.

· · · · · · · · · · ·

We are always searching, yearning for something better, because we
haven't yet touched the center, the source of love. We will be going back
and forth between sun and moon, I-It and I-Thou, until we reach comple-
tion, ten. Even in moments of perfect oneness, we cannot hold onto the
I-Thou. We inevitably slip back into the I-It, the position of the observer.
In Hebrew, the word relation is *kesher,* link, which sounds suspiciously
like *gesher,** bridge, implying a going back and forth. In the romance languages, "to relate" comes from the Latin *relatus* (*re* back + *latus* carried),
to carry back. We will have to go forth and carry back, weaving know-
ingness with naming, until the two worlds become one. A relationship
always implies a risk, a surrender to an unknown, whose essence, once
revealed, is carried back for the enlightenment of the seeker. Pay attention to your emotions as you do this next exercise. Do it to remember the
truth of the partner you are struggling with, or to discover the essence of
your future soul mate, if you haven't yet met in person.

Exercise 93

· · · · · · · · · · ·

Cup the Cheek

Breathe out slowly three times, counting from three to one. See the
one as tall, clear, and bright.

Stretch your arm out to reach and touch another's cheek. Feel

---

*We could speculate on an ancient etymological connection. A contemporary investment
company, Gesher l'Kesher, which means Bridge to Connection, has used the close
soundings of both words to make its point.

how your hand becomes receptive to the contour of the other's cheek. What shifts in you emotionally?

Breathe out. Take your hand away.

Breathe out. If there was a problem stretch your arm out again to reach and touch the other's cheek. This time, wait and ask for permission to touch. When you have received it, cup the other's cheek. What is different?

Breathe out. Bring your hand back. What has changed?

Breathe out. Open your eyes.

· · · · · · · · · · ·

What if you are not able to cup the other's cheek? What if that other doesn't like what you are bringing to his or her face with the palm of your hand? Accepting the other with an unprejudiced hand (and mind) may prove more difficult than you are admitting to yourself. Einstein said there are only curves in this universe, only relationships that must be cupped, or received in the curve of your surrender to their reality. Accepting to become receptive will make your life in this dual world much easier. Be patient. We are just beginning to decipher where your blocks to relationship may be.

Exercise 94
· · · · · · · · · · ·
Carrying Back

Breathe out slowly three times, counting from three to one. See the one as tall, clear, and bright.

Visualize someone you're experiencing difficulty with standing a few feet away from you. Stretch your hand toward that person, and see what is in your hand that you are offering to that person.

Breathe out. See if the person accepts your gift.

Breathe out. See what the person chooses to offer back.

Breathe out. If the person doesn't accept your gift, or doesn't offer one back, examine what you have given, and how. See what it is you need to change. Do this until you receive something back from the other.

Breathe out. Carry the gift you've received back to your place. What do you feel now looking at the other?

Breathe out. Open your eyes.

· · · · · · · · · · ·

While it is customary as a sign of goodwill to exchange gifts, we are not talking about material gifts here, but rather subconscious offerings. What we give the other, and what the other gives us sub rosa, will make or break a relationship. In *A Little Book on the Human Shadow*, Robert Bly, the poet and Jungian, describes the situation: As their son and daughter get married in the church above, the mothers exchange their families' hidden agendas in the crypt below.[9] Here is an evocative story of diverging agendas that ends well, at least for two of the protagonists. While King David generously let King Nabal's army cross his lands, when it came time for Nabal to return the favor, he refused.[10] This provoked great animosity among David's men, and the two armies prepared for combat. Abigail, whom we shall encounter in the following exercise, is Nabal's wife.

Exercise 95
. . . .
King David and Abigail

Breathe out slowly three times, counting from three to one. See the one as tall, clear, and bright.

Imagine that you are King David, surrounded by your men, eager to fight King Nabal's army, who are lined up opposite you. Feel the anger rising in you, the desire to make war.

Breathe out. A beautiful lady carrying a large red pomegranate in the palm of her hand suddenly steps forth between the two armies.

Breathe out. Take the fruit she offers you. Hold it delicately so as not to bruise it. What are you feeling now?

Breathe out. Open your eyes.

. . . .

If you have done the exercise, you know why the battle didn't take place. Hearing what his wife had done, King Nabal, who preferred killing to conciliation, had a heart attack and died. Two weeks later David married Abigail. While "Make love, not war" always seems to be a better solution, it may not be that easy or advantageous of an approach. As we have already pointed out, our brains are dual. The sun brain illuminates boundaries, favors naming, sees us as fundamentally antagonistic and at war; and the moon brain blurs all boundaries, sees us holistically, and favors merging and oneness. While the sun brain shines forth with ego and pride, the moon brain reflects back with surrendering acceptance. Who has more power, the I-It or the I-Thou, the male or the female? If we want to enjoy a good relationship, we cannot let the moon brain's lovingness obscure what the facts tell us. On the other hand, we can't let the sun brain's acuity destroy our feelings of acceptance and compassion. This was the unfortunate story of Adam and Lilith, his first wife. She was exact and unforgiving in her pure mirroring, a true image of God. Because her conscious and subconscious worlds were one, she could come face-to-face with God and not die. Even Adam found it a trifle too taxing. "And I find woman bitterer than death."[11] So God gave him Eve, fashioned from his dreaming side, his subconscious moon brain. Like Adam, we cannot bear facing the cutting sword of revelation without a mirror to shield the impact of the truth. Being mercilessly cut down by an angry partner is too hurtful and serves no positive outcome. We need justice with mercy. But can we ask it of another? The sages say that each of us has *deyo partzuf panim,* two faces, male and female, that are "back-to-back," unrecognized.[12] Since you cannot force the other to recognize what he or she is doing or, for that matter, to change, your only option is to recognize how you err, and how you can change yourself.

Exercise 96
. . . .
Back-to-Back

Breathe out slowly three times, counting from three to one. See the one as tall, clear, and bright.

Be Adam. See the world through your male eyes.

Breathe out. Turn to the other side, and see the world through your female eyes.

Breathe out. See and feel how "back-to-back" means that the male and female in you cannot see each other;

Breathe out. Have different goals;

Breathe out. Have their own respective interests at heart.

Breathe out. Open your eyes.
. . . .

Two warring types of consciousness will inevitably create relationship problems, and you certainly can't correct love problems that way. So let us try to reconcile **your** male and female sides. Remember that Adam and Eve were back-to-back and could not see each other. It took a splitting in two for them to be able to turn and face each other. It takes your sun brain looking into your moon brain to come face-to-face with what really animates you.

Exercise 97
. . . .
Face-to-Face

Breathe out slowly three times, counting from three to one. See the one as tall, clear, and bright.

Look into one side of a two-sided mirror and see your male side.

Breathe out. If there is something you don't like about your male side, lift your index finger to the sun, fill it with light and bring it down to the mirror.

Breathe out. Use your index finger of light to correct whatever you don't like in the mirror about your male side.

Breathe out. Turn the mirror to its other face. See your female side in the mirror.

Breathe out. If there is something you don't like about your female side, lift your index finger to the sun, fill it with light, and bring it down to the mirror.

Breathe out. Use your index finger of light to correct whatever you don't like in the mirror about your female side.

Breathe out. See the two sides of the mirror become one inner space. See how male and female turn face-to-face. See how they greet each other. If they are still antagonistic, correct some more until they can greet each other, embrace, and become one.

Breathe out. Have the merged one look at you. What are you feeling now?

Breathe out. Open your eyes.
. . . .

We have seen how negative naming (criticizing, attacking) could break a relationship. But if they merge, will the merging be a subordination of one by the other?

They are trying to become one creature . . .
they are an almost animal,
washed up on the shores of a world
or huddled against the gate of a garden.[13]

Or will the memory of their soul roots act to bring the two together? Rectifying those two parts of yourself can go far toward rectifying issues you may have in your couple or in relationships. This androgynous being you are contemplating is what you were in the embryonic phase before the split happened, and you became gendered in the fetal phase. Anatomically, you are clearly (at least in most cases) of one gender or the other, but psychologically, mentally, spiritually? The "sex of your soul"* may conflict with your gender. You are female but behave more like a warrior, or you're male, behaving more empathically. Correcting what you don't like about your male, or your female, then returning them to a sense of oneness will help when trying to achieve *shalom bayit,* peace in the home, a concept the Hebrews give great weight to. For how can you make peace in your home if there is no peace within you? The secret of a peaceful home is hidden in the words "*ish*" and "*ishah,*" man and woman.

Ish = Aleph yud shin = man
Ishah = Aleph shin heh = woman

Take away the name of God, Yah, which is written yud heh, and you're left with aleph shin, pronounced *esh,* which means "fire." "If they merit, the Divine Presence dwells between them, but if they do not merit, fire devours them."[14] What does it take for fire not to devour you? Adam brings Lilith into the tent, and they have their first quarrel about, guess what? Who's going to be on top, who'll subdue the other. You cannot bring an "alien fire" into the tent, the space of God's dwelling on Earth, as did Nadav and Avihu, the sons of Aharon, without "a fire coming forth from before the Lord that consumes you."[15] We have all experienced how our anger, fear, jealousy, envy, bitterness, rebellion, lust, greed, power, weakness, dependency, disappointment, fear of

*See also Charles Mopsik's 2005 book *Sex of the Soul.*

uncertainty, or of differentiation have turned love into a battleground and sweetness into a devouring fire.

Exercise 98
. . . .
Alien Fires

Breathe out slowly three times, counting from three to one. See the one as tall, clear, and bright.

Go through your life, from the beginning to today, identifying repetitive alien fires you have indulged in.

Breathe out. Standing on the cliffs of the Pacific Ocean, breathe those fires out, and see them roll up into a red ball that travels out over the ocean.

Breathe out your soul. See it as a white ball. See it traveling fast over the ocean, reaching the red ball, and pulverizing it.

Breathe out. See the white ball coming back over the ocean.

Breathe it in, and see the white light gently filling every part of you.

Breathe out. Open your eyes.
. . . .

To keep the space in between your male and female, or in between your couple free from garbage depends entirely on your attitude. Will you love the other one inside of you or the other one in your couple as yourself? Or will you continue on a combative and egocentric path? This reminds me of a student I hadn't seen in a while who called and asked to see me urgently. When she walked in, I could see she was very angry. Her husband had lost his job six months before, and she couldn't bear to even look at him or let him touch her. I let her spew about her husband for a few minutes, then when she least expected it, I said, "Close your eyes."

Exercise 99
. . . .
Remember Love

Breathe out slowly three times, counting from three to one. See the one as tall, clear, and bright.

Remember the first time you fell in love (with your husband).

Breathe out. Open your eyes.
. . . .

She opened her eyes, and now she was very angry with me, which served my purpose. She hadn't expected this, but in the light self-hypnotic trance of counting backward, she felt the love. For a moment she wasn't consumed in a devouring fire, but felt the joyous fire. All it took was turning her eyes in another direction. The space opened up, and the next day her husband got a job! Clearing the space allows for the creative to happen.

We are told that God speaks in the space atop the Ark of the Covenant "from between the two cherubim."[16] You and your partner are meant to be like those two cherubim guarding the space. But as we know, an empty space can feel eerie, for you never know what will pop up. Loving puts us in that empty space.

Exercise 100
. . . .
Fear of Loving

Breathe out slowly three times, counting from three to one. See the one as tall, clear, and bright.

Ask yourself what frightens you most about loving?

Breathe out. When frightened, what do you usually fill the space with?

Breathe out. Open your eyes.
. . . .

The fear of loving is closely related to the fear of death. Death is the ultimate surrender. Orgasm is called *la petite mort,* the little death, because it requires complete surrender. To accept that losing control can be good and is, in fact, part of falling in love, we must loosen the ties to nefarious emotional attractions we are all too familiar with, such as anger, impatience, rebelliousness, fear, humiliation, and control.

Exercise 101
. . . .
Like Attracts Like

Breathe out slowly three times, counting from three to one. See the one as tall, clear, and bright.

See, feel, and resonate like to like by remembering an instance where you answered:

anger with impatience;
control with rebelliousness;
fear with wrath;
self-hate with humiliation;
weakness with power.

Breathe out and find a way to forgive yourself. What is the new quality that emerges? Is it loving-kindness, humility, or some other quality?

Breathe out. Answer anger, control, fear, self-hate, and weakness with that quality.

Breathe out. Open your eyes.

· · · · · · · · · · ·

The rebellious force called Lilith is trying, as my student was, to control the inner space. The self-gratifying force called David fills the space with transient lusts. The twin peaks of rebelliousness and impatience are the adversaries, the little devils, against which, k'negdo, we must measure ourselves. Our work is to trick them into becoming our allies. When rectified, these forces are said to usher in the messiah, whose realm is love and peace. Doing this next exercise every day for a month* will help to clear our residual temptations, our little devils that corrupt the integrity of the space. Respectful waiting and allowing are the necessary ingredients of love. What love requires is sovereignty, the freedom for the other to be fully who he or she is.

Exercise 102
· · · · · · · · · · ·
The Scrub Wheel (Formal)

Breathe out slowly, releasing all that disturbs you, tires you, or obscures you.

Breathe in the blue light from the sky. See it traveling through your nostrils, down your throat, and down your back as a great river of light. When it reaches your pelvic floor, see it switch to the front of your body, travel up to your throat and back down your back to your pelvis, then go up again, inscribing an oval of blue light in your body. Let this oval become larger and more circular until it becomes a great wheel of light circulating back to front,

---

*See Introduction.

to back again. Continue watching the wheel turn until it becomes brilliant white.

When the wheel is brilliant white, see it begin to spiral toward and into the secret chamber of your heart. Follow it in and face the portal to the divine (or mystery) that is open at the back of your heart.

Breathe out. Bow to it, prostrate yourself fully on the ground, promising to submit to the mystery inherent in the space.

Breathe out. Turn and sit facing forward, sending the brilliant white light out in all directions.

Breathe out. Slowly reintegrate your whole body, seeing yourself emanating light in all directions.

Open your eyes, seeing this with open eyes.

· · · · · · · · · · ·

✳

The story goes that Adam dreamed about Eve before she was created.[17] When your imagination is rectified, like an ocean cleared of its garbage, you too will have the insight, and you will see your soul mate. They are your dream come true, or about to come true. What your soul mate needs to be able to manifest, or if they're already in your life, to come toward you, is your patient, expectant love. Being empty of love, a victim coveting what others have, will not bring love. Instead, the sages say, to attract love, you have to have a little bit of love inside you. This is not about being passive or empty, but about actively turning your conscious mind into your subconscious dreaming, like the tarot Emperor lovingly looking toward his Empress, learning to remember.

Exercise 103
· · · · · · · · · · ·
Calling Your Soul Mate

Breathe out slowly three times, counting from three to one. See the one as tall, clear, and bright.

Look inside yourself and feel the fire of love that is inside of you. Stoke it by your looking.

Breathe out. See the door of relationship closed in front of you.

Breathe out. When the fire of yearning blazes up within you, blow it out of your mouth to push open the door.

Breathe out. Step through, and feel who is coming toward you. Do not worry about the person's appearance. Just feel the qualities emanating from him or her.

Breathe out. Hold this insight preciously in your heart.

Breathe out. Open your eyes.

· · · · · · · · · · ·

If you want to see the date at which you will meet, go to exercise 42: Deadline. One of my students told me a story that gave me the goose bumps. Long before she met me, she was at a workshop where the teacher asked the participants to choose a partner and go for a half hour walk hand in hand. She felt very uncomfortable about the exercise and was determined to walk out with the girl sitting next to her. But a man signaled to her, so she went with him. When she took his hand, she recognized the touch. Four months later they were married. So keep your heart free and in expectancy.

The burning in you must always be kept alive. Do not despair. Don't be afraid to long and yearn. The meeting, whether it is meeting a soul mate or meeting the partner you are already with, must be called forth each time anew. Let your attitude be one of openness to wonder. One of my students who had come to me to unblock whatever was stopping her from meeting her partner came into the office one day telling me she had gotten a phone call from an important business contact but wasn't returning the call although she knew she should. "Do it now!" I insisted. I gave her the phone, she called him, and now he is her husband. Imagine if she hadn't called back? Be alert. Cultivate the same care, the same intent, the same waiting. Think of it as taming a wild deer.

Exercise 104
· · · · · · · · · · ·
Taming the Wild Deer

Breathe out slowly three times, counting from three to one. See the one as tall, clear, and bright.

Imagine you are in the woods where the wild deer roam. You have come prepared with food to lure the deer out. You have no idea where the deer might be, but you know it's somewhere nearby. What is your attitude?

Breathe out. When the deer comes close, what changes for you, if anything?

Breathe out. When the deer nuzzles your hand, what changes for you, if anything?

Breathe out. When the deer leaves, what do you feel?

Breathe out. Open your eyes.

. . . .

I knew a man who could do that. He was a longtime student and friend. He stood quietly in the forest, his outstretched hand filled with seeds, and the birds came and ate out of the palm of his hand. He taught my son how to feed the wild stag and the angry swan that came at his call. The Prayer of Saint Francis, who tamed the wild wolf and talked to the birds, comes to mind.

> *Lord, make me an instrument of your peace.*
> *Where there is hatred, let me sow love;*
> *where there is injury, pardon;*
> *where there is doubt, faith;*
> *where there is despair, hope;*
> *where there is darkness, light;*
> *and where there is sadness, joy.*
>
> *O Divine Master, grant that I may not so much seek*
> *To be consoled as to console;*
> *To be understood as to understand;*
> *To be loved as to love.*
> *For it is in giving that we receive;*
> *It is in pardoning that we are pardoned;*
> *and it is in dying that we are born to eternal life.*[18]

The bottom line is that you cannot enter the space unless you're invited to, but you must stand vigilant like the faithful virgins of the parable who kept their lamps and oil in readiness for when the bridegroom should come.[19]

Love as a revelation, as the perfection of the garden, the radiance in which we are one, is called the Tree of Life. Love as a walk, as a process of slow gestation and maturation, like a seed in the womb, is the result of eating of the fruit of the Tree of the Knowledge of good and evil. Can you hold them both in your heart without comparing? To address the mix of good and bad, while keeping the flame of insight alive, practice the following exercises. You will need them when the temptation to give in to "he said, she said" seems overpowering.

Exercise 105
· · · · · · · · · ·
The Blue Pillow

Breathe out slowly three times, counting from three to one. See the one as tall, clear, and bright.

Stand in front of the partner you are having issues with. Feel what is happening in your body.

Breathe out, and take three steps back. What do you feel now? What do you see? If need be, take three more steps back, and again, three more. Feel the difference.

Breathe in the blue light from the sky. Fill your mouth with the light. Now blow it out to create a pillow of light between you and the other. See and sense this buoyant space between the two of you.

Breathe out. Open your eyes.
· · · · · · · · · · ·

Practice keeping the buoyant blue pillow between you. See it whenever you think of the other. That space is called love. Then, when you want to say something, say it across the buoyant blue space. To communicate, it is best not to communicate directly. You will only rehash the same grievances. Return into your room and practice communicating through the dreaming.

Exercise 106
· · · · · · · · · ·
The Bridge

Breathe out slowly three times, counting from three to one. See the one as tall, clear, and bright.

Look into your heart, and see the color of your love for your partner. Send this color as a bridge of light to the other's heart. See it traveling through the buoyant blue space. What happens when it touches the other's heart?

Breathe out. Using images or words, relate through the bridge of light what you need to say to the other.

Breathe out. Watch and listen. See and hear what the other sends back to you through the conduit of the bridge.

Breathe out. Continue the conversation until there is peace and love between you.

Breathe out. Open your eyes.

. . . .

I remember a distraught mother who hadn't seen her seven-year-old son for many months. After his parents' divorce he moved in with his father and refused to see his mother. We did the exercise, and she went home. On arriving home, there was a message on the answering machine: "I miss you, Mom. When can I see you?" Remember quantum dreaming? Instantaneous communication. While your sun mind can only rehash its anger, pain, and grudges, your moon mind is your dreaming reminding you of how you really feel. Mother and child in that moment gave form to the divinity.

If you haven't yet met your soul mate, take consolation in the fact that any act of love between partners (mother and son, friends, business partners) calls down the presence of God—or if you don't believe in God, the presence of the mysterious vivifying creative space. Ahavah, love, and *ehad,* which means one, have the same numerical value.* The magical act requires the spell of soft words of praise, acceptance, and love; and the imagining of the other, stretching out to encompass the other, and to become one with them. Forgetting yourself for a moment to experience the other totally is the highest form of love.

Exercise 107
. . . .
Eyes and Oneness

Breathe out slowly three times, counting from three to one. See the one as tall, clear, and bright.

---

*13. This is done by adding up the value of each letter of the word "ahavah": aleph 1+ heh 5 + bet 2 + heh 5 = 13 and of the word "ehad": aleph 1+ het 8 + dalet 4 = 13

See your beloved standing in front of you. Sense all the changes in your body and heart.

Breathe out. Come closer and closer. Embrace.

Breathe out. Plunge your eyes deep into your partner's eyes. Feel your whole being plunging into the ocean of luminosity that is your partner's eyes. Sense, see, feel, and live yourself becoming one.

Breathe out slowly and open your eyes.

. . . .

The act of love cannot happen without duality. Use the split instead of fighting it. Stoke each other's fires until your flames merge and rise ever higher. In the act of finding your soul mate, or in the act of love, timing is all. Love plunges us into deep time, where time as we know it stops, and we enter a blissful state of no-time, we enter paradise on Earth. How to handle time and the acceleration of time is our next chapter.

12

Time and Choice

God wove the beginning to the end and the end to the beginning.

SEFER YETSIRAH 1:9

Once in Judea, an old man was planting a fig tree. The Roman Emperor Hadrian passed by and asked him, "Do you really expect to live long enough to eat the fruit of these trees?" The old man answered, "My ancestors planted for me, and now I plant for my children." On the surface, this is a simple story. But as conscious dreamers, are you fooled? What is happening that merits bringing together an old Jew and the emperor of the world? Is it a story about figs, trees, or linear time? Let us look for the Remez,* the pattern, starting at the first mention of a fig tree in Genesis. After they eat of the fruit of the Tree of Knowledge, Adam and Eve use fig leaves to cover their nakedness.[1] Before that, they were unashamedly one timeless being of light, "extending from one side of heaven to the other."[2] After their expulsion, as we know, they contracted, and "God made skins to cover their nakedness."[3] No longer one with all, but now bodies bound by form, constrained by their new reality to move through space, "toiling . . . all the days of their lives." Why toiling? Toil comes when things do not

---

*See chapter 1.

happen instantly. The old man is planting by the sweat of his brow and presumably won't see the fruits of his labor.

"If you live long enough, bring me figs from your tree," says the emperor. The man was one hundred years old when this encounter happened. But a number of years in the future, he appears before Hadrian with a basketful of plump figs. We can imagine him sprightly and grinning happily. What did he toil for? The Drash* question is answered by the emperor's gesture. He fills the old man's basket with gold, fulfilling the Sod level of the dream. What has the old man's dreaming done for him, which the emperor recognizes? Has the old man tricked time? Incorruptible gold shining in all directions seems to indicate so. Does he, like primordial Adam, live in a timeless present? Is that the treasure? Has he escaped linear time altogether, or simply prolonged his life?

To us who hear this story, can we, like the old man, hope to master time? Many have wasted their life's blood searching for the famed fountain of youth. Are we dreamers or idealists, as so many accuse us of being? Do we really think we can escape the toil and sweat of our daily lives? Can we break away from the corrosiveness of doubt that leads us to question why should we live, since inevitably we will die? If the answer to longevity and maybe eternal life is hidden in the subconscious realm of dreamtime, wouldn't you want to know?

✳

Our greatest complaint today is that we have no time for anything. No time for our children, our spouses or lovers, no time for our friends and community. No time even for ourselves! "How did it get so late, so soon?"⁴ Overworked for too little reward, either of money or leisure, and separated from our environment by a fog of busyness (our busy dream) that's become a habit of the mind, we've lost our taste for life. Few today remember God's exhortation to Abram, lekh lekha, go to yourself, or Horace's simpler prompting: Carpe diem, seize the day. We tell ourselves our "time poverty" is a fact. Well, in fact, it's not. We have more leisure time than ever before, but do we use it? "Time is the stuff that money is made of"⁵ unfortunately has become a truism many of

*See chapter 1.

us live by, in a world where needs are carrots, fabricated for the sole purpose of tricking the consumer into spending money. And if you want things, you must take the time away from other things to make the money you need to be able to afford them. We've come full circle. Keeping up with the stuff we think we need is a stressful occupation, and stress is the biggest cause of the physical and psychic diseases that afflict us and shorten our life spans.

So then is it all simply about learning to control our impulses? If we need less, we'll need less money, and we'll have more time for life.

But then we must know what we want to do with our lives. The meaning of our life is intimately connected to the fact that time exists. If we use time productively—whatever that means to each of us—our life will feel meaningful. If we squander our time, our life will feel empty. Trying to find our way to the gold that the emperor, the ruler of our inner world, wants to give us is a quest only our subconscious can map out for us. Therefore this chapter is not an expose about time, but an experiential journey through time's different manifestations, and the challenges they offer us. The aim is to discover how to combine and use these different time experiences to rise out of our time addiction and despair, and into timeless wisdom, which is "a tree of life to those who embrace her."[6]

As we speak, the rumor going around town is that time is accelerating. But even our cosmologists disagree. They may receive a Nobel Prize for saying that the universe's expansion is accelerating, and time with it,[*] but others are already questioning these findings and may yet get their own Nobel Prize.[†] But how would we really know? If the world is going faster, everything in the world is also accelerating, and we have nothing to compare it to. We would need clocks outside of our universe to measure it. We're all one giant ship of fools traveling together. Having eaten of the fruit of knowledge of good and evil, many of us believe that time, toil, and pain are inescapable companions on the road to dust and ashes, a sad attitude that science has so far only served to exacerbate.

---

[*]2011, Adam Riess of Johns Hopkins University, Brian Schmidt of Harvard, Saul Permutter of the Supernova Cosmology Project.
[†]Professor Subir Sarkar, and teams at Oxford University's Department of Physics and at the Niels Bohr Institute in Copenhagen.

Leaving science aside, the mystical traditions have another explana-tion. Follow the trail of indigenous cultures around the world, and you will find their traditions unanimous in predicting an imminent massive awakening, a shift in consciousness that will greatly quicken our rates of vibration, the rate of passage of our energy from dense matter to light. Here is what the Zohar has to say: "In the six hundredth year of the sixth millennium,* the gates of wisdom above, together with the wellsprings of wisdom below will be opened up, and the world will prepare to usher in the seventh millennium."[7] We are now in the year 5782 (2022 CE) and are fast approaching the seventh millennium. But even the 218 years left in this millennium are subject to acceleration! With "arousal from below"—which means with our active participation—the process will speed up, and the "Lord will accelerate it in its time."[8] Is this change in the rate of our vibrations what we are experiencing as time speeding up?

The Gaon of Vilna, eighteenth-century Talmudist and Kabbalist, prophesied that science and mysticism, having turned global, and publicized their innermost secrets, would seem to fundamentally diverge and go their separate ways, but would ultimately rejoin in a grand unified worldview, ushering in the new awakening. He urged his followers to engage in and learn about the sciences, as a way to hasten the coming of the new consciousness, which in Jewish thought is called the Messianic Age. Meanwhile, believers in science and believers in mystical truth muddle along, generally disdaining each other. Will the twain meet again? If, according to Alfred North Whitehead,† "what has accelerated is the rate at which novelty enters the world,"[9] can we learn to adapt fast enough? Since the Industrial Revolution, we have seen an explosion of inventions that have revolutionized our lives. The pace of change is shrinking from an indeterminate thousands-of-years span (the wheel), to thirty years (cars and planes), to seven years (the information explosion with the computer, the iPhone, the internet, etc.), and now we are seeing a three-year span at which novelty enters the world. As an Apple technician told a lady who sought repairs for her three-year-old computer, "Your machine is vintage, Madam." Moore's law, which

---

*That's 1840 CE or 5600 in the Jewish lunar calendar.
†1861–1947, mathematician and defining figure of process philosophy.

predicts that microchip performance would double every two years, is "causing an increase in the pace of change that is challenging the ability of the human being to adapt."[10] Should we relinquish all technology and return to nature? Knowing that the changes we are experiencing in every sphere of life today are not separate phenomena, but part of a unified changing consciousness, and that trying to hold back the tide will only make the changes more painful, how can we participate in the "arousal from below"? To hasten the coming of a new age predicted to be one of "universal peace and brotherhood," we must learn to extricate ourselves from time's addiction, and the various emotional patterns and belief systems that block our way to becoming masters of time.

"The only reason for time is so that everything doesn't happen at once,"[11] said Albert Einstein. It might be a quip, but think of it for a moment. Without time, the world as we know it wouldn't exist. The secret is entwined in the meaning of the Hebrew root SFR, which can be read as *SeFeR,* space, universe, book; or as *SeFaR,* time, number, year; or as *SiPuR,** soul, story. *Sefer* is the shape of space or things that create our universe. *Sefar* is sequence, walking through space, counting our footsteps, creating time. *Sipur* is the story the soul makes, the lines and curves it draws as it traverses the space-time continuum we bathe in.

Exercise 108
The Continuum Space-Time Story

Close your eyes. Breathe out slowly three times, counting from three to one. See the one tall, clear, and bright.

See and feel that without space you can't define time.

Breathe out. See and feel that without time, space freezes.

Breathe out. Tell the story of your passage through space and time. Have one image of what that story looks like.

Breathe out. Open your eyes, seeing that image with open eyes.

Does having a concentrated image of our story line actually collapse our space-time continuum? Can linear time cave in to mysterious other

---

*As previously mentioned, the sounds "pe" or "fe" are represented by the same letter P, pei in Hebrew.

forces? Are we not inexorably moving toward the moment of our death? "Time is passing, time is passing, Madame/Alas, time is not. It is we who are passing."[12] Who is the *we* that is passing? Is it all of us, or only our bodies, fashioned of clay and water? Let us see if we can loosen up our unshakable belief that time, like the anthropomorphic Saturn in Goya's famous painting, will swallow all of us up.

Exercise 109
• • • • • • • • • • •
River of Time

Close your eyes. Breathe out slowly three times, counting from three to one. See the one tall, clear, and bright.

Imagine that you are spinning out of control in the river of time, being buffeted and pulled along by the rapids and currents you have no control over.

Breathe out. Find a way to step out of the river, and stand on the embankment overlooking the river. What has changed for you?

Breathe out. When you step back into the river, what is different?

Breathe out. Open your eyes.

• • • • • • • • • • •

If we can experience stepping out of time, there is more nuance to the experience of time than appears on the bare page. Just now, your mind may be occupied with the past, remembering what your grandmother told you when you were four. Or is it envisioning a future in which you are driving a flying car? Your time may be deep within, contemplating your beloved, or just on the surface of things, wondering if you'll have time to finish your report before you must pick up the children. Chronology is something we hang onto to grasp the journey of life. But as we've seen with dreaming, there are four levels of reality within, which are simultaneously many revolving realities that we experience all at the same time. We have the reality of P'shat, the past, our story line; the reality of Remez, our Now configuration; the reality of Drash, our hopes and fantasies about the future. The fourth level is Sod, the response, a No-Time everlasting beingness "that is not passing" and that we call PRDS, the Garden of Eden. Past, present, future, and No-Time. The Talmud's astounding statement that "there is no chronological order to the Torah"[13] can just as well apply to a human life.

While it is indisputable that our bodies walk sequential time, our inner experience weaves back and forth, leaping ahead, or reversing time at will. Time has many ways of manifesting, as well as many directions, sounds and colors.* Time is an ever-expanding Now.

Exercise 110
The Time of Trees

Close your eyes. Breathe out slowly three times, counting from three to one. See the one tall, clear, and bright.

Live the time of trees.

Breathe out. Live the time of leaves.

Breathe out. Live the time of birds.

Breathe out. Live the time of grass.

Breathe out. Live the time of butterflies.

Breathe out. Live the time of stones.

Breathe out. Live the time of oceans.

Breathe out. Live the time of clocks. What changes?

Breathe out. Look into yourself and live your inner time.

Breathe out. Open your eyes.

The time of trees or birds or stones reverberates as an experience in your dreaming mind. Whereas, by living in clock time, you fall right back into your causal mind. Can we relinquish clock time and, using the dreaming mind, learn to expand time (ocean time), contract time (grass time), or even stop time (stone time) at will? But before we go there, let us mention this amazing fact: There is no evidence whatsoever of any force that makes time flow. Time as a force doesn't exist. So what is this illusion that is so real we live and die by it? "If I am not asked about time, I know what time is. But if I am asked I do not," said Saint Augustine† in the fifth century.[14] Today we are equally in the dark, and time rules our lives to the hour, minute, and second. Our digital clocks

---

*Inspired by Jay Griffiths's book, *A Sideways Look at Time*, Harper Collins, 1999.

†354–430 CE, theologian, philosopher, and one of the most important of the Church Fathers; author of *The City of God, Confessions,* among other works.

proclaim a time cut loose from any pretense to natural cycles. With the first appearance of mechanical clocks in the fourteenth century, a slow divorce process was set in motion between man and his environment. We no longer needed to consult our biological time, or the heavenly cycles. Artificial time began imposing an unnatural rhythm on our biological time, disrupting our subconscious body processes, and affecting our health that, as we will see in the next chapter, is based on rhythm. To trick clock time, we must move away from time as a constrictive force imposed on us.

Exercise 111
. . . .
Breaking Clock Time Addiction

Close your eyes. Breathe out slowly three times, counting from three to one. See the one tall, clear, and bright.

What is the first thing you ask when you get up in the morning?

Breathe out. See, feel, and recognize how you are addicted to clock time.

Breathe out three times slowly. Roll back time. Hear the cry of the rooster waking you up. How does your consciousness move?

Breathe out. Roll back to nighttime, and hear the wolves howling.

Breathe out. At dusk hear the bullfrogs singing.

Breathe out. At the sun's zenith hear the piercing cry of the hawk, the swish of his wing cutting through the blue sky.

Breathe out. In the morning sunlight hear the hens clucking in the yard.

Breathe out. What has changed in your consciousness?

Breathe out. At dawn feel the first rays of the sunlight touching your body.

Breathe out. Open your eyes.
. . . .

The idea that the past and the future are irrevocably set in space is another illusion, a convention that some tribes in the Amazon see reversed. They experience the past before them—they know what it looks like—and the future behind them—they can't yet see it. The Hebrews also see the past before them, for at the moment they see it, it's already slipping into the past!

Exercise 112

· · · · · · · · · · ·

Directionality

Close your eyes. Breathe out slowly three times, counting from three to one. See the one tall, clear, and bright.

You stand on a vast, empty plain. There are no visible landmarks. Ask yourself, Where is your past?

Breathe out. Where is your future?

Breathe out. Switch directions, putting the past where the future was and the future where the past was. What happens to you?

Breathe out. See the sun in the sky. Where is it in relation to you? Position yourself to face the sun. What have you gained?

Breathe out. Open your eyes.

· · · · · · · · · · ·

Since the tyranny of time is mainly lived as one of inevitable historicity, systematically reversing the arrow of time will help to further loosen the hold this addiction has on you. We have done some reversing in the last exercise. Here is the formal reversing exercise taught in my lineage. It is based on the idea of *t'shuvah*, TSHVH, which is often translated as "repentance" but really means "return." What are we returning to? A more innocent time, a timeless present, "extending from one side of heaven to the other," the Emperor's basketful of luminous Sod gold.

Exercise 113

· · · · · · · · · · ·

Reversing

Do this every night without fail. Do it in bed, with your eyes closed, just before going to sleep: Look at your day backwards, as if rewinding the tape of your day. When you come upon a difficult encounter with someone, go stand in that person's shoes. Look at yourself from that person's vantage point. When you see clearly how you were behaving, return to your body and continue reversing the day's events. If you fall asleep, remember that the brain doesn't sleep, and it will continue reversing. You will wake up refreshed, your burdens lightened.

· · · · · · · · · · ·

My son once complained I hadn't taught him about reality. "Which reality?" I asked. Going back through time allows us to access the roots of the reality we're stuck in. Switching places opens up new perceptions, new realities, in our space-time construct. It loosens our belief system that there is only one way of seeing things, thus breaking open the specific space-time relationship we conceived of as a fact. The belief that there is only one reality fixes time more than anything else. There are other realities. And one of those is cyclical time.

The cyclical nature of time is evident to the smallest child. Day follows night, and spring follows winter. The sun rises in the east and goes down in the west. The waxing and waning moon affects ocean tides and also affects our inner waters and moods. From time immemorial, people around the world have based their understanding of time on the cyclical nature of planets and stars in our sky. Rituals celebrating the cycles form an integral part of all religious ceremonies. Shavuot and Sukkot are harvest feasts.* Christmas is the shortest day and longest night of the year and, to children's delight, comes back every three hundred and sixty-five days. The ancients imagined the stars and planets to be fixed in rotating celestial spheres. Is the universe a giant mechanical clock? This was Isaac Newton's† contention: absolute time, flowing at a consistent pace, unaffected by any observer or outside influence. The inevitability of the recurrence of days and seasons is both a comfort and anxiety producing.

Exercise 114
. . . .
Cyclical Time

Close your eyes. Breathe out slowly three times, counting from three to one. See the one tall, clear, and bright.

---

*These Jewish feasts of spring and fall are the pilgrimage feasts and include Passover. The ancient Israelites would mark the feast by making a pilgrimage to the Temple in Jerusalem. Shavuot (Pentecost) is a harvest festival and commemorates the giving of Torah and the Ten Commandments on Mount Sinai. Sukkot, the festival of booths, is also a harvest festival (fall) and commemorates how the Israelites were sheltered in booths and protected by God during their forty years in the desert.
†Sir Isaac Newton (1643–1727) was an English mathematician, physicist, and astronomer.

Hear and see that "what has been will be again, what has been done, will be done again. There is nothing new under the sun." (Ecclesiastes 1:9) What do you feel?

Breathe out. Imagine that you die and return to the very same life and live it exactly the same way as you lived it before. What do you feel? Can you embrace this eternal return and grow stronger? What do you gain? What is missing?

Breathe out. Open your eyes.

· · · · · · · · · · ·

If we unequivocally believed in Solomon's sad words, or Newton's absolute time, there would be nothing for us but to bow to the reality of a deterministic universe. Nietzsche* said it more plainly: "Escape is impossible,"[15] an attitude that would likely lead us, as it did him, to madness. And while we cannot know why he went mad, this leaves us with a sour taste. His idea of "recurrence as a selective principle in the service of strength (and barbarism)"[16] destroys all hope of a world of peace and brotherhood. At which point, what reason is there to go on? Job, the proverbial victim of horrendous afflictions, asks this very question. His name, which means "persecuted" or "hated by life," may signal to us that a corrosive doubt had already insinuated itself into his mind and heart. The storm that turned everything he held dear to ashes and dust may only have been in his mind. When he finally recognizes a power greater than himself, One who commands linear, cyclical, and everlasting time, his loved ones and his possessions are all returned to him. Jolted out of his despair, Job's vision of reality opened and changed him.

Exercise 115
· · · · · · · · · · ·
Clearing Chronophobia

Close your eyes. Breathe out slowly three times, counting from three to one. See the one tall, clear, and bright.

See, feel, and live your fear of losing what you have.

Breathe out. Recognize how it is an impediment to your enjoyment of life.

---

*Friedrich Nietzsche (1844–1900) was a philosopher, classical philologist, and author.

Breathe out. Lift your hands up to the sun, feel them becoming warm, and turning to light.

Breathe out. Bring them down into your feet, and pull the fear up and out of your body through your mouth.

Breathe out. Lift the fear up to the blue sky. See your hands disappearing in the blue.

Breathe out. Feel the weight in your hands diminishing. Bring your hands down. What do you have in your hands now?

Breathe out. Stretch your hands with their gift toward the east and the rising sun. What do you feel? What do you hope for? What happens to the gift in your hands?

Breathe out. Open your eyes.

. . . .

Luckily, Heraclitus* reminds us that "no man ever steps in the same river twice, for it's not the same river and he's not the same man."[17] Which means that our cycles are not really cycles. Our lives, our planets, and our galaxies, in fact, describe a spiraling pattern. The spiraling pattern is ensuring that we can never step in the same river twice, nor do two things in exactly identical ways. If it were otherwise, we would be like machines spitting out the exact same copy every time. Free choice wouldn't exist, and we would never evolve. Our creative purpose, which is the living breath within us, wouldn't manifest. Even if the same events were to repeat endlessly, the person reliving those same events has the capacity to respond differently, as is so perfectly illustrated in the film *Groundhog Day*. Neutrality doesn't apply here. We choose to be despairing or to respond to the necessity of the situation. Tikun, the same maneuver we used in the correction or amelioration of dreams, can be consciously applied to life's challenges.

Exercise 116
. . . .
The Serene Hours

Close your eyes. Breathe out slowly three times, counting from three to one. See the one tall, clear, and bright.

You are walking in a garden and come upon an ancient sundial

*Heraclitus (535–475 BCE) was a Greek philosopher.

that says: "I count only those hours that are serene." What happens to time? To you?

Breathe out. Open your eyes.

· · · · · · · · · · ·

We have heard much about the evolution of matter. What about the evolution of soul? It is just as significant, or more so, according to the Kabbalists. This leads us straight to the agonizing question: Does every part of us die? Does a part of us survive and live on in the uterine paradise of eternity? Do we continue the cyclical movement that is the law of this universe? Or can we use that added (YSF, the root of Joseph's name*) time to dream ourselves higher up on the ladder of transformation? Meet Death, the mysterious lady in red, who bumped into the grand vizier in the gardens of the sultan one evening and looked surprised. Horrified at his impending doom, the grand vizier begged the sultan for his fastest horse to gallop off to Samarkand. But as the story tells us, time and space are arranged for the meeting of the grand vizier with nothingness. The sultan, curious, went out into his gardens to meet the lady in red. "Dear lady, why did you frighten my grand vizier? He's off to Samarkand on my fastest stead." "Ah! Now I understand," said Death. "Indeed, I have him on my tablets for tonight in Samarkand."[18] The inescapability of death, the impending horror of the void, can paralyze the mightiest. Death is an unknown we must all face, let loose into, and trust that the cyclical law of the universe applies, if not to our physical envelope, at least to our souls, and will bring them cycling back into new bodies. Dr. Ian Stevenson's meticulously conducted interviews with children around the world claiming recollections of past lives is fascinating reading. But if that doesn't convince you, take a wager, like Pascal did, on the truth of God's existence. You will be in good company, since so many traditions around the world believe in reincarnation. The hope of rebirth will confer much solace and buttressing against the fear of death "for death cometh with the next-life key."[19] It will change your life.

---

*See chapter 2.

Exercise 117

· · · · · · · · · · ·

The Origami Flower

Close your eyes. Breathe out slowly three times, counting from three to one. See the one tall, clear, and bright.

You have in front of you a transparent bowl filled with clear water. Throw into the water a folded origami flower, and watch it unfold, petal by petal, until it is fully open.

Breathe out. See its petals curling under, until the whole flower folds back into itself.

Breathe out. See the flower begin the unfolding all over again.

Breathe out. Watch this process happening three times. What are your feelings?

Breathe out. Open your eyes.

· · · · · · · · · · ·

In the Kabbalistic universe, the wheel of death and rebirth is called *gilgul*. Isaac Luria, the Ari,* the great Kabbalist of sixteenth century Safed† says that we all have *gilgulim* but that the righteous have many more, because they are active "transformers" whose true destiny is to repair the world. While we may not be righteous ones, what stops us from responding to the necessity of life's challenges? One sunny morning in August 1980, a man stepped into Colette's garden. He had had a dream that night that showed him his tombstone. It read September 17, 1980. He was understandably shaken. "Close your eyes, breathe out." Colette had him erase the date with chisel and hammer and replace it with a new date. On September 17 his car was hit by a huge truck and totaled. He came away without a scratch or a bruise on his body.

If "man is the perfecting agent in the structure of the cosmos,"[20] then what stops us from choosing to perfect our own lives each time at a higher level of consciousness? And for that matter, what prevents us from intending a rebirth at a higher level of the ladder? We have nothing to lose, and everything to gain. We can surmise that the arousal that triggers rebirth comes only with our soul's desire—or that of the

---

*The lion.

†Israel.

universal DreamField , pushing us to try again, to engage a larger challenge. To the Buddhists, the wheel of rebirth allows the soul to correct its karma. To the rabbis, gilgul gives us another change at enlarging our consciousness through tikun. "When mind becomes greater, time becomes lesser . . . until it is ultimately nullified."[21] Tikun initiates t'shuvah, the return back to light and unity (yehidah) that shines atop the ladder of dreaming.

Exercise 118
. . . .
360-Degree Vision

Close your eyes. Breathe out slowly three times, counting from three to one. See the one tall, clear, and bright.

You have walked deep into the countryside. You come upon a great tree.

Breathe out. Embrace the tree. Put your left ear to the tree, and listen to its murmuring life.

Breathe out. Become the tree.

Breathe out. Become the roots.

Breathe out. Become the trunk.

Breathe out. Become the branches.

Breathe out. Become each and every leaf of the tree.

Breathe out. Observe how wide a vision you have. Can you see 360 degrees all around?

Breathe out. Pay attention to your sense of time.

Breathe out. Become yourself again, now sitting at the summit of the tree. Can you still see 360 degrees all around?

Breathe out. Climb down and walk away, seeing 360 degrees all around you.

Breathe out. Open your eyes.

. . . .

In many legends and myths, and in the Hebrew Bible, there exist heroes who manage to transcend time. Serah, granddaughter of Jacob, lives on century after century, reappearing at the passage of the Red Sea, at King Solomon's judgment, and in the concentration camps. It is the rhythms of her melody's coming and going, as does all music, that comforts and appeases Jacob, as she sings to him of the reappearance of his son Joseph, whom he had mourned for twenty years. For the consolations of cyclical time that she represents, he blesses her with eternal life. Serah is the personification of the never-ending cyclical law. But it is the prophet Elijah who actually transcends time. He goes up to heaven in a chariot of fire and becomes the Angel of the Presence,* the man of light, "extending from one side of heaven to the other."[22] The chariot of fire, like Moses' burning bush that doesn't burn, turns linear time to an intensity of experience that nullifies all time as we know it. In a vertical present, "time is measured not by lengths, but by intensities."[23]

Exercise 119
. . . .
Vertical Time

Close your eyes. Breathe out slowly three times, counting from three to one. See the one tall, clear, and bright.

See and live the fears, doubts, regrets, and guilt that have kept you from transforming your life and have pushed you to emptiness and loneliness.

Breathe out. See and live how these fears are fears of the unknown and fear of death.

Breathe out. See, feel, and know that to fight against these fears, we need to settle out of the horizontal line of everyday life and go into such an intense present that it is lived as a vertical eternity.

Breathe out. See and sense yourself constructing the vertical line instant by instant. See each instant as a point. See and feel how you are living point after point, as though reborn.

Breathe out. Open your eyes, feeling this with open eyes.

. . . .

Moving "from the multiplicity of our natures to the Oneness from which we originated," we land on a point that we call NOW. It cannot last, for just thinking about Now it is already past. But what can last is presence spreading in every direction, as an expansion of feeling (joy, peace, serenity) that has nothing to do with pain, toil, or bondage. Presence exists in the realm of the matrix, the superconscious mind that

---

*Metatron.

knows "a depth of beginning, a depth of end; a depth of good, a depth of evil; a depth of above, a depth below; a depth east, a depth west; a depth north, a depth south."[24] It has nothing to do with the individual self, but all to do with the timeless source of being. By recollecting this oneness, we stop time.

Exercise 120
. . . .
The Sun Drop

Close your eyes. Breathe out slowly three times, counting from three to one. See the one tall, clear, and bright.

Imagine that you are standing in your meadow looking up at the blue sky. See where the sun is. If it's to the left, watch it traveling across the sky until it is above you.

Breathe out. Watch as a sun drop falls from the sun, stopping at the level of your eyes, three feet away.

Breathe out. See the sun drop, slowly expanding sideways, becoming a long oblong. What becomes of time?

Breathe out. Decide how long you want to remain in this extended No-Time.

Breathe out. Open your eyes, holding the image and the intent in your mind for a few seconds.

. . . .

Here, two seemingly incompatible things are happening simultaneously: the infinite light extending like the firmament "from one end of heaven to the other" and the measurable corollaries of space and time interacting. As prophesied by the Gaon of Vilna, divergent thought processes are finding common ground: Einstein tells us that space and time are not separate dimensions, but corollaries to "the speed of light which is absolute, invariable and cannot be exceeded." Kabbalistic thought says that merging with the light is the only way to be united with Oneness. While light extends everywhere, it is also traveling past and through us in all directions. You can visualize these two concepts as one, in the image of a hummingbird vibrating so fast (that's the intensity of the light) that it appears to be still (its movement has corollaries that fix it in space and time).

In practical terms, a collaboration between our two brains is the only way forward. We need them both if we are to reconcile our physical experience of a limited life span, with our soul's experience of eternity, our conscious brain living in linear time and our subconscious brain living in No-Time intersect where intent exists. Intent or kavanah is the burning desire for self and goal to be instantaneously one. The conscious act of dreaming is our best tool, both ancient and at the cutting edge of modern thought, to manifest a goal without toil or pain. As described in midrash,[25] after Jacob wakes from his great ladder dream,* he resumes his journey toward the land of his uncle Laban, his mother's brother. But, we are told, not by walking: The land compresses under his feet, and he is instantly at the well in Haran, Laban's land, where shepherds come to water their flocks and women to fill their water jugs.

Exercise 121
. . . .
Love Conquers Space-Time

Close your eyes. Breathe out slowly three times, counting from three to one. See the one tall, clear, and bright.

Visualize in front of you someone you love. Feel and see the light of love emanating from you toward that person.

Breathe out. See the light of your love surrounding and encompassing the one you love. What happens to the space between you? What happens to the time separation?

Breathe out. Open your eyes.
. . . .

Jacob's love arousal magnetizes a soul mate at just the crossroads of space and time corresponding to his first meeting with Rachel. Space-time collapses, and movement slows to a snail's pace. With the intensification of energy that signals he's tapping into the everlasting No-Time source, Jacob finds the superhuman strength needed to lift the great stone blocking the well. Waters start gushing from the well, and also from his eyes. He cries. Here is the fabled fountain of youth! Rabbis call this state deep reality. "In deep reality, space and time are abolished."[26] Athletes call it the zone. You can also enter into the

---

*See chapter 2.

zone by consciously practicing this slow motion while seeing yourself effortlessly and perfectly reaching your goal. Try it when you are very late to an appointment across town and know that there is no realistic way that you'll be able to get there on time.

Before learning the main exercise on how to consciously collapse space-time, here are two simple practices.

Exercise 122
. . . .
Wake-Up Time

Set your alarm to 8:05 a.m.

Lying in bed, close your eyes. Breathe out slowly three times, counting from three to one. See the one tall, clear, and bright.

Give yourself the order to wake up at exactly 8 a.m.

On awaking, don't immediately open your eyes, instead visualize the time on your bedside alarm clock.

Open your eyes. Check the time.
. . . .

If you're able to do this, then move on to the next exercise.

Exercise 123
. . . .
Anticipate Clock Time

Close your eyes. Breathe out slowly three times, counting from three to one. See the one tall, clear, and bright.

Look at your watch imaginally, seeing the precise time, both hour and minute.

Breathe out. Open your eyes and check the time on your physical watch.
. . . .

Do this many times a day until you are able to tell time precisely without having to look at your watch. Once released from the tyranny of the clock, you can begin trusting that plunging into deep time won't take you dangerously out of sequential reality. You will come out of it at exactly the time you set.* Your two brains can easily function

---
*See Chapter 7.

simultaneously. You need the deep insights of the subconscious mind to effortlessly create the goal you are envisioning. And you need the deadline that your sequential mind sets, to manifest your dreams into this everyday reality. To this effect, I suggest you add something to your practice: Never complain about time!

Here is the main exercise for teaching yourself how to collapse space-time.

Exercise 124
. . . .
Collapsing Space-Time

Close your eyes. Breathe out slowly three times, counting from three to one. See the one tall, clear, and bright.

Knowing that you are very late, slowly breathe out all your panic.

Now visualize the place where you must be and the exact time you must be there.

Breathe out. Do everything in slow motion—clean up your bedroom, put away discarded clothes, straighten up your papers—before leaving the house.

Breathe out. Hold in mind the place where you want to be and the place you are, merging to become one.

Breathe out. Hold in mind your arrival at exactly the planned time.

Breathe out. Open your eyes.

. . . .

It is good to try this exercise in your mind before practicing it in your daily life. You may need to practice this a few times before getting it right. Don't give up. One day it will just happen effortlessly, without pain or toil.

There are many phenomena that can be easily explained when you understand and practice plunging into the subconscious mind. The subconscious realm lives in No-Time. Past and future exist in its deep cauldron. Telepathy (seeing in actual time something happening at a distance), precognition (seeing future events), time travel (peering into another time frame, as if you were dropped into the garden of Marie Antoinette, a famous case), visionary space travel (the Dogon people of

Mali described Jupiter's moons long before any telescope or spaceship could confirm their existence), bilocation (the Baal Shem Tov, founder of the Hasidic movement, was often seen in two different places at once), levitation (the effects of gravity change when your energy transforms to light: Father Pio and Saint Teresa of Ávila were reported levitating by many eyewitnesses) all begin to make sense when the space-time corollary breaks down. If you have experienced a similar phenomenon, write it down in your DreamBook. While these phenomena are valuable milestones, do not pursue them, for your avid curiosity will immediately set you back. You will fall back into emotion, and emotion belongs to sequential time. What you must pursue is light. Light and feeling are one. They transcend space-time and story.

Remember the four rabbis who decided to go to PRDS, the Garden of Eden? The first one saw only the story line, and died of the shock. The second one saw only the pattern in the story and went mad. The third asked the question but dismissed the answer as simplistic.

Only Rabbi Akiva came and went in peace.

Therefore strive to remember the serene hours, and let them become all your hours.

13

Healing
Will It Be Leprosy, Wellness, or Wholeness?

And his heart shall understand, and he shall return and become healed.

ISAIAH 6:10

For God prepared the remedy before He brought on the disease.

MEGILLAH 13B

How can we live serene hours when we're ill or in pain? Why is it that as soon as we perceive ourselves as ill, we are already alienated from the world? The trees aren't as green, the water not as blue, the sunlight disturbs us, even our loved ones irritate us. Their health is a flaunting insult. We've become lepers, exiled forever to the colony of the wounded ones. Hopelessness, alienation, and isolation are our lot. Leprosy, *tsara'ath*, the Bible tells us, is an impurity that separates us from others. I understood how disastrous that was one day, as I was visiting a friend in the hospital. He had severe arthritis and walked on crutches. The prognosis wasn't good, and he looked to end his days in a wheelchair. The man sitting in the next bed was paralyzed from the waist down. He called me over and loudly whispered how much he hated my friend. I had two healthy legs; why didn't he hate me? The abyss between the healthy and the sick is huge, and seemingly impassable. Are there indeed two separate worlds? Is there a way back to the world of wholeness and health? Can we leap over the abyss and plant our feet squarely back in the healthy camp called wholeness? Or is there an in-between phase? Let's call it wellness. Wellness is not as stable a condition. Maybe we're on a precarious bridge that links the two worlds. We're walking in the right direction, toward health, but some symptom could pull us right back into the lepers' camp. Wellness is a changeable state that requires effort on our part. Supplementation, diet, exercise, medicines, and regular visits to the doctor may be insurance against a dire diagnosis, but they are no effortless assurance of health.

Shouldn't we be satisfied with wellness? Playing the balancing act to remain on the right side of the boundary that separates health from illness is a common enough tactic. But it is said that "there is no left in that Ancient One; all is right."[1] God has only a right side. And we are made in God's image. So how should we visualize wholeness? As an irrepressible fountain, a cornucopia of goodness, or a seamless abundance of riches both physical and spiritual? That, it seemed, was Job's happy fate. He could boast health, wealth, family, homes, cattle, and land. Grateful to God for his blessings, he showed it, by tithing 10 percent of his earnings to charity. Yet some midrashic sources place him in Egypt, as advisor to Pharaoh at the time of the plagues, at the time Moses was making a nuisance of himself, demanding that Pharaoh let his people go. This implies that Job might have been motivated as much by self-interest as by love for God. What if Job were to lose everything? Would he still remain whole? Or was he simply mimicking wholeness? Job was God-fearing. On hearing of God's warning of hail (plague seven), he rushed his laborers and cattle under protective shelter. But how could he escape the dark wind (so black that light was totally extinguished, plague nine) that swept away all his wealth, homes, children, and cattle? In his dark despair, he broke out in boils (plague six) all over his body, causing his wife to urge him to curse God. The truth was out: Job's good health had been wellness, not wholeness, and when he was stripped bare, he tumbled straight into the lepers' colony and was overwhelmed by despair. Whether sudden or slow in onset, when illness strikes, like the ten plagues combined, it can wipe away everything we've labored for. We are flung far from the land of milk and honey we took for granted and brought face-to-face with who we really are.

Shockingly, we are told that Jacob, the third patriarch, demanded of God that He give us illness. "Why?" asked God. "So that we would feel the urge to put our house in order," said Jacob. God thought it a good idea, and Jacob was the first man to die of illness.[2] Does this reconcile us? Did it reconcile Job, the everyman who is good but maybe not "very good," having not yet plunged to the mysterious source of wholeness. Like Job, we could manage less fierce adversaries than disease and disaster. And while we are in good health, we happily ignore that we are all terminally ill. Our complacency, our enslavement to our self-interests, comforts, and status are shaken up by an unknown adversary, our k'negdo, called Satan in the Job story. Satan can take on many forms and anonymous faces that we don't always recognize. What are the plagues, if not catastrophic pointers illuminating our exile from wholeness?

✳

Like Pharaoh of the stiff neck, we are very stubborn. While we may see the writing on the wall, we don't necessarily accept it. Though our throats are sore, our coughs persistent, our headaches worsening, and our pouches growing, we continue steadfast down a path that pits us, like Pharaoh, against the voice of God. "I'm not going to live on a diet for the rest of my days. That's not my kind of life," remarked a young man who likes to live it up but is dangerously overweight. As I told him, "It's not what you want; it's what your body wants!" If the young man persists in eating rich foods and drinking alcohol, the arteries and veins of his body will get clogged, bringing on the plagues. High cholesterol, palpitations, or a heart attack may be the crescendo sound of God's voice in his body. For if indeed, as Job says, "In my flesh I will see God,"[3] then the God in his body is crying out for him to return to balance and order. The body's warning is, in effect, its homeostatic urge to return to tov m'od, the very good state of Adam haRishon, the first human.

Many would say that God is punishing the young man for his sin of gluttony. It's an easy assumption to make through simple cause and effect, but in fact, the young man doesn't understand why he struggles to stop eating and drinking so unhealthily. Job, too, is in the dark: Why was he so afflicted? Job's three friends have it conveniently settled: Since God, in their view, causes no one to suffer innocently, it goes to prove that Job sinned and is being justly punished. God reproaches "those miserable comforters" for having spoken wrong and adding guilt to the sufferer's pain. In disease let's leave morality out of the equation and focus on natural laws. The Tower, the sixteenth tarot trump card, shows what happens when we are not in alignment with natural laws. Thunder and lightning hit the tower summit, knocking down its (our) crown, and tossing us out of the tower. It could happen to any one of us. Attributing blame is adding insult to injury. Job vehemently refuses to repent, for he has nothing to repent, and he is right. God chose to afflict Job for His own inscrutable reasons. When rivers overflow, locusts swarm, pestilence kills, and darkness persists beyond the demarcation of dawn; something is out of order. Who knows where the unbalance started? Was it from an outside trauma or on the inside? Was it triggered by an ancestral pattern, an emotional entanglement, or a betrayal? We have five bodies, from dense to energetic, from physical, emotional, mental, spiritual, and beyond. Any one of these levels, or multiple levels, could have been impacted and contributed to unbalancing our fragile ecosystem. Whenever we are called on to sit with someone afflicted, we shouldn't jump to conclusions, but instead bow to a complexity that is beyond our comprehension. There is no known logic for ill health, nothing to explain why—though we both bake in the sun, you get melanoma and I don't. If there are subconscious reasons, we are not privy to them; only the afflicted one knows. Through our imagination, through stretching out to hold the other in love, and becoming one for a moment, we can come close to the other's mystery but never pierce it. Respect for the other's suffering, even when you think you know what they did wrong (He wouldn't stop eating; what do you expect? Now he's got diabetes!) is a prerequisite attitude to attempting any healing work. There is some kind of poetic twist in the biblical text when it declares that the cause of tsara'ath, leprosy, is gossip!

Let us all consider ourselves in need of healing, for we have all gossiped and disregarded mystery. Dis-ease puts us in the leper's colony, the narrow land of Egypt, where stress, hard work, and time constraints repress our life force and instigate the slow decline toward illness. We have all been there and may still be embedded in that chaotic and constrictive world. If we want to leave pressures behind, like the Hebrews, we must pack lightly: What weighs on us? What can we do without? What burden can we drop to facilitate our way back toward ease and well-being? This is not unknown work to you. You have been practicing this uncluttering and letting go all along. In chapter 2 you learned how to clean up your dreams by applying tikun (correction) to disordered images. In chapter 7 you threw doubt over your left shoulder to allow for what you see in your dreaming to manifest. In chapter 8 you cleared complex emotional knots, and in chapter 9 you cleared old family patterns. In chapter 10 you left behind beastly emotions and obstructive parental figures, to make your way back to the child of light at your core. In chapter 11 you dropped old grudges, resentments, guilt, and anger and freed your inner space to relate joyfully to your partners in life. In chapter 12 you conquered the pressures of time and learned how to sink into deep time. All this work guides and informs you back to our model for wholeness, Adam haRishon, the first human.

Exercise 125
· · · · · · · · · · ·
Drop Your Clothes

Close your eyes. Breathe out slowly three times, counting from three to one. See the one tall, clear, and bright.

Imagine that you are standing before a very tall and majestic pine tree, whose branches start very close to the ground.

Breathe out. Start climbing the tree. Climb up five branches, and drop an article of clothing.

Breathe out. Climb up five more branches, and drop another article of clothing.

Breathe out. Climb up five more, and again, drop an article of clothing.

Breathe out. Continue this way until you are completely naked.

Breathe out. Now drop your first skin.

Breathe out. Climb up five more branches, and drop your second skin.

Breathe out. Climb five more, and drop your third skin.

Breathe out. If anything is left of your body, continue climbing and dropping (your musculature, your skeleton), until your body is only light.

Breathe out. Climb to the nest at the summit of the tree, and sit there, seeing 360 degrees all around you.

Breathe out. Stand, and catch a multicolored ray of sunlight. Wrap yourself in rainbow light.

Breathe out. Climb down the tree in your rainbow robe, and walk away feeling refreshed and unburdened.

Breathe out. Open your eyes.

· · · · · · · · · · ·

Having established that we are everyman in need of healing, we can accept, like the Hebrews, that there are many tests or health challenges on the inescapable trajectory from birth to death. As we have said, wellness is not a static state but one in constant flux. There are four worlds, Atsilut (Emanation), Bri'ah (Creation), Yetsirah (Formation), and Asiyah (Manifestation), and our physical bodies belong to the lowest, Asiyah, the world of manifestation. The common approach to restoring wellness and health starts at the bottom with Asiyah, with the physical body and its diseases. Symptoms call for a remedy. It is a logical approach, represented by allopathic medicine, and also in part by holistic medicine. But is curing the symptom the way back to wholeness? One of the great errors of modern medicine is thinking that erasing the symptom will ensure the healing. The body is not a dense piece of meat but an energetic whole. Many things can happen on the way from the big bang (Atsilut), through the first inklings of consciousness (Bri'ah), to the unfolding of blueprints and images (Yetsirah), and finally to manifestation (Asiyah). As you experienced in the last exercise, the body is capable of moving up and down the ladder, from dense to energetic and back. The return approach addresses Yetsirah (your images), Bri'ah (your intentions), and Atsilut (your burning desire). We'll call this approach soul healing (as opposed to body healing). We need both approaches. The healing must happen at the soul level as well as on the physical level for us to truly heal and be whole. The soul (top down) approach is different from the body (bottom up) approach. Wholeness is a pathless land; symptoms will not guide us here. We can only plunge and hope for instantaneous revelation and restoration to who we really are.

Because our body functions mostly on a subconscious level, both approaches (bottom up or top down) benefit from imaginal remedies. What the body understands is experience, and images provide that.

Let's start with **the bottom-up approach.**

Exercise 126
· · · · · · · · · · ·
Cutting a Lemon

Close your eyes. Breathe out slowly three times, counting from three to one. See the one tall, clear, and bright.

Imagine cutting a lemon in two. Smell it. What experience is happening in your mouth?

Breathe out. Open your eyes.
· · · · · · · · · · ·

By using this simple imagery, you were able to activate your salivary glands. This proves two things: first, that the body is conscious; second, that it understands the language of images. By using appropriate images, you can direct your body to do specific and well-defined tasks. I call these exercises P'shat, which means simple story line, or visualization.* I am giving simple directions to the body in images. There is no jolt involved, and no transformation. I am simply reminding the body of what to do. The exercise helps to reinforce the body's known trajectory toward healing. I am using my consciousness to support and enhance its natural ability to heal. Dr. Carl Simonton made news by having his cancer patients visualize a video game character named Pac-Man coursing through their bloodstream

---

*Note that I distinguish between visualization, which I consider to be P'shat exercises, and imagery exercises, which contain a jolt.

and eating up the cancer cells. With exercise 31: The Waterfall* you have an example of a P'shat exercise. I give it to cancer patients to use after chemo sessions to clear their bodies of toxic chemicals. You can use it if you've been stung by a poisonous animal. I haven't tried it on snakebites, but two people who had been stung, one by a poisonous urchin, another by a stingray, both causing horrible pain, got immediate and spectacular relief. The exercise is a special favorite with my son and his friends, as well as all my Russian students, as it helps to clear hangovers. Here are a few examples of P'shat exercises.†

Exercise 127
· · · · · · · · · · ·
The White Staircase (to lower high blood pressure)

Close your eyes. Breathe out slowly three times, counting from three to one. See the one tall, clear, and bright.

Imagine that you are standing at the foot of a large white marble staircase. You are wearing the clothes you have on now.

Breathe out. As you start climbing, your clothes become paler and paler, and finally, as you come to the top of the staircase, you see them turning white.

Breathe out. Come down the staircase in your white clothes.

Breathe out. Walk away in your white clothes.

Breathe out. Open your eyes. See yourself with open eyes wearing all white clothes.

· · · · · · · · · · ·

I chose this exercise, as you can easily check whether your blood pressure has gone down. Verification is important. If you don't verify, you'll never be able to trust that you can move your body using images. Practice it three times a day for three days.‡ Remember that the physical body is habit forming. A habit must be replaced by another habit. By teaching your body on a regular schedule to do this, you are changing its bad habit and replacing it with a better habit. Here's an exercise for

---

*See chapter 5.

†In my book *DreamBirth,* you will find many P'shat exercises that tell the body what to do during pregnancy and labor. For more examples, read *Healing Visualizations* by Dr. Gerald Epstein, a longtime student and collaborator of Colette Aboulker-Muscat.

‡Or more if needed.

clearing the blood, for if we are to believe the Talmud, "I, blood, am the primary source of disease."[4]

Exercise 128
. . . .
Star Horse

Close your eyes. Breathe out slowly three times, counting from three to one. See the one tall, clear, and bright.

Imagine standing under the starlit dome of the sky. Look among the thousands of stars, and find your very own star.

Breathe out. Watch it twinkling in the sky. As you watch, see that a spark of light jumps from your star straight into your heart.

Breathe out. See the spark in your heart becoming a horse of light. See it galloping throughout your circulatory system, dissolving all impurities and bringing starlight wherever it goes.

Breathe out. See the horse returning into your heart where it returns to being a spark of light.

Breathe out. Look at your blood stream; what does your blood look like now?

Breathe out. Open your eyes.
. . . .

I gave this exercise to a student of mine whose partner had died of AIDS, who was, himself, HIV positive. His horse kept on bumping into rotten potatoes and turning them to light. One day he came into the office with a photograph of an HIV molecule that looked exactly like a rotten potato! He said he now understood what we had been doing and left after that on a mission, he told me, to teach his community how to heal themselves.

Here's a simple exercise for the heart. It has helped many people with heart disease. Do it even if you don't have a heart problem. It works emotionally as well as physically. Pay attention to what you feel, in and around your heart.

Exercise 129
. . . .
The Green Leaf

Close your eyes. Breathe out slowly three times, counting from three to one. See the one tall, clear, and bright.

Imagine that one fall day, you are walking down a country lane. You see a beautiful dried leaf on the ground and bend to pick it up.

Breathe out. Hold the dry leaf between your two palms. Feel how the moisture from your hands and the heat slowly softens the leaf.

Breathe out. When it feels very soft, open the palms of your hands and see that the leaf has returned to be a very soft young green leaf.

Breathe out. Place the green leaf over your heart.

Breathe out. Open your eyes.

· · · · · · · · · · ·

All illness begins with constriction. You could have been betrayed in love, have an ancestral pattern of heart attacks, or be overtaxing yourself at work. This simple exercise will help your heart muscle to relax and the vessels around your heart to expand.

One of the most common side effects of illness is pain. Pain starts with sensation. Something you saw, heard, smelled, tasted, or touched can trigger emotional or physical dis-ease. Go back to the sense opening exercises in chapter 10. While they are P'shat exercises, they work, as do all the exercises, on many levels at once. Issues with sight, hearing, smell, taste, and touch are greatly helped by these simple visualizations. Let's restore the goodness of smell by using it like a homeopathic remedy to cut the pain. Take a lavender sachet, and pass it swiftly under the nose of the one in pain. Or you can do it with imagery.

Exercise 130
· · · · · · · · · · ·
The Lavender Field

Close your eyes. Breathe out slowly three times, counting from three to one. See the one tall, clear, and bright.

Imagine standing before a vast lavender field that stretches out as far as your eye can see. Let the purple color fill your vision.

Breathe out. Now breathe in the scent of lavender. Feel how every cell in your body is suffused with the scent and the color of lavender.

Breathe out. Open your eyes.

· · · · · · · · · · ·

Taste, touch, sound, and image work equally well to stop pain. Counting backward will also do it. For a few seconds, the body is free. **Pause is the secret to healing.** Getting out of the body's way restores it to itself, which effectively allows it to re-pair itself. We'll come back to this concept soon. Remember that when your consciousness pays attention to your body, your body starts reconfiguring. It can only reconfigure to what it *knows* (Adam *knows* Eve) and remembers subconsciously. It returns to its blue pattern, what the Zohar* calls its wisdom. Lekh lekha, "Go to yourself," says God to Abraham.

Exercise 131
. . . .
The Body Reconfigures

Close your eyes. Breathe out slowly three times, counting from three to one. See the one tall, clear, and bright.

Look into your body, and see where your pain is.

Breathe out. Imaginally stretch your index finger up to the sun, and fill it with light.

Breathe out. Bring it down. With your index of light, touch the point of pain. What other point responds in your body?

Breathe out. Imaginally stretch your other index finger up to the sun, and fill it with light.

Breathe out. With your two index fingers filled with light, simultaneously touch the two points. Watch what unfolds and reconfigures in your body. Take your time and observe, so that you can describe to yourself exactly what is changing.

Breathe out. See the new configuration.

Breathe out. Open your eyes.
. . . .

I used this exercise with a woman who found it hard to visualize but could see two points. She had severe scoliosis. Repeating the exercise again and again with different points along her scoliosis, she was able to gain two inches. With a straightened spine, she looked like another person.

But would she be able to hold onto her two inches? We had dealt

---

*The Book of Splendor, thirteenth-century Spanish Kabbalistic masterpiece.

with the symptom, not with the source. Observe that I'm not using the word "cause." Disease is an exile from wholeness. "Illness (or any type of affliction) implies a lack in the sufferer's connection with the Source of Life."[5] Because she had a hard time with imagery, we didn't pursue source. But as long as I knew her, she kept her added two inches.

Let me make the distinction clear between the two approaches with another example. A man came to see me to ask if we dream only at night or all the time. I said, "All the time." He wanted me to prove it to him, and he asked to be the guinea pig. So using one of his dreams and his morphological (body) shape, I told him about himself. I ended the session by saying, "By the way, there's a plague of mice in your house." I could see them scurrying about in his DreamField. This was such a jolt to the man that he jumped out of his body—or at least, his DreamBody jumped out of his physical body and floated up to the ceiling (I have very high ceilings in my office). "Come down!" I called. "I can show you how to get rid of them!" But he was too frightened to listen and ran out of the office. Was I going to tell him to sweep all the mouse droppings, wash and clean every item in the house, discard all mouse-attractant foods, plug up every hole in the house, and call the exterminator? Yes, of course, we must always make use of allopathic means. But that would still only be dealing with the symptom. He may have stepped out of the lepers' colony, but he'd still be in the recovery room, beseeching the powers that be for the plague not to reoccur. In wellness, we are still living with anxiety: Logic says if it happened once, it can happen again. Would it be too much to say that mice were coming to his house, attracted by his energetic form, a DreamField whose emanations fit the mouse colony perfectly? Carl Jung called these types of acausal events synchronicity. We could say that the outside perfectly mirrored, energetic form to energetic form, what was happening inside him. To clear the house of the plague once and for all, something radical had to happen. I didn't have the occasion to help him with his mouse problem, because he didn't come back. He sold the house and moved away. But did he heal the rift to source that left him open to the mouse invasion? To leap from precarious wellness to wholeness requires an anarchistic disregard for the logical. Wholeness is a revolutionary plunge or leap into otherness.

The Top-Down Approach

Returning to the story of Moses, Pharaoh represents the stubborn persona in us who holds on tightly to all of his bad habits. When that part of us lets go, it's as if we've suddenly been ejected from a constrictive womb onto a desert-like expanse. There are no signposts to show us which way to go: left, right, back, forward, up, or down. How do we reach the pathless land? Simcha Benyossef, a longtime student of Colette's, wrote in her important book, *Reversing Cancer Through Mental Imagery*:

> If you asked me what is the single most important concept needed to understand Colette's remarkable success in healing incurable diseases, I would immediately reply: Reversing to restore yourself to wholeness. Simply put, reversing means making a turn in life away from habitual attitudes and distressing emotions toward new possibilities. We go "sur-nature," or above our nature.[6]

At the foot of Mount Horeb,* amidst the rumblings and the smoke, something extraordinary happens: six hundred thousand people† look up and "see the voices."[7] A synergic coming together of the senses! For a moment, personal afflictions are forgotten. Beyond the humdrum of cause and effect, the veil tears open, revealing a hitherto concealed reality, sur-nature. Wholeness healing is instantaneous. We re-pair ourselves: I and Thou come together as one. The revelation is an event newly born in us, that both creates and cures.

Revelation doesn't require a massive show of light and sound. All it takes is moving things out of order, and creating the unexpected. Laughter is provoked through unexpected juxtapositions. Here's a

---

*Also called Mount Sinai, where Moses receives the Ten Commandments and the Hebrew Bible. Horeb means "desolation" or "dryness." It's also translated as "glowing" or "heat" and is associated with the sun, whereas Sinai, sometimes seen as another peak nearby, is associated with the moon.

†Six hundred thousand men by census count, plus all the women, children, and old men were at Mt. Horeb and witnessed the giving of the Ten Commandments and the Hebrew Bible.

funny one told me by Rodger Kamenetz, who studied with Colette one summer.

> Rodger: "Can I be your student?"
> Colette: "I only work with the terminally ill. . . . Come next Wednesday."

Twenty-five years later, Rodger is still pondering this!

Poets are adept at catapulting us from a commonplace to radiance.

> Your eyes behind your veil are doves. Your hair is like a flock of goats descending from the hills of Gilead.[8]

It is poetry that shakes Job out of his doldrums, not reasoning.

> *Who shut up the sea behind doors*
> *When it burst forth from the womb,*
> *When I made the clouds its garment*
> *And wrapped it in thick darkness*
> *When I fixed limits for it*
> *And set its doors and bars in place,*
> *When I said this far you may go and no farther,*
> *Here is where your proud waves halt?*[9]

Awe, wonder, and trembling are Job's response.

> "I understand nothing. It is beyond me. I shall not know!"[10]

All he had lost is returned to Job and more: God doubled his blessings. What is the meaning of this? He is gifted with more creativity, more life, more abundance, because he has gained greater consciousness, humility, and gratitude he didn't have before. The story remains current today, five thousand years later. I had two dear friends who both fell ill at the same time, one with cancer and the other with leukemia. The one with cancer cursed God. Hadn't she given all her time and attention to a sick husband? Why was she not recompensed with time of her own now that he was dead? Her bitterness was great. Though she knew the work, she refused to do any exercises. What for? God had betrayed her. The other saw life with new eyes. Every moment of her life had become precious. Simple objects around her acquired a special glow, and people who helped were angels of mercy. She gladly did the exercises. Her heart was filled with gratitude, and she expressed it. My first friend died two months after her diagnosis. This one is alive five years later. Is the attitude everything? No, you can't simply decide to be grateful, but the exercises will allow you to get there on your own. There is an emotive movement to the jolt exercises that brings its own transformation. Transformation signifies that you have tapped into the source of creativity; in effect you have reconnected with "the Source of Life." **It is creativity that heals.** We can't force ourselves, of course. Most of us wouldn't know how. Losing sight of all that made us happy before the diagnosis, we get very focused on the rigid routines prescribed by our doctors. All laughter, wonder, and joy fly out the window. Covered in soot and ashes, our senses veiled, our energy dampened, we forget there are magical slippers, coaches, and princes in the cornucopia of our subconscious.

Reversing 1. Closing leaks

Whenever anyone experiences a traumatic event, it's as if the door to the solar plexus is thrown open, and the life force, like a gushing river, leaks out. Many describe the event as falling into an abyss or darkness. As I've mentioned, the first thing you can do after a trauma is to close the solar plexus. This can be done simply, by placing a pillow on the solar plexus, or a folded coat, or your hands. Use whatever is immediately available.* Later on, you can teach the person how to close his or her solar plexus imaginally. For those of you who get too easily flooded with impressions from the outside, or who have a lot of nervous energy, place your hands over your solar plexus at night just as you're falling asleep.

---

*Of course, don't get in the way of the paramedics. If it's impossible to approach the person, visualize placing a golden pillow on their solar plexus, or your two hands filled with light.

Exercise 132

. . . .

Closing the Solar Plexus

Close your eyes. Breathe out slowly three times, counting from three to one. See the one tall, clear, and bright.

Imagine you are in a meadow. Pick the long grasses and rays from the sun, and weave them together into a green and gold pillow.

Breathe out. Weave a sash with the grasses.

Breathe out. Place the pillow over your solar plexus, and wrap the sash around your chest to hold it tight.

Breathe out. Open your eyes.

. . . .

Any serious trauma will blow a hole in the energetic field of the body. Have the person breathe in the blue light from the sky, and see it gently filling their body until it emanates from every pore of their skin.* If the person cannot do this themselves, imagine filling your hands with blue light and passing them over the person's body, from head to toe, an inch away from the skin. You can also pass your palms over them physically, while visualizing blue light in your hands.

Reversing 2. Rebuilding the life force

Having dealt with the immediate energetic danger, the next task is to rebuild the life force that was depleted and constricted by the medical diagnosis or catastrophic event. The senses, as you know, close down, and the outer world turns dark and dull. When a friend who had recently lost her partner came to visit, some close friends and I took her to a restaurant that offered a tasting menu. We tried seventeen different dishes. Opening up her taste buds again gave her a modest boost (but even modest is good enough if there is some progress away from the dark) to get through the mourning process.

---

*"The Blue Vase Exercise" is described in detail in my book *Kabbalah and the Power of Dreaming*.

Exercise 133
· · · · · · · · · · ·
Making Tea

Close your eyes. Breathe out slowly three times, counting from three to one. See the one tall, clear, and bright.

Imagine that you are in a tea shop and the shopkeeper has given you permission to smell the different teas.

Breathe out. Choose the teas you like, and place a teaspoon of each together in a teapot. Pour the hot water over the tea leaves, and smell the fragrance of your tea.

Breathe out. Pour a cup of tea for yourself. Smell it, and taste it.

Breathe out. If you are satisfied, pour another cup of tea, and take it to someone you love. Offer it to them, and watch them smelling and tasting the tea.

Breathe out. Sit together, sipping your tea companionably.

Breathe out. Open your eyes.
· · · · · · · · · · ·

The life force can be rebuilt in many different ways, but gardens, trees, and rivers can be especially replenishing. Exercise 32: Breathing with the Tree* is very helpful.

Reversing 3. Restoring light

Opening up the senses means opening up to the light. Everything starts with light. God's first creation, "Let there be light," happens on the first day. But the sun, moon, and stars are not yet created (they will be created on the fourth day), so what kind of light are we talking about? God creates through looking into Himself and igniting His own light, and so do you. Turning your eyes inward ignites the light in the darkness. Kabbalists call this the light of creation.† Since at every moment you are creating yourself, if you allow darkness to overcome you, you are courting death. Colette, who had congestive heart disease, told me that whenever she felt close to dying, she visualized a vertical ray of light in the darkness and stepped into it, becoming the ray of light. To bring life back into someone, even someone comatose, you must help

---

*See chapter 5.
†See chapter 1.

the person visualize light, whether a sunrise, a bright yellow flower, a blue vase filled with light, or simply a meadow where the grass is very green and lit up by the sun. It was midnight in Hadassah Hospital in Jerusalem, and I was sitting next to a comatose young girl who, the doctors said, was not going to last the night. Although she was in a coma, I was talking to her and having her visualize a green meadow. Suddenly she sat up, to our terror and amazement (there were two doctors and her mother in the room), said, "The frog jumps!" and laid herself back down to sleep. The next morning when I came in to see her, she was sitting up and having breakfast. Later she told me that the frog that jumped came from a puppet show she remembered watching as a kid. When every puppet in the show was beaten by the bad one, the frog jumped up and saved the day.

Exercise 134
· · · · · · · · · · ·
The Column of Light

Close your eyes. Breathe out slowly three times, counting from three to one. See the one tall, clear, and bright.

Imagine standing in your meadow with heaven above and Earth below your feet.

Breathe out. Now see yourself spanning heaven and Earth.

Breathe out. See yourself becoming a hollow column of light.

Breathe out. Sense and see the blue light from the sky pouring into your column.

Breathe out. Sense and see the red fire from the Earth rising up in the hollow of the column.

Breathe out. What is happening when the blue light and the red fire meet? Where in your body do they meet? What happens?

Breathe out. Return to your natural size and body form, keeping the light in your body.

Breathe out. Open your eyes.
· · · · · · · · · · ·

Reversing 4. T'shuvah, return or repentance

When a student told me she dreamed she was rubbing salt in her wound, I wasn't shocked (although the image itself was painfully raw), because alas, it is quite common. People cannot stop scratching a bite, nor can they stop obsessing over their guilt. If only . . . But only when we turn our eyes in another direction can something new reveal itself. I'm speaking again of the concept called t'shuvah, return. It's often translated to mean repentance, but it's important not to dwell on the *sin* aspect, which only intensifies guilt. You must do everything to correct the wrongs you've done; if that can't be done, giving to charity is a great help in lifting the burden of guilt. Start with confessing your sins to get them out of your way, so that you can create yourself anew.

Exercise 135
· · · · · · · · · · ·
The Sacrificial Ram

Close your eyes. Breathe out slowly three times, counting from three to one. See the one tall, clear, and bright.

Imagine walking into the desert holding a red ribbon and a black pen in your hands.

Breathe out. Write all of your sins, large and small, in black ink on the red ribbon.

Breathe out. When you are done, call each one out loudly in the desert.

Breathe out. Watch as a mighty ram appears out of the buzzing heat.

Breathe out. Wrap your red ribbon around one of his horns. Thank him, and send him away.

Breathe out. See his image sizzling and dissolving in the heat of the day.

Breathe out. Walk out of the desert.

Breathe out. Open your eyes.
· · · · · · · · · · ·

Reversing 5. Distancing yourself from the illness or trauma

The great drama of your wounding is attracting all eyes to it, as if it stood in the spotlight of a theater stage. T'shuvah means "turning away." What you need to do is walk away from the drama.

Exercise 136

· · · · · · · · · · ·

Walking Away from Drama

Close your eyes. Breathe out slowly three times, counting from three to one. See the one tall, clear, and bright.

Imagine that you are on stage with other actors and props, acting out your drama.

Breathe out. Walk backward and offstage.

Breathe out. Walk backward down the aisle. When you encounter the door, push it open with your back.

Breathe out. Walk through and into the theater lobby.

Breathe out. Turn around, and walk out of the theater. Walk away.

Breathe out. Open your eyes.

· · · · · · · · · · ·

It is not always easy to turn away. I was once called to the side of an Israeli soldier who had been wounded by a cluster bomb in the Lebanese campaign. It was reported to me that he hadn't slept for three weeks. He wouldn't even close his eyes. I asked him what he was guarding so preciously. He said the photo of his wife and kids. When he was wounded, the photo flashed before his eyes, and he knew, he told me, that if he closed his eyes, he would never see them again. If we could put the photo in a safe place, I asked, would he close his eyes? He said, "Yes, for a short while." We placed the photo in the secret chamber in his heart, and his body agreed to sleep two hours. After that he improved very quickly.

Reversing 6. Dissolving the dis-ease

You are no longer the victim whose tyrannical need to be the center of attention holds you and your audience spellbound. You are regaining some freedom. It's time to dissolve the dis-ease. You have many inner helpers. One is always watching out for you.

Exercise 137

· · · · · · · · · · ·

Exchanging Parts with the Guardian Angel

Close your eyes. Breathe out slowly three times, counting from three to one. See the one tall, clear, and bright.

Stand in your meadow, and look up into the blue sky. Let your eyes wander across the sky until you land on the deepest blue of the sky.

Breathe out. Let your eyes gaze into the deepest blue, and call on your guardian angel to appear.

Breathe out. See your guardian angel in all the glorious light he is composed of.

Breathe out. Ask for permission to exchange your diseased parts with your guardian angel's parts.

Breathe out. See your diseased parts rising up to be transformed into light, and your angel's parts of light descending to replace your body parts.

Breathe out. See your body filled with the goodness of your angel's light.

Breathe out. Open your eyes, seeing this with open eyes.

· · · · · · · · · · ·

If you have lost a part of your body to surgery or illness, do not abandon that part to the darkness. Your body is made of light. You can re-create your physical parts in light, as you re-create your emotional or mental bodies with light. Phantom limb pain tells us the truth about our bodies: While a physical part may be lost, the blueprint remains very much alive, continuing to emit light and nerve impulses. Maybe one day we'll learn to regrow our missing parts as the lizard regrows his tail. I have treated many amputees and patients who lost a limb, whether an organ, a breast, or a tooth. Light diminishes or completely wipes away phantom limb pain. Always remake every lost part of your body in light.

Exercise 138
· · · · · · · · · ·
Reversing Phantom Limb Pain

Close your eyes. Breathe out slowly three times, counting from three to one. See the one tall, clear, and bright.

You are standing in your meadow. Look up at the radiant blue sky filled with sunlight.

Breathe in the blue light through your nose. Fill your mouth with the blue light.

Breathe out the light inside your body to remake your limb or organ in light. See it being made perfectly in light.

Breathe out. Open your eyes, and see this with open eyes.

· · · · · · · · · · ·

If the problem is emotional, reverse backward through your past to find the root of the problem.

Exercise 139
· · · · · · · · · · ·
Poisoned Arrow

Close your eyes. Breathe out slowly three times, counting from three to one. See the one tall, clear, and bright.

Imagine going backward through your life to the very first time you experienced the emotion that is disturbing you.

Breathe out. See it as a cyclops towering over you and blocking your way.

Breathe out. Look in a mirror, and see that a poisonous arrow has pierced your heart.

Breathe out. Remove it slowly with your left hand. Place it in a blowgun that you hold in your right hand.

Breathe out. Breathe in the blue light, and blow it out through the blowgun, sending the arrow through the eye of the cyclops. See him collapsing and dissolving.

Breathe out. The path is clear, and you can now follow your heart's desire. See yourself reaching it.

Breathe out. Open your eyes.

· · · · · · · · · · ·

Reversing 7. Return to the life source

God cured Job by directing his gaze to the awesome beauty and majesty of nature. Nature is both olam, the visible world, and ne'elam, the concealed world. To gaze upon the natural world and its mysterious order, to know you are a part of it and feel for a moment that you are one with it is astonishing in and of itself. But what God shows Job is that there is a mysterious and awesome power concealed behind its marvels that creates and regulates this order. To understand this is to become humble. Your body is made of God's light, and in you, as in Adam Kadmon,* is all the universe concealed. Go to exercise 36: Becoming the Creatures in the Garden,† to experience transformation, or do the following exercise.

---

*See Glossary.
†See chapter 6.

Exercise 140
· · · · · · · · · ·
Transformations

Close your eyes. Breathe out slowly three times, counting from three to one. See the one tall, clear, and bright.

Become a fountain and each and every drop of the fountain.

Breathe out. Become a rock, and live the infinitely slow movement of its atoms.

Breathe out. Become a tree. Stretch your roots out into the land, sucking up the minerals and water. Stretch your branches up to the sun, drawing in the light and warmth.

Breathe out. Become yourself sitting at the foot of the tree, listening to the sounds of nature. What is nature telling you?

Breathe out. Open your eyes.
· · · · · · · · · ·

The source of all life is a mysterious and ever-flowing river that, we are told, overflows from the Garden of Eden and irrigates the myriad different life-forms. Returning to the source, we are nourishing not only our physical bodies, but our souls.

Exercise 141
· · · · · · · · · ·
Drinking at the Source (Formal)

Close your eyes. Breathe out slowly three times, counting from three to one. See the one tall, clear, and bright.

Imagine that you've walked up into the mountains. You come upon a mountain river. Take off your shoes and socks, roll up your pants, and step into the river.

Breathe out. Walk up the river, always staying in the river. If there are tree trunks or boulders, climb over them. If there are waterfalls, climb up the waterfalls.

Breathe out. Notice the change in landscape as you climb higher and higher.

Breathe out. Climb all the way up to the source. When you get there, cup your hands, and drink very slowly of the pure mountain water.

Breathe out. Watch the water flowing inside your body, see its shimmering light, feel its coolness, and see how it is irrigating your body.

Breathe out. Cup your hands, and drink a second time, following the pathway of the water in your body.

Breathe out. Cup your hands, and drink a third time, feeling
refreshed and renewed.

Breathe out. Take a look at your body; how do you look now?
Describe it to yourself exactly, the color of your skin, your hair, your
expression, and your body.

Breathe out. Come down the mountain, following the bank of
the river. Don't step into the river. Go all the way down to where
you left your shoes.

Breathe out. See that your old shoes are gone and new shoes
are waiting for you. Put them on, and try walking in them.

Breathe out. Walk all the way back home in your new shoes.

(If you haven't found shoes and you're barefoot, that's fine too.)

· · · · · · · · · · ·

Reversing 8. Changing perspective

We can drink at its source, but we cannot create the source ex nihilo.
Returning to drink at its source means we accept a changed perspective. Dreaming allows us to switch perspectives easily. We could be on
a flying carpet looking down at the world or at the bottom of a lake
looking up through the verdant waters. God teaches Moses, when he
speaks to Pharaoh, to switch the natural order of the ten creations. The
ten plagues shuffle up that order. Changing perspectives can change
our situation. We can travel and see the world from many different
perspectives.

Exercise 142
· · · · · · · · · · ·
Travels on a White Cloud

Close your eyes. Breathe out slowly three times, counting from three
to one. See the one tall, clear, and bright.

You are lying down in green grass, looking up at the blue sky.
Feel very relaxed and heavy on the ground.

Breathe out. A small white cloud floats by. Feel yourself floating
up out of your body into the white cloud.

Breathe out. Lie facedown on the cloud, and look down. See
yourself on the cloud, floating above a clear blue lake. See your

reflection on the white cloud, looking up at you from the lake.

Breathe out. Feel yourself in both places at once.

Breathe out. The small white cloud descends to Earth and returns you to your physical body.

Breathe out. Look up from your physical body, watching as the white cloud floats up into the sky and moves away.

Breathe out. Open your eyes.

. . . .

Moses plays magical tricks before Pharaoh. He changes his wooden staff into a snake. Then he picks it up, and it becomes a staff again. Because the order of creation is that trees are created before creepy crawlies, a staff comes before a snake. Throw it to the earth, and it becomes a snake. But then pick it up off the ground, and it becomes a staff again. Does it make sense? Not really, not in the world of Asiyah, the world of doing. But in the imagination, the world of Yetsirah, it does. Playing with forms is *making* (which is our way of creating with the forms we've been given), and we are enjoined to la'asot, to make.[11]

Exercise 143
. . . .
Two Hands

Close your eyes. Breathe out slowly three times, counting from three to one. See the one tall, clear, and bright.

Imagine that in the palm of one hand, you hold a dream object representing your physical body and its needs.

Breathe out. In the other palm, have a dream object that represents your soul's needs.

Breathe out. Bring the two palms together, as in a prayer position. Feel the warmth and the moisture. Feel the two hands becoming one.

Breathe out. Cup open your hands. What do you have in your cupped hands?

Breathe out. Open your eyes.

. . . .

Reversing 9. Changing time

The past is gone; the future doesn't exist. Learning to live in the present is returning to a fullness of presence in which dis-ease doesn't exist. Exercises 119: Vertical Time, and 120: The Sun Drop* put you in the Now. Here's another exercise to show you what the Now looks like.

Exercise 144
. . . .
The Train Ride

Close your eyes. Breathe out slowly three times, counting from three to one. See the one tall, clear, and bright.

Imagine you have left your old life. You've stepped onto a train with a suitcase containing the few belongings you are taking with you.

Breathe out. Watch as the train stops at different stations and passengers get off.

Breathe out. You are the only passenger left on the train. Get off at the final station.

Breathe out. Walk out into the open landscape. There are no buildings, no trees, no bushes, no rivers. You are alone between Earth and sky.

Breathe out. Throw open your suitcase to the sky, and watch as your belongings fly out and up into the sky. Watch what happens.

Breathe out. Open your eyes.

. . . .

Reversing 10. Joy

The ancient rabbis decreed that no crippled or diseased body could enter the temple. You can read this as a most unfair dictate, or you can read it as a metaphor. If metaphor, your work is to return all your bodies (physical, emotional, mental, spirit, and beyond) to what Nahman of Bratslav, the great eighteenth-century Hasidic master, called the deep chant (*niggun*) of the ten vital rhythms. Why ten? Because ten is the wholeness we've been pursuing, ten is the mirror image of one (the zero doesn't count; we're back to one). When the two come face-to-face, I and Thou are re-paired (become one, in the image of God), and there is joy. "Joy is a great remedy. One must find in oneself, a single positive point that makes us joyful, and attach ourselves to it."[12]

---

*See chapter 12.

Exercise 145

· · · · · · · · · · ·

The Music of the Deep

Close your eyes. Breathe out slowly three times, counting from three to one. See the one tall, clear, and bright.

Imagine sitting on the beach watching the sunset. Watch each color, and imagine it as the string of a musical instrument.

Breathe out. Elongate your arms, and play the many colored strings of your sky instrument.

Breathe out. Feel the music vibrating in all the cells of your body. Hear your cells singing, Hallelujah, Hallelujah, Hallelujah.

Breathe out. Listen as all the creatures on Earth and in the sky join with you to sing, Hallelujah, Hallelujah, Hallelujah.

Breathe out. Open your eyes, keeping the joy preciously in your heart.

· · · · · · · · · · ·

God said: "I have given you life and death, blessing and curse. Choose life."[13] When you pursue joy in the face of calamity, you are saying no to death. You are actively choosing life. Joy will come to you and re-pair you, as it is said, "Heal me O Lord and I will be healed."[14] Even though we may "walk through the valley of the shadow of death,"[15] knowing leprosy and wellness, our souls can choose to cleave to the realm of wholeness. And if we do, we prolong our life span, if not always through days, weeks, or years, but through aliveness, pure joy, and gratitude.

His students asked: What is Holem?

He replied: It is the soul—and its name is Holem.

If you listen to it, your body will be vigorous (Halam) in the ultimate future. But if you rebel against it, there will be sickness (Holeh) on your head, and diseases (Holim) on its head.

They also said: Every dream (Halom) is in the Holem. Every precious white stone is in the Holem. It is thus written with regard to the High Priest's breastplate (Exodus 28:19), ["And in the third row . . .], a white stone (aHLaMah)."[16]

The light of creation brought about by your dreaming heals all. In wholeness, you are at the very core, the heart of your being-in-relationship. You are allowing for sur-nature, the great beast of the deep, the Leviathan, to rise in all his rainbow splendor and radiance. The veil parts, and the concealed becomes revealed. Your soul revealed is Leviathan.

PART III

Raising the Leviathan

*The Serpent of the Deep,
Your Superconsciousness or, as the
French Like to Call It, Your Sur-nature*

How many are the things you made, O Lord;
You made them all with wisdom;
The Earth is full of your creations.
There is the sea, vast and wide,
With its creatures beyond number,
Living things, small and great.
There go the ships,
And Leviathan that you formed to sport with.

PSALM 104:24–26

You have learned some simple techniques to tap into the subconscious and harness its powers. In the process, you have responded to the necessity of your images and cleared the second tier of your consciousness, the subconscious garbage. You are taming your beast. Your subconscious waters are becoming transparent, allowing you to peek in and begin consolidating your experience of the third layer of the subconscious, the superconscious or sur-nature. You are being shown your soul in action.

Your soul, the immortal part of you that is woven into the vast oceanic DreamField, upon which the world is created, and which the texts call Leviathan,* needs you to be able to awaken and shine.

By hovering over the inchoate mass of Leviathan, the awesome beast of the deep, you are coaxing order out of the chaos. By then responding to the necessity of the images that appear, you enable ever more fluid and lively creativity. But the end game is not about cleaning, nor is it about fixing an image of your soul. These basic maneuvers open up a path toward a far greater achievement hinted at by God playing with Leviathan.

Forget reason and logic. Chop off your head! The third layer of the subconscious is calling you back to joy. It's asking you to enter into the

---

*"He is the beginning of the ways of God." Job 40:19.

play of give and take wholeheartedly. And as the Egyptian hieroglyph for heart shows, the heart is a vase whose handles are ears. Listen to your heart. It speaks the subterranean language of rhythm. Is your heart rhythm harmonious or discordant? Either way, it brings forth in your primordial mind colors, smells, shapes, and images. Play with them! Your greatest achievement is to play. Let go, flow, accept, relax, enjoy, be happy, and laugh! Learn to cavort in the waves with the many-headed hydra of your personal Leviathan until, like the dancing figure of the twenty-first Arcana of the tarot, the World, it rises to become your axis mundi* and food for your delectation and delight. In their interaction, both the sinuous female Leviathan, "who surrounds the whole world,"[1] and the risen male Leviathan, "vertical as a bar,"[2] paradoxically sustain your luminous true presence ever more fluidly and cohesively.

---

*The axis of the rotation of the planetary spheres.

14

The Heart-Centered Way

A broken and humbled heart can burst open all the gates,
and all the heavenly palaces.

BAAL SHEM TOV

Have we asked to be born? Have we signed up for the bittersweet adventure that is life? We are dropped into this world and must make do with what we're given, whether it's health or infirmity, beauty or plainness, cleverness or simplicity. At the very onset, we could find ourselves plunged into heartbreaking circumstances. Are we not entitled to ask why, and more poignantly, why me? The Bible tells us that "The Lord God took Adam and set him down in the Garden of Eden."[1] Why? If Adam wasn't created in the Garden, why then put him there? "He (Lord God) took him (Adam) with beautiful words and **seduced** him to enter the garden."[2] Is God in love, yearning for the beloved? Is God seducing each of us, like Adam, into His heart, enticing us to play with Him? Imagine all that you have ever longed for, abundance, flow, bliss, all of God's many creations, being offered for your delectation, free of charge. Except that, having been seduced, you are now engaged for better or worse in the game of love. "I opened to my love, but he had slipped away."[3] The game of love is dangerous. Of the fruit of the tree in the middle of the Garden, "you shall not eat of it or touch it, lest you die!"[4] Lest your heart should break and you can't put it together again, like the king's men with Humpty Dumpty.* "Where are you?" God calls out, after Adam and Eve have burst the bubble of bliss and perfect merging. It is a call that resonates down the halls of time and knocks on the door of our hearts. Will you risk your small heart to reach out and engage God's great heart? You are being stirred up by your dreaming, and by a longing you can't even explain to yourself. Can you endure the chaos, confusion, fear, wounding, and loss of self? Can you live through the whirlwind of uncertainty that promises paradise?

The Garden is called PRDS in Hebrew (pronounced "pardes"). We have seen that these four letters reveal the way back to the Garden, to the beloved, for "my love has gone down to his garden."[5] P is P'shat, the story line, the visible world; R is Remez, the patterns, the clues hidden within the story line; D is Drash, the questioning, the search for the deeper meaning; S is Sod, the treasure hidden in the folds and waves of the concealed world. Touch this hidden treasure and you're instantly filled with bliss. The fall and exile away from the Garden is the original wounding, and you are on a treasure hunt to return to your beloved in the Garden, to cleave to the burning core of love. When the chaos becomes play, and the games of love become delight, you have reached the superconscious. Every moment is a blissful frolic with God, in complete safety and trust. The great beast of the deep, no longer chaotic, rageful, or destructive, has become a tame puppy looking up at you with soulful, loving eyes.

✳

The Torah's first letter is B, bet; its last letter is L, *lamed*. LB reads *lev* and means "heart." The text of the Torah, every single one of its letters, is considered to be God's great name. God is love. When we come to the end of Torah, we rush to start reading all over again. What happens in between the last letter of Torah, the lamed, and the first letter, bet? *Tehom*, an abyss of not knowing, opens up. All journeys of the heart must cross the tehom, otherwise known as the tohu va'bohu, the great abyss of the subconscious, that we have encountered before. Hovering above it through our dreaming, we help bring order out of chaos. The lamed illustrates our

---

*English nursery rhyme.

hope, for it spirals up into space, towering above all the other letters of the alphabet, reminding us that the journey is never the same twice. By taking the journey again and again, we have a chance to expose ourselves to God's heart, and to grow ever closer to the burning center. As Avivah Zornberg's translation of the Bereshit Rabbah tells us, "a man was traveling from place to place when he saw a castle on fire. He said 'Would you say that the castle is without a lord?' The lord of the castle glanced out at him and said 'I am the Lord of the castle.'"[6] The midrash is telling us that if we are to reach the Garden, the heart of God's creation, the source of all creativity and joy, the journey is necessary.

What is holding us from completing the journey? Until PRD finds its final letter S, Sod, its treasure, it is still only PRD, *parad*, which sounds like *pahad*, fear.* There is fear in all great love affairs. To cross what separates I from Thou is to cross the tehom, where the great beasts of the deep live. Will this movement awaken them? Will all the furies of existence suddenly grab at me, my anxiety, my fear of rejection, my jealousy, my rage, my envy, and my guilt? Will I be able to endure not knowing whether Thou accept or reject me? Seduced into the garden, we enter on tiptoe into a love affair with our creator, a world of bliss and communion, from which, as with all love affairs, we know we will be thrown out, for we cannot long endure oneness. We fall back into separateness and must take up the journey again, and yet again, until we learn to live in oneness and separateness simultaneously. Only after moving from the conscious (separateness) to the subconscious (oneness) worlds and back again, "traveling from place to place," will we be able to conquer our fear when seeing the burning castle.

Fear is our greatest enemy. She is Leviathan entangling the sleeper in her nightmarish coils, the red lady consulting her files for her meeting with the grand vizier tonight in Samarkhand, or Sphinx blowing her hot breath on Oedipus. "Who is the one who walks on all fours at dawn, on two feet at noon, and on three feet at dusk?" Don't answer, or death will come rushing at you to swallow you up. Mortal fear shortens our life expectancy and dilutes our joy in the present. While living on

---

*In pahad the R, *resh*, is replaced by H, het, but parad and pahad have the same pronunciation in Hebrew.

a linear trajectory adds pathos to all our love affairs, it ignores other realities, just as powerful, that cycle, spiral, and expand time, serving to dissolve fear. Our logical mind knows we will die, but our subconscious mind has something else to offer us.

Cyclical journeys, seasonally recognized, remind us that what dies will flourish again. Cycles suggest that, like nature, our lives flourish, then shrink and disappear into the unknown to be reborn in a new springtime. Contemplating cyclical time, we can hope for rebirth, whereas with its final spiraling lamed, Torah tells us that we are given another chance, in this or another lifetime, to rise ever closer to the beloved. Our choice to confront our fears sets us journeying from the torments of hell to heavenly bliss, on a journey mapped by seventeenth-century French writers as *la carte du Tendre*, the map of love. Osiris, who takes such a journey into the underworld and resurrects from the dead, is called the lord of love. Jesus of Galilee, who spends three days in hell before he resurrects, is the great teacher and master of love. Dante, in *The Divine Comedy*, must travel through hell and purgatory to merit reaching the heavenly city where his beloved awaits. *The Pilgrim's Progress** reminds us that we all start in the City of Destruction. Only the choice to leave sin behind and transform our hearts will lead us to the Celestial City. The driving force behind transformation is love: love of God, love of the beloved, or, if you prefer to call it by another name, love of the self, speaking to us with the still, small voice within the whirlwind, the earthquake, or the fire of our emotions.[7] Our intuition, telling us what is right and good for us, is the voice of our heart that we must listen to, if we want to be guided back to the Garden.

How is that done? How does the subconscious help us to transform our hellish emotions into feeling? We have covered the transformation of emotions into feeling in exercise 48: The Pathways of Emotion; exercise 49: Switching from Emotions to Feeling; and exercise 89: Emotions and Feelings.† But let me remind you here of a story that illustrates

---

*John Bunyan's 1678 Christian allegory.

†In chapters 8 and 10, and in great detail in my first book *Kabbalah and the Power of Dreaming*.

the journey of love, the story of the temptation of Joseph—the great dreamer of the Bible, who was the overseer of Potiphar's household. Potiphar's wife lures Joseph with seductive and bold words* into the house when "no man is there."[8] She gets close enough to him that she can grab at his garment. At that moment of greatest danger, when we can presume that his heart is beating in his ears with the disturbed sound of his emotions, the midrash tells us that Joseph turns his head to the window and sees his father's face. His father Jacob is miles away in the land of Canaan, and Joseph is in Egypt. His beloved father's face reminds him of everything good and true that he had lost when he was sold into slavery. "The heart follows where the eyes go."[9] And Joseph runs out of the house. She will accuse him, and he will be sent to jail, but his hell will soon be followed by a phenomenal rise to the highest court and gardens of the pharaoh. Our journey is made of similar choices, the lesser for the greater, that only we can undertake. "Every human being has the freedom to change at any instant."[10] Our choices for the greater boosts us up the spiral until finally the gap between the loss of the Garden and its return is spanned in the blink of an eye.

Exercise 146
. . . .
The Quest

Close your eyes. Breathe out slowly three times, counting from three to one. See the one tall, clear, and bright.

See and know that to be a seeker is to be looking for something more.

Breathe out. Know and see that your quest is not about something unknown, but about something you have lost or forgotten.

Breathe out. Listen to this lost chord. Hear it resounding in you, and know how the restoration of your wholeness is possible.

Breathe out. Open your eyes.

. . . .

We can understand the journeying better if we look at Adam, ADM, the first human. A is the Hebrew letter aleph, numerically worth

---

*"Lie with me!"

one, an unpronounceable and mysterious letter. DM, read "dam," means "blood." Kabbalists, interpreting the name of Adam, often add a final letter, ADMH, which reads *adamah*, earth. Blood journeys between mystery and earth, linking our two worlds, soul and body. It is a closed circuit whose only window opens onto the lungs, where it deposits carbon dioxide and picks up oxygen. The inside links to the outside through our heartbeats and through our breathing. By focusing on the interconnection between the closed blood circulation and the open loop of our breathing, we stimulate our vital energy.

Exercise 147
· · · · · · · · · · ·
Closed and Open Circulations

Close your eyes. Breathe out slowly three times, counting from three to one. See the one tall, clear, and bright.

Look at the color of your blood.

Breathe out. See, feel, and live the closed circulation of your blood.

Breathe out. Live the open circulation of the air.

Breathe out. What is the color of the blood now?

Breathe out. Open your eyes.

· · · · · · · · · · ·

The fierce joy of vitality is called nefesh, liveliness. Our liveliness and our stamina depend on this double circulation of blood and breath. The pulse of the heart and the rhythm of breathing communicate energy and information, instructing our cells and telling us how we're doing. A shock will change our breathing and heart rates. We call it an emotion, from the Latin *ex,* going out, and *motion*. We move out, reacting to an outside shift, change, or stimulus. Our best friend betrays us, our spouse leaves us, a loved one dies, or a trusted teacher humiliates us in front of the whole class. Breathing and heartbeat leap out of their habitual grooves, changing the deep chant (niggun), of our rhythms that keeps us healthy and vital.

Why do we have emotions? What are they for? Charles Darwin (1809–1882), the English naturalist best known for his theory of evolution, tells us that emotions help in the evolutionary fight for survival.

They are our survival mechanism against a perceived danger. We call it fight or flight (anger or fear). But William James (1842–1910), an American philosopher and psychologist, reminds us that the body trembles even before we are aware of fear. So does body apprehend danger before our brains can register it? According to him, emotion is the result of a physiological change. James is recognizing, de facto, the larger range of the body's receptors. Whereas Epictetus (55–135 CE), a Greek Stoic philosopher, says that we are moved because we think. Change our thinking, and our emotions disappear. Margaret Mead (1901–1978), a cultural anthropologist, insists that an emotion is acquired early on in life and stems from a learned social role. She does not see emotion as a universal phenomenon.

What do you think emotion is for?

Exercise 148
. . . .
Why Emotions

Close your eyes. Breathe out slowly three times, counting from three to one. See the one tall, clear, and bright.

Imagine that your father has left his house to your sibling and nothing to you (Epictetus, think).

Breathe out. Imagine being attacked by a tiger (Darwin, survival of fittest).

Breathe out. Imagine trembling all over and not knowing why (William James, physiological).

Breathe out. Imagine being a macho man who catches his estranged wife in adultery (Mead, cultural).

Breathe out. Open your eyes.
. . . .

Having experienced all four theories about emotion, you'll agree, I'm sure, that all four have merit. The body's reactions are complex. All obstacles, whether physical, mental, cultural, moral, or spiritual, act adversarially, as k'negdo, to the body's well-being, provoking a body reaction that we call emotion.

Before continuing, it is important once again to emphasize the difference between an emotion and a feeling.* The two have generally been confused except in biblical literature. Observe in yourself the difference between anger and love.

Exercise 149
· · · · · · · · · · ·
In Anger

Close your eyes. Breathe out slowly three times, counting from three to one. See the one tall, clear, and bright.

Relive a moment when you experienced strong anger. Follow its movement in your body.

Breathe out. Hear the prophet Habakkuk's words: "In anger, remember love."[11] How does love move in your body?

Breathe out. Open your eyes.
· · · · · · · · · · ·

When speaking of anger, the French say, "La moutarde me monte au nez," mustard rises to my nose. Anger rises up and projects out, through a fist, or through an explosive stream of insulting words. When you switch to love, concentric circles expand from your body outward. An emotion has a jagged pathway through the body. A feeling is always expansive.

With that clarified, I'd like to propose another theory for why we have emotions. Emotions crack us open. They free our energy, and if we are fast enough to catch the moment before the emotion starts on its pre-destined pathway, we can redirect that energy to love or to creativity, or to any focused direction we have chosen. Emotions are there to free us from slavery. They are there to push us, k'negdo, to transformation. "The entire purpose of creation, and the interlinking of all the worlds is in order to reveal His wholeness exactly from its opposite."[12] As the physical chemist and Nobel Prize winner Ilya Prigogine puts it, coming to a point of bifurcation, a system either collapses—from instability, stress, and pain—or reorganizes itself in a new way.[13] Emotion is our chance to reorganize and, for an instant, to leap back into the garden. "My lover, my king has brought me into his chambers."[14]

---

*See chapter 8.

Do not rebel against your emotions. Do not repress them. Accept them and use them. Use your separateness, your broken heart, your agony—"Why have you forsaken me, O Lord?"[15]— to turn your eyes toward what you love and long for most, and lo and behold, the Garden will appear before you in all its expansive radiance and bliss. Will it last? No, but every time you leap into feeling, you are helping to stabilize within you the trust that the Garden is here for you now, anytime, all the time. You will be able to switch more and more easily. The more you practice the switch, the more you enlarge and stabilize your consciousness. You are building what Abraham Heschel calls "a temple of light."[16] Your emotions are the chaotic beast of the deep, but switched to feelings, they stabilize and raise the Leviathan. In other words, the tohu va'bohu of your subconscious is being reconfigured to reveal the magnificent order of the superconscious rising for your delectation and delight. This is the great work of the imagination, to bring order out of the chaos.

Exercise 150
. . . .
Pain, a Holy Spark

Close your eyes. Breathe out slowly three times, counting from three to one. See the one tall, clear, and bright.

Live that "everything that we are, in a positive sense, is by virtue of a limitation."[17]

Breathe out. See and feel that in every pain there is a holy spark from God.

Breathe out. Open your eyes.
. . . .

Pain is not good, but it can be used for the good. This is why it is more important to have a nightmare than a good dream. It breaks open your heart, and you find yourself standing on the brink of the abyss. Pain, confusion, despair, grief, anger, and fear jolt you out of repressed, frozen emotions (frustration, sadness, self-hate, anxiety, guilt, resentment, jealousy, envy, etc.). They are the keys to igniting and setting in motion what the Hebrew Bible calls your *merkabah*, the vehicle, or chariot, of your body. As the great sage Rabbi Akiva tells us, any setback, however painful, is for the good: *Gam zu l'tovah*.

Exercise 151
. . . .
Your Worst Nightmare

Close your eyes. Breathe out slowly three times, counting from three to one. See the one tall, clear, and bright.

Live your deepest, most persistent nightmare. Ask yourself, until when? Until what?

Breathe out. Say: Gam zu l'tovah, that too is for the good.

Breathe out. Visualize your nightmare as a black egg cracking open, revealing its treasure.

Breathe out. Open your eyes.

. . . .

Thus we see God sending a great Flood, the tehom, to destroy all those caught in repetitive habits and frozen emotions. To build a new world, he recruits Noah, whose name means "comfort" or "rest."

Exercise 152
. . . .
In Honor of Tagore

Close your eyes. Breathe out slowly three times, counting from three to one. See the one tall, clear, and bright.

Imagine that you are thrown overboard into a turbulent ocean. Imagine trying to stay afloat.

Breathe out. Instead of fighting the waves, let yourself sink into the ocean. Sink deeper and deeper to the very center of the ocean.

Breathe out. Become the ocean.

Breathe out. Slowly reconfigure, and rise up toward the surface of the ocean.

Breathe out. When you reach the surface, how is the ocean?

Breathe out. Swim to shore. Rise out of the waters. Dry yourself in the sun.

Breathe out. Catch a ray of light and cocoon yourself in light.

Breathe out. Open your eyes.

. . . .

If you have become the ocean in all its vastness and quiet, and risen again, your ocean surface should now be calm and peaceful. This tells us something about emotions (turbulent) and peace (concentric quiet and expanding). The tohu va'bohu is smoothed out. The beast of anger is tamed into playfulness.

Exercise 153
. . . .
Taming the Beast

Close your eyes. Breathe out slowly three times, counting from three to one. See the one tall, clear, and bright.

Choose someone in your daily life that represents for you a dangerous obstacle, like an angry boss, a rebellious student, a panicked clerk, or another example more relevant to you. Find a way to tame that person. You can use the Solar Plexus exercise,* or any exercise that comes to you in the instant. Watch the change.

Breathe out. Open your eyes.
. . . .

Do this exercise in real life. Practice it again and again, and see how, in taming the outer beasts, you are taming your inner beasts.

✳

Imagine that you are Moses going up Mount Horeb to meet with God. You are gone forty days and forty nights into the cloud of unknowing. Another part of you, impatient and fearful, gives vent to your repressed emotions by building a golden calf, a solid, visible god to support your uncertainty. When you finally come down the mountain holding the two stone tablets on which God's own finger has inscribed the new rules for joy, bliss, and happiness, you are confronted with what you have done to yourself, and in your rage, you break the tablets. Later you humbly go up the mountain again to entreat God's forgiveness, and to write new tablets.

The complete new set of tablets Moses wrote at God's dictation were placed in the Tabernacle, the Holy of Holies. The broken tablets were also placed there, to ensure that we would never forget the value of a broken heart.

---

*Exercise 45: The Solar Plexus.

Exercise 154

· · · · · · · · · · ·

A Broken Heart

Close your eyes. Breathe out slowly three times, counting from three to one. See the one tall, clear, and bright.

See, feel, and live that "nothing is more whole than a broken heart."[18]

Breathe out. Open your eyes.

· · · · · · · · · · ·

In the play with your beloved whom you have seduced, and who has seduced you into the garden of marriage, remember that you broke a glass under the *hupah* (marriage canopy) to remind yourselves that "emotions provide the opportunity for us to practice behaving well."[19] In love and in marriage are many emotions, and the opportunity to practice behaving well! And while the nursery rhyme is pessimistic about Humpty Dumpty's future, we can imagine a new and more powerful scenario where all the king's men do put king Humpty Dumpty together again. He cannot be re-paired exactly as he was, but he can come out of his experience with interesting and artful cracks and scars. He is no longer the naive egg of the nursery rhyme, but one who has tamed the Leviathan and can play in the ocean of creativity with his beloved. He has learned to trust all the kings' men, God's helpers, (or if you prefer, his inner helpers) to put him back together again. Trust, gratitude, and the humility to let oneself be helped are our last and most triumphant conquest.

15

Prayer and the Leviathan

When you make the two one,
and when you make the inside as the outside
and the outside as the inside,
And the upper as the lower,
And when you make the male and the female into a single one,
So that the male is not male and the female not female,
And when you make eyes in place of an eye,
And a hand in place of a hand,
And a foot in place of a foot,
An image in place of an image,
Then shall you enter . . . (the Garden or the kingdom)

GOSPEL OF THOMAS 22

Once upon a time, no time, no place. "Arise, my love, My fair one, and go forth. For the winter of bondage has passed, the deluge of suffering is over and gone."[1] Cloaked in a muted splendor, the Master of the Garden awaits **you**, with your hearing, and your seeing, and all your other senses, to enliven His colors and revive His radiance. Shema, listen with the ears of your heart, what do you sense, see, feel, know? The Master cannot do without you. "O My dove . . . show me your powerful gaze, let me hear your supplicating voice."[2] The Master is calling his beloved to Him. Is He praying **to you**? Supplicating you? Is He teaching you how to weave a garland of prayers, a tenuous bridge, to cross the tehom, the abyss, toward Him?

What, in fact, is prayer? Is it the art of seducing the other with sweet words, supplications, and powerful gazes? Is prayer a counterpoint, a duet between I and Thou? Is it a form of intercourse, as the Baal Shem Tov, the founder of Hasidism, suggests? Is prayer God? For most people, prayer is an institutionalized and formal set of words, recited out loud together or internally at fixed intervals.* It has a soothing and repetitive quality like a lullaby and is a powerful reminder to return within. But for you who have already learned to turn your eyes inward, who have developed a relationship to your inner world and your images, would you talk to your beloved in formulas? Prayer is *avodah she'balev,* the work of your heart. Your heart doesn't speak in rote words, but rather in rhythm and image. Your heart sings, as did Miriam's in gratitude at the crossing of the Red Sea,[3] and Hannah's in supplication for a child.[4] Your heart intercedes, like Abraham or Moses who begged for mercy and forgiveness for their people. True prayer springs from the wellspring of creativity that is love of creature to creator. Praying in words is strong. But praying with your whole being in body movements, in song, in images arising from the depths of the subconscious, is what "raising the Leviathan" is all about.

✳

"You shall serve God with all your heart."[5] How to do this? To pray, *hitpalel,* is a reflexive verb in Hebrew and comes from the root word PLL (*palal*) meaning "to judge." The work of prayer is judging oneself, which is everything we have done so far in these chapters. The act of watching the images rise to be judged according to their necessity, and transformed through tikun, is prayer. Prayer changes the DreamField, first your own and then that of those connected to you by blood. Ultimately this great work of transformation clears the universal DreamField. This is called tikun olam, the correction of the world. Kabbalah considers that each one of us has a specific part to play in

---

*Generally three times a day.

the repair of the world. If you have done the exercises, you have done your work of personal, family, and world tikun, and now you are cleansed, cleared, stripped bare, and can stand on your own two feet in what is called the Amidah, the standing posture prayer. Having tamed your beasts (your emotions), and calmed the ocean of the deep (your subconscious), you can look within to the bubbling creative spring, the God within, speaking to you in images and through the still, small voice that tells you all you need to know. At this point, your work is not to do, since all obstacles have been removed, but to let go and let God, or if you prefer, to let your superconscious, your bubbling fountain of creativity, take over and guide you.

Exercise 155
. . . .
The Garden of Eden

Close your eyes. Breathe out slowly three times, counting from three to one. See the one tall, clear, and bright.

You are walking toward the east and the rising sun. See in the distance the flashing colors of the great revolving sword held by the angel guarding the entrance to the Garden of Eden.

Breathe out. Come close and find in your heart the word that, when whispered in the angel's ear, will grant you entry.

Breathe out. Enter the Garden and walk to the center, where the primordial source of creative flow springs forth. Peer into the source.

Breathe out. Pull yourself away, and retrace your steps back toward the entrance to the Garden.

Breathe out. Walk out of the Garden. Thank the angel as you walk past.

Breathe out. Open your eyes.
. . . .

I was walking in the mountains with the abbot of the Yamabushi hermit monks of Japan, Mr. Oshino. I had a bad knee, but he never looked back. He blew on his conch, calling for us to follow him. There was nowhere else to go, so I followed him up the mountain, climbing 2,446 steps to the main shrine. When it seemed too hard, we were instructed to call out UKETAMO, I accept. Secretly I called out, HEKABEL from the word Kabbalah, surrender or receive. I received the step below my foot, I received the trees surrounding me, I received the air that rang with the prayers and chanting of the pilgrims and the blowing of the conch. I received the vibrational field of the Mountain of the Moon, the mount of the subconscious, mount of death. On the next day, I would climb the mount of resurrection, the Mount of the Sun, having been granted new life from the annihilation of my ego, the small death I experienced on my climb up the Mountain of the Moon.

Later Mr. Oshino and I compared traditions. He trains his students through the rigors of the body, climbing mountains, standing under powerful waterfalls, accepting the rain and the rock. He showed me the soles of his feet that were not calloused at all. Indeed they were smooth and white as baby skin. It's a love affair, he told me, a dance between the mountain and the climber. I told him that Kabbalah likewise is a love affair. We surrender to the teaching, and the teaching is done by creating a circle (using the dream induction) through which the students leap into the unknown, yielding to the Ein Sof, the void. It's not easy to take the mortal leap, trusting that "Thou opens thy hand and satisfies the desire of every living being."[6] As much as we are conditioned to fear the cold and the dangers of nature, we are conditioned to work and to struggle to reach our goals. Suffering is part of the plan we have been brainwashed into believing will bring about the desired effect. Alas, we are not taught to trust that the subconscious will serve up to us "all that we desire." We do not know, or we forget, that we are not in charge. God (or if you prefer, the universe or the subconscious) is in charge. The work of students of Kabbalah is to get aligned to God's truth, as Mr. Oshino's students get aligned to the truth of the mountain or the waterfall.

In the Hebrew Bible God has many names. One of them is Elohei Tsevaot, the God of hosts or armies. What armies? The armies of the angels, the galaxies, stars, planets, seasons, life and death, that revolve in a perfect order reflecting the order of the divinity. Will you become a part of God's armies? You already are. But you have been given free choice. You can decide to rebel, to take a detour away from your true path. When you fail to act on the guidance of your inner voice or images, everything becomes more difficult. The Tarot (Torah when read backward) tells us that if we do not align to God's purpose, which is also our soul purpose, we will be thrown off balance, as shown in the sixteenth Major Arcanum, the Tower. Your sole (soul) aim should be to fit into God's (the universe, your subconscious) purpose like a hand in a glove. God is in charge, not you. What do you think you can control? Relax and let Him move you. God lives within you. He is the still, small voice, the revelation that rises up to meet your dazzled eyes, the light, the bliss, the joy, the presence of the beloved in His many splendored forms. Do this, and all becomes easy. Life flows, full of happy surprises. So don't struggle, but learn to frolic, like Leviathan, with your beloved.

God is prayer. Prayer puts you in a relationship of faith to the unknown. Prayer is a radical shift in consciousness. Pray in images, pray with your senses, pray with enjoyment, with tears, with supplications, with shakings, with inspiration. "Is prayer preposterous? Yes, but so are all the stirrings of the heart, and the heart has eyes through which the mind cannot see."[7]

Once upon a time there was an illiterate man. He never went to synagogue because he was ashamed of his ignorance. Yet God answered all his prayers. At the synagogue, the learned rabbis were perplexed: Their prayers weren't being answered. Finally, they decided to visit the man. "How do you do it?" they asked. The man was embarrassed. "I am but a humble man and cannot read. So I throw all the holy letters of the alphabet up into the heavens and pray, God in Your infinite mercy, arrange the letters in the configuration which is most pleasing to You!"

Prayer is your most creative act, an act in which you need do nothing but gaze into the Ein Sof, the void, waiting until nothingness takes form and rises like the axis mundi, the great beast of the deep, Leviathan, leaving in its "wake . . . a luminous path."[8] The more you turn your eyes inward, the more luminous your Leviathan becomes until even "his sneezings flash lightning, and his eyes are like the glimmerings of dawn."[9]

Exercise 156
. . . .
The Empty Bowl

Breathe out slowly three times, counting from three to one. See the one as tall, clear, and bright.

Imagine that you hold in your hands an empty bowl. Look in and wait.

Breathe out and open your eyes.

. . . .

But the material world is so alluring in its variety and challenges that we forget to look inward. Looking inward requires dedication. We must consciously bend our will to the task again and again, day after day, and night after night, like Jacob who stayed in tents (a metaphor for looking within) while his brother Esau went hunting. We must look inward every day and declare **in images, for words are not sufficient,** our intention to serve God (the universe, your subconscious).

Exercise 157
. . . .
Dedication

Close your eyes. Breathe out slowly three times, counting from three to one. See the one tall, clear, and bright.

Imagine dropping all your burdens and starting your climb up a steep mountain before dawn. You have donned a white robe, and your feet are bare. Feel your effort, your exhaustion, your dusty feet and achy limbs.

Breathe out. You encounter a very verdant little valley halfway up the mountain. In the valley is a bubbling fountain.

Breathe out. Leave the path, and step onto the thick green grass. Feel the moisture and the comforting wetness of the grass beneath your feet.

Breathe out. Go to the fountain. Put your hands and arms up to your elbows into the cold spring waters. Lift them up to the first rays of sunlight. Dedicate your hands to works of goodness and life.

Breathe out. Put your hands in the water, and touch your eyes, to clear them. Dedicate your seeing to piercing the veil of conceal-ment, and to seeing only goodness and life.

Breathe out. Put your hands in the water, touch your ears, and feel the water clearing away all discordant sounds. Dedicate your hearing to goodness and life.

Breathe out. Put your hands in the water, touch your nos-trils, and feel the water clearing your passages of all impurities. Dedicate your breathing to the flow of spirit entering your body,

traveling through and coming out into the world to serve only goodness and life.

Breathe out. Put your hands in the water, and touch your lips, to
clear all that goes in and out, and dedicate the work of your mouth
and throat to goodness and life.

Breathe out. Put your hands in the water, and sprinkle the water
all around your skin to clear its pores and dedicate its feeling and
touch to goodness and life.

Breathe out. Step away from the fountain. Step back onto the
dusty path, and continue on your way up the mountain.

Breathe out. Open your eyes.

. . . .

Each night for at least one minute, cry all the tears of your body,
washing your eyes with your tears, blowing your nose to clear the path
for spirit, unblocking your ears, cleaning your tongue with songs of love,
moving your body in rhythm forward and back, left and right, up and
down. "Happy is the man who finds refuge in you. . . . O Lord of hosts,
happy is the man who trusts in you."* In other words, turn inward, and
fervently pray for help, and you will receive it.

Exercise 158
. . . .
Surrender

Breathe out slowly three times, counting from three to one. See the
one as tall, clear, and bright.

Ascend to the higher reaches of the mountain. Come upon a
meadow as the first rays of light illuminate the meadow. See the
meadow turning to radiant light.

Breathe out. Step on the meadow so lightly that the blades
of grass do not even bend. See and feel how your body turns to
rainbow light.

Breathe out. Come to the center of the meadow. Take a piece
of white chalk out of your pocket and draw a circle in the grass.

Breathe out. Step into it. Call on all your angelic beings,
guides, protectors, and ancestors to do for you what needs to be
done now.

---

*As did King David in Psalm 84:6 and 84:13.

Breathe out. Watch and surrender to their ministrations. Do nothing; just let go and let God.

Breathe out. When all is done, erase the circle. Humbly thank your helpers.

Breathe out. Open your eyes.

· · · · · · · · · ·

Just as you can never heal yourself through willpower, but only by surrendering to inner alignment, so too you cannot heal another. You can only create the space for the other to be. Draw the circle, and step out. Call the one who has asked for prayer to enter the circle. Then call for their helpers. Watch what is happening in the circle. You are the caller, and you are the witness. You are not the doer, the helpers are.

A note of caution: Never engage in this formal prayer unless the other has specifically asked you for prayer. The other's free will must be respected. Of course, you may keep the other in what I call a prayer pouch, a secret space within your heart, or in the back of your neck. From time to time, send them some light. This is permitted. In fact it is impossible to stop oneself from praying. O Lord, help so and so. . . . But the formal prayer is a powerful ritual that must be respected.

Exercise 159
· · · · · · · · · ·
Prayer of Intercession

Breathe out slowly three times, counting from three to one. See the one as tall, clear, and bright.

Imagine a tent of blue light. Call into the tent the person you are interceding for.

Breathe out. Call in the person's angelic helpers, guides, protectors and ancestors. Watch them, full of light, trooping into the tent. Do not enter the tent.

Breathe out, knowing that whatever this person needs will be taken care of by her helpers.

Breathe out. Open your eyes, knowing that she or he will leave the tent when all is done. Feel grateful for the help that is always available.

Breathe out. Open your eyes.

· · · · · · · · · ·

For many years I've had a prayer group where we formally pray for others. Our prayers are not in words but in images that unfold naturally before our eyes from the supplicant's subconscious DreamField. Our only contribution is lending our presence and attention to helping the supplicant realign to his or her truth. For years we have verified the results of our prayers. Prayer works, but it must be undertaken only when we ourselves are clear and humble conduits, seeking nothing but to be of service to another's truth. We also pray for families and for the world.

Prayerful attentiveness, waiting empty-handed, empty-minded, and agenda-free, is the work of the Kabbalist. It is said that a Kabbalist, to be accomplished, must become a woman. In other words, be a womb, offering your empty space for the other's comfort and growth. Be a woman before God, your beloved. Let yourself be totally filled with Divine presence.* And never ever, at any moment of day or night, forget your beloved.

We are two until we are one. When we are one, we cease to exist. Ecstasy fills us to the brink. Like the holy ones at the great feast given in their honor in the world to come, we are given a foretaste of the delectations of Leviathan. So sweet, so heavenly is his flesh. This is called dveikut, cleaving to the Divine. Tasting Oneness.

Exercise 160
. . . .
Oneness

Breathe out slowly three times, counting from three to one. See the one as tall, clear, and bright.

See and live that you are the smaller part of a greater circle that is the Divine.

Breathe out. Open your eyes.
. . . .

*Again, if the word doesn't sit right with you, think of the universe or subconscious presence.

As Colette once wrote,

> *As much as I need you*
> *God*
> *You need me*
> *Our no-separation*
> *Is Oneness . . .*
> *As you are everywhere*
> *And everything,*
> *Here and now*
> *You are me.*[10]

✳

I wish you well as you plunge. Your heart will reveal treasures far surpassing the treasures of the mind. Trust your subconscious, for it will always show you Truth. When the S (Sod) returns to PRD, fear becomes ecstasy, radiating out in all directions; sending its warmth, light, and love into the world; and calling the same to itself. Then you can truly play and frolic in the waves of the subconscious with your beloved beast, who has become your playmate. God will bless you, and your life will become effortless.

Glossary

'ad ko, עד־כה—beyond, yonder.

Adam haRishon, אדם הראשון—the first human.

Adam Ḳadmon, אדם קדמון—the first spiritual World that came into being after the contraction of God's infinite light. In Lurianic Kabbalah, descriptions of this world are anthropomorphized. In the four Worlds concept, Adam Ḳadmon represents a fifth World beyond or above that of Atsilut.

adamah, אדמה—Earth, or more generally, the earth (or soil) of the land.

ahavah, אהבה—love; devotion.

Ashkenazi, אשכנזי—European Jewry descended from the Jewish communities of France and Germany. The geographic name is derived from the biblical name of Ashkenaz, a son of Gomer in Genesis 10:3.

avodah she'balev, עבודה שבלב—contemplative worship; i.e., tefillah (prayer, for example, in the Amidah). Lev means heart, but as the heart was understood as the locus of the mind, this reference to the heart suggests mental effort.

bara, ברא—(as in bereshit bara Elohim), "in the beginning of Elohim's creation" from Genesis 1:1. "Bara" is often translated "to create"; i.e., ex nihilo, asserting a theological position. A closer translation would be "to shape"—with an organic valence, especially in relation to the growth of living things over time, fruits and infants, trees and human beings.

benoni, בינוני—average, medium. A benoni is an average, unremarkable person, not exceptionally righteous or wicked.

bikkurim, בכורים—first fruits, specifically in the context of the early summer agricultural festival of Shavuot (also called Pentecost).

binah, בינה—understanding. in Kabbalah, the sephirah opposite that of ḥokhmah, wisdom.

bnei ha-nevi'im, בני־הנביאים—disciples of the prophets, a group referred to in 2 Kings 4:38 and 2 Kings 6:1.

Canaan (K'naan), כנען—also known as Canaan, the son of Ham, and the eponymous ancestor of the Canaanite peoples.

da'at, דעת—knowledge; in Kabbalah, the integration of wisdom and understanding.

deyo partzuf panim, דיו פרצוף פנים—from Eruvin 18a: "Rabbi Yirmeya ben Elazar also said: Adam (was first created with) two [deyo] faces, (one male and the other female)." Compare Eruvin 18a with Aristophanes's tale of the first person as hermaphrodite in Plato's Symposium.

drash, דרש—a Torah insight derived from interwoven interpretations of scripture, its early translations, and glosses. See, PaRDeS.

dveiḳut, דבקות—cleaving to the divine, an aspirational state of love for God, by which the aspirant is nourished and sustained. From the root דבק, to adhere.

eḥad, אחד—one, unique, inimitable.

ehyeh asher ehyeh—a Divine name introduced in Exodus 3:14. Literally, "I will be that I will be" but often translated in different ways. For example, Rashi on the verse explains, "I am (—with Israel in their subjugation in Egypt) who I will be (—with Israel under future oppressors)."

Ein Sof, אין־סוף—the Infinite, a divine epithet in the Kabbalah; literally, "without end."

Elohei Tsevaot—a divine epithet, elo'ah of hosts (or legions) referring to the vast numinous angelic powers that YHVH commands.

etsev, עצב—the pain of sadness, sorrow, and grief.

gam zu l'tovah, גם זו לטובה—"this too (gam zu) is for the good," the common response of Naḥum of Gamzu upon hearing even bad news. For the full story in the Talmud, find Taanit 21a.

gilgulim, גלגולים—metamorphoses, after galgal (wheel). In later Kabbalistic terminology, gilgulims refer to the recycling (transmigration) of souls that are either too righteous or deficient to be processed in the normal way. The fate of the soul of the uniquely righteous (tsadiḳ) is to be born again as a righteous individual, as their continued activities help to sustain the continued existence of a world constantly imperiled by wickedness. The fate of the soul of the uniquely deficient is to become a gilgul, the spirit of which is reborn in the body of a nonhuman creature, to humble them through that experience, so that their spirit may continue to be processed in Gehennom after their demise.

ḥalom, חלום—a dream.

Ḥam, חם—one of the three sons of Noah introduced in Genesis 5:32. Ḥam is one of the surviving remnants of humanity after the generation of the Flood and thus one of the common fathers of humanity in the Hebrew Bible.

ḥamor, חמור—donkey.

hataḇat ḥalom, הטבת חלום—lit. the betterment, or amelioration, of a disturbing dream, by means of a particular ritual and prayer. For the text in the Talmud, find Berakhot 55a.

Ḥavah, חוה—a/k/a Eve, the first human's name for his partner ("because she was the mother of kol ḥai"—all the living or all life), given during the expulsion from the Garden of Eden, in Genesis 3:20. Before this moment she is simply named Ishah (woman), apart from Ish (man), and distinct from ha-Adam (the Earthling).

ḥayah, חיה—a living creature. A wild creature; i.e., a creature that makes its own living (in distinction to a behemah—a domesticated animal); pl. ḥayot.

hineni, הנני—"Here I am" as, for example, in response to God's call in Genesis 22:1.

hitpalel, התפלל—to pray, to worship; to hope.

ḥokhmah, חכמה—wisdom. in Kabbalah, the Sefirah opposite that of Binah, understanding.

ḥomer, חמר —material, substance.

Ḥoreb חרב—dryness, aridity. Mt. Ḥorev might translate to "desert mount."

ḥupah, חפה—the wedding canopy used for Jewish marriage ceremonies.

ish, איש—a man.

ishah, אשה—a woman.

Ivri, עברי—in the Torah, referring to a person belonging to the Hebrew people. The term is first applied in Genesis 14:13 to Avram ha-Ivri (Abram the Hebrew), dwelling at the terebinths of Mamré the Emori.

Kabbalah, קבלה—the "received (hidden tradition)." The term derives from the root, קבל (ḳibel), to receive, meaning the received hidden tradition within (or transmitted in parallel to) rabbinic Judaism, something of a conceit in a tradition that in part embraces innovative interpretations, creative derivations, and even, through specialized praxes, communications from numinous entities (for example, Eliyahu haNavi). Academically, the term refers to an esoteric Judaism that began to be publicly revealed in the late middle ages through the teachings of thirteenth-century Jewish scholars in Gerona, Spain, after the death of their teacher, Moshe ben Naḥman (Naḥmanides, 1194–1270). Popularly, the term is synonymous with esoteric Jewish teachings as a whole, transmitted since the time of Adam and part and parcel of the Oral Tradition (Torah she'bikhtav) received by Moshe at Mt. Sinai. In this latter understanding, kabbalah includes earlier cosmogonic, midrashic, and magical works including Heikhalot literature, the Sefer Yetsirah, and the Sefer Bahir. Transmitters of kabbalah are referred to as mekubalim.

kavanah, כונה—intention (also, concentration and conviction), from "kiven," כִּוֵּן— to aim, to direct toward a target. A kavanah may be a declaration of intention, as with many kavanot (pl.)—statements of one's intention prior to perform- ing a mitsvah or ritual. Kavanot are a familiar part of Kabbalistic explanation for prayer literature that provide an esoteric explanation for otherwise exoteric prayers and ritual activities.

keruv, כרוב—a type of angel, the angelic manifestation of cloud (Patai). Mainly appearing in pairs (keruvim), but in Psalms 18:11, offered in singular.

kesher, קשר—a knot, connection. relationship.

kibbutz, קבוץ—modern Hebrew for a collective settlement. In Hebrew, a kibbuts is an ingathering, a collection (a k'vutsah is a group). In the twentieth century, kibbutzim (pl.) were founded as socialist-communist intentional communities for settling the land of Israel while providing a sustainable agricultural economy for the new state of Israel.

ki tov, כי־טוב—"that it was good," as exclaimed by God in (almost) every day of creation in Genesis 1. Find, for example, Genesis 1:4.

k'negdo, כנגדו—lit. "against him," in the context of Genesis 2:18–20, the creation of Ḥavah (Eve).

la'asot, לעשות—lit. to do; i.e., a statement of poesis, making.

lehem, לחם—bread.

lekh lekha, לך־לך—take yourself or go you forth; in Genesis 12:1 the first words communicated from YHVH to Avram (later, Aḅraham).

levanah, לבנה—(the) Moon.

leviathan, לויתן—Heb. Livyatan, a primordial mythical creature of cosmic enormity, possibly synonymous with Tiamat. In the book of Job, it is paired with another such creature: Behemōt (the Behemoth). In a myth preserved in the Talmud, the two are destined to slaughter one another at the end of this world, whereafter they will be served at the Feast of the Righteous. However, other sources indicate there are at least two Leviathans, one male and one female, and that they may be differentiated also in their form, coiled and straight. Speculation on the significance of these distinctions is further explored in the Zohar.

maḥshavah, מחשבה—thought, philosophy.

merkavah, מרכבה—the Divine chariot.

midrash, מדרש—broadly, midrashim (pl.) are expansions of the biblical narrative (midrash aggadah) or legal text (midrash halakhah) by way of exegesis. Part of the Oral Torah in rabbinic Judaism, midrashim may be derived by manner of exegetical rules, but the term is often used as a synonym for aggadot (stories) and nonlegal texts in general.

Mitsrayim, מצרים—Egypt.

ne'elam, נעלם—unknown, in the sense of hidden or concealed. from the same root as olam.

nefesh, נפש—spirit, person, neck. In the tripartite, pneumatic concept of soul in esoteric Judaism, nefesh is synonymous with the most immanent, animating level of spirit.

neshamah, נשמה—breath, soul. In the pneumatic metaphor of the tripartite soul in esoteric Judaism, the neshamah is the most distant aspect of the soul still attached to our animate physical selves (through the ruaḥ and nefesh), requiring an effort for it to be directly experienced, and through it, a sense of the lofty realms in which it is more familiar.

niggun, נגון—a tune, as for a liturgical prayer or song, or by itself, as a wordless melody (pl. niggunim).

Noaḥ, נח—also known as Noah, from naḥ, comfort, relief. The son of Lemekh, Noaḥ becomes the common father of all humanity after the tragedy of the generation of the Flood.

olam, עולם—world, but in a sense also connoting a period of time with a fixed beginning and end; i.e., a cosmos.

Olam Asiyah, עשיה—in the four Worlds concept in Kabbalah, the World of Action, the lowest of the four. Based on Isaiah 43:7.

Olam Atsilut, אצילות—in the four Worlds concept in Kabbalah, the World of Emanation, the highest of the four.

Olam Bri'ah, בריאה—in the four Worlds concept in Kabbalah, the World of Creation, the penultimate world below Atsilut. Based on Isaiah 43:7.

Olam Yetsirah, יצירה—in the four Worlds concept in Kabbalah, the World of Formation, the world above that of action. Based on Isaiah 43:7.

PaRDeS, פרדס—Pardes (the Orchard), as from the Song of Songs 4:13, but here referring to a mnemonic acronym for four ways of deriving meaning from Torah study: via P'shat (the explicit meaning), Remez (allusions), Drash (an intertextual exegesis), and Sôd (the esoteric, secret meaning). The use of "PaRDeS" as an acronym first appears in the writings of Moshe de Leon, the central author or redactor of the Zoharic texts in the late thirteenth century.

pataḥ, פתח—to open.

patar, פתר—to solve, to decipher.

p'nei tehom . . . p'nei hamayim, פני המים . . . פני תהום—the face or surface of the abyss (or the deep), the primordial waters, a cosmological term found in Genesis 1:2.

poter, פותר—one who solves (riddles, conundrums, etc.).

P'shat, פשט—the explicit meaning or the simple interpretation. See PaRDeS.

ra, רע—an evil, wicked, or otherwise villainous individual. Ra also describes anything that is bad or malicious.

Remez, רמז—a hint. In rabbinic hermeneutics, a literary allusion. See PaRDeS.

ruaḥ, רוח—wind, spirit. In the pneumatic metaphor of the soul, ruach is the middle portion, mediating between the immediate animating portion (nefesh), and the distant and rarefied portion connected to the spiritual realm (neshamah).

safar, ספר—to enumerate; safur, counted.

sefer, ספר—a book, scroll, or tablet; sefarim (pl.)

Sepharadi, ספרדי—Jewry of the Iberian Peninsula, Spain and Portugal, surviving after their expulsion beginning in 1492 in many lands to the east and west. The name is derived from the biblical name of Sefarad, in Obadiah 1:20.

shalom bayit, שלום בית—lit. peace of the home, a euphemism for a happy domestic (sexual) relationship.

Shema, שמע—one of the core prayers of Jewish liturgy, the incipit of Deuteronomy 6:4, "Listen Yisrael . . ."

shemesh, שמש—(the) Sun.

shnei panim, שני פנים—two faces.

sipur, ספור—story, tale; sippurim (pl.)

sod, סוד—a secret or mystery, a familiar term in ḳabbalistic writings for describing a divine activity, as well as the description of that activity often using specialized terminology.

tafar, תפר—tailor.

tehom, תהום—(the) Abyss. find Genesis 1:2.

tiḳun, תקון—repair, correction. from the root tiḳen תקן, to repair, to fix.

tohu va'ḇohu, תהו ובהו—primordial chaos and void, the creative matter from which the world was organized in the cosmology described in Genesis 1:2.

tov m'od, טוב מאד—lit. "very good" or "excellent." Find Genesis 1:31 for God's declaration at the end of the sixth day of creation.

tsadiḵ, צדיק—a uniquely righteous individual.

tsara'ath, צרעת—a skin affliction described in Leviticus 13:2 requiring the inspection and intervention of a kohen (priest)

tsela, צלע—rib, side. For other rabbinic explanation of the meaning of tsela, find Eruvin 18a.

t'shuvah, תשובה—repentance, lit. to return.

yeḥidah, יחידה—unification.

yeridah, ירידה—descent. Practice of "ascent" seems to be preceded by an experience of "descent." An early school of esoteric Jewish practice were the Yordei haMerkavah, the descenders to the chariot, authors of the Heikhalot literature who described these ascents.

yetser, יצר—inclination.

yud, יוד—(also pronounced "yod"), the tenth letter of the Hebrew aleph-bet.

Notes

Preface

1. Ex. 20:15.
2. 2 Kings 4:38 and 6:1.

Introduction

1. Gen. 2.
2. Zohar 2:179a.
3. Rashi, *Rashi on Baba Bathra* 74b.
4. Pesiqta Rabbati 48.
5. Gen. 1:9.
6. Gen. 7:11.
7. Johanan bar Nappaha, Babylonian Talmud, Baba Bathra 75a.
8. Isa. 27:1.
9. Ps. 104:24–26.
10. Job 41:17 and 41:24–26.
11. Baba Bathra 75a.

Part I. The Leviathan, Great Beast of the Deep

1. I Ching.
2. "Ali Baba and the Forty Thieves."

Chapter 1. The Mystery of Dreams

1. Crick and Mitchison, "The function of dream sleep."
2. Hobson and McCarley, "The Brain as a Dream State Generator."
3. Shainberg, *DreamBirth.*
4. Keleman, *Your Body Speaks Its Mind.*

5. Berakhot 55b.

6. Pushkin, "The Tale of the Fisherman and the Fish."

7. Berakhot 55a.

8. Chagigah 14b, Zohar 1:26b, Tikkunei Zohar, Tikun 40.

9. Berakhot 55b.

10. Berakhot 55b.

11. Berakhot 55a.

Chapter 2. Tikun and a Ladder to the Light

1. Gen. 1:12.

2. Gen. 1:31.

3. Chagigah 12a.

4. Exodus 20:18.

5. Gen. 37:10–20.

6. Gen. 37:5.

7. Gen. 37:9.

8. Gen. 37:11.

9. Berakhot 55b.

10. Campbell, *The Hero with a Thousand Faces*.

11. Keleman, *Myth & the Body*.

12. Ginzburg, *Legends of the Jews*.

13. Berakhot 55b.

14. Gen. 40.

15. Gen. 40:8.

16. Gen. 41.

17. Gen. 41:55.

18. Campbell, quoted in Keleman, *Myth & the Body*.

19. The Emerald Tablet.

20. Gen. 28:14–15.

21. Gen. 39:1–20.

22. Eccles. 5:4.

23. Ginsburgh, *Body, Mind and Soul*.

Chapter 3. Incubation and Saphire Imagery

1. Eccles. 1:9.

2. Gen. 22:2.

3. Genesis Rabbah 67:8.

4. Shir HaShirim Rabbah 6:2.

Chapter 4. The Creative Act

1. Chagigah 12a.
2. Gen. 2:20.
3. Gen. 3:16.
4. Job 41:18.
5. Job 28:12.
6. Job 28:23.
7. Hullin 60b.
8. Rosenblit, "Midrash on the Moon."
9. Weizmann Institute of Science, "Quantum Theory Demonstrated."
10. Gen. 1:28.
11. Dickens, *Oliver Twist*.
12. Isa. 30:26.
13. 1 Kings 19:12.
14. Gen. 2:3.
15. Gen. 2:10.

Chapter 5. Signs of Transformation: The Grammar of the Imagination

1. Keleman, *Myth & the Body*.
2. Job 38:11.
3. Ex. 20:18.
4. Num. 22:31.

Chapter 6. Symbol or Metaphor

1. Berakhot 55a.
2. Berakhot 56b.
3. Bereshit Rabbah 68:12.
4. Baudelaire, *Flowers of Evil*.
5. Michel Foucault, "Dream, Imagination and Existence."
6. Ex. 3:14.
7. Gen. 40: 9–13.
8. Berakhot 55b.
9. Berakhot 55b.

Chapter 7. Playing with Manifestation

1. Wolfson, *A Dream Interpreted within A Dream*. Wolfson is referring here to Maimonides' opinion. His own view is that "In the dream, there is an

amalgamation of the real and the unreal to the point that the real is presumed to be unreal inasmuch as the unreal is presumed to be real."

2. Rig Veda X.177:1–3, Trans. Laurie Patton.
3. Rabbi Shimon bar Yo'chai, *The Zohar,* Vol. 3, folio 152a.
4. Gen. 2:3.
5. Gen. 3:16.
6. Gen. 2:3.
7. Foucault, "Dream, Imagination and Existence."
8. Hill, *Think and Grow Rich.*
9. Hill, *Think and Grow Rich.*
10. Hill, *Think and Grow Rich.*
11. Hill, *Think and Grow Rich.*
12. Berakhot 55 b.
13. Gen. 37:12.

Chapter 8. Dreamfields and Complexes

1. Winkler, *Daily Kabbalah,* Day 85, Rabbi Ben Abraham.
2. Job 38:11.
3. Gen. 2:1.
4. Gen. 2:15.
5. Va-Yaqhel 2:210b.
6. Gen. 11:1–9.
7. 3 Baruch 3:5; on the Tower of Babel.
8. 3 Baruch.
9. Keleman, *Myth & the Body.*
10. Deut. 6:21.
11. 1 Kings 19:12.
12. Bettelheim, *The Uses of Enchantment.*

Chapter 9. Ancestral Patterns

1. Gen. 1:28.
2. Gen. 9:25.
3. Ex. 20:5.
4. Jung, *Aion.*
5. Ex. 20:5.
6. Keleman, *Myth & the Body.*
7. Blake, "From Blake's Engraving of the Laocoön."

Chapter 10. The Inner Child: From Duality to Singularity

1. Matt. 18:3; Sermon on the Mount.
2. Bereshit Rabba 85:7.
3. Jodorowsky and Costa, *The Way of Tarot.*
4. Chesterton, *The Illustrated London News.*
5. Gen. 18:13–14.
6. Matt. 6:22.
7. Gen. 2:23.

Chapter 11. Misery and Splendor: Restoring Relationships

1. Gen. 2:18.
2. Gikatilla, *Le Secret du Mariage de David et Bethsabee.*
3. Sanhedrin 22a, Sota 2b, Moed Qatan 18b.
4. Ginsburgh, *The Mystery of Marriage.*
5. Gen. 2:23.
6. Gen. 11:4.
7. Lev. 19:18.
8. Buber, *I and Thou.*
9. Bly, *A Little Book on the Human Shadow.*
10. 1 Sam. 25.
11. Eccles. 7:26.
12. Eiruvim 18a; also Shlomo Yitzchaki, known as Rashi, 1040–1105, French rabbi and commentator of the Tanakh and Talmud.
13. Robert Hass, "Misery and Splendor."
14. Sotah 17a.
15. Lev. 10.
16. Ex. 25:22.
17. Bereshit Rabbah 18:4.
18. "Prayer of Saint Francis."
19. Matt. 25:1–13

Chapter 12. Time and Choice

1. Gen. 3:7.
2. Deut. 4:32.
3. Gen. 3:21.
4. Attributed to Dr. Seuss.
5. Franklin, "Advice to a young tradesman."
6. Prov. 3:18.

7. VaYeira 117a.

8. Isa. 60:22.

9. Whitehead, *The Harvard Lectures of Alfred North Whitehead.*

10. Moore, "Cramming more components onto integrated circuits."

11. Attributed to Albert Einstein.

12. de Ronsard, "Sonnet to Marie."

13. Pesakhim 6b:7; Rashi on Exodus 31:18:1.

14. Saint Augustine, *Confessions,* Book 9, 14:17.

15. Nietzsche, *The Will to Power.*

16. Nietzsche, *The Will to Power.*

17. Heraclitus, *On Nature.*

18. *Tales from the Thousand and One Nights.*

19. Yeats, "Kanva on Himself."

20. Scholem, *Kabbalah.*

21. Nachman of Breslov, *Likutei Moharan.*

22. 3 Enoch 9:2.

23. Bonder, *The Kabbalah of Time.*

24. Sepher Yetsirah 1:5.

25. Targum Yerushalmi 28:10; Sanhedrin 95b; Hullin 91b.

26. Rabbi Shneur Zalman of Liadi, *Tanya.*

Chapter 13. Healing: Will It Be Leprosy, Wellness, or Wholeness?

1. Zohar 3:129a.

2. Genesis Rabbah 97.

3. Job 19:26.

4. Bava Batra 58b.

5. Ginsburgh, *Body, Mind and Soul.*

6. Benyossef, *Reversing Cancer Through Mental Imagery.*

7. Ex. 20:18.

8. Song of Sol. 4:1 and 4:4, 6:7 (A New Translation).

9. Job 38:8–11 (New International Version).

10. Job 42:3 (Tanach: the Stone Edition).

11. Gen. 2:2.

12. Nahman of Bratslav, quoted in Greenbaum, *The Wings of the Sun.*

13. Deut. 30:19.

14. Jer. 17:14.

15. Ps. 23:4.

16. Aryeh Kaplan, *The Bahir.*

Part III. Raising the Leviathan

1. Ben Meir, *Commentary on Baba Bathra* 74b.
2. Ben Meir, *Commentary on Baba Bathra* 74b.

Chapter 14. The Heart-Centered Way

1. Gen. 2:15.
2. Rashi, *Commentary on the Tanakh.*
3. Song of Songs 5:6.
4. Gen. 3:3.
5. Song of Sol. 6:2.
6. Bereshit Rabbah 19:1–2, quoted in Zornberg, *The Murmuring Deep.*
7. 1 Kings 19:11–13.
8. Gen. 39:11.
9. Bereshit Rabbah 98:20.
10. Viktor Frankl, *Man's Search for Meaning.*
11. Hab. 3:2.
12. Rav Menakem Mendel Morgensztern, quoted in Raz, *The Sayings of Menahem Mendel of Kotsk.*
13. Ilya Prigogine, quoted in Sarbajit et al., "Ordered Complexity from Dissipative and Chaotic Systems."
14. Song of Sol. 1:14.
15. Ps. 22:2.
16. Heschel, *The Sabbath.*
17. Attributed to José Ortega y Gasset.
18. Rav Menakem Mendel Morgensztern, quoted in Raz, *The Sayings of Menahem Mendel of Kotsk.*
19. Alessandri, "It's a Terrible Day in the Neighborhood, and That's O.K."

Chapter 15. Prayer and the Leviathan

1. Song of Sol. 2:10–11.
2. Song of Sol. 2:14–15.
3. Ex. 15:1–18.
4. 1 Sam. 1:10–18 and 2:1–11.
5. Deut. 11:13.
6. Ps. 145:16.
7. Michaelson, *Everything Is God.*
8. Job 41:24.
9. Job 41:10.
10. Aboulker-Mouscat, *Alone with the One.*

Bibliography

Aboulker-Muscat, Colette. *Alone with the One.* New York: ACMI Press, 1995.

Aboulker-Muscat, Colette. *Life Is Not a Novel.* Trans. Francoise Coriat. Sharon, Ma.: Black Jasmine, 2008.

Alessandri, Mariana, "It's a Terrible Day in the Neighborhood, and That's O.K." *New York Times,* November 11, 2019. Available at New York Times online.

Baudelaire, Charles. *Flowers of Evil.* Trans. Jacques LeClerq. Mt. Vernon, NY: Peter Pauper Press, 1958.

Benyossef, Simcha. *Reversing Cancer Through Mental Imagery.* New York: ACMI Press, 2017.

Bettelheim, Bruno. *The Uses of Enchantment: The Meaning and Importance of Fairy Tales.* New York: Knopf, 1976.

Blake, William. "From Blake's Engraving of the Laocoön" in *The Prophetic Books of William Blake: Jerusalem.* Ed. E. R. D. Maclagan and A. G. B. Russell. London: A. H. Bullen, 1904.

Bloch, Ariel, and Chana Bloch. *Song of Songs: A New Translation.* Berkeley: University of California Press, 1995.

Bly, Robert. *A Little Book on the Human Shadow.* San Francisco: HarperOne, 1988.

Bonder, Nilton. *The Kabbalah of Time: Teachings on the Inexistence of God.* Bloomington, Ind.: Trafford Publishing, 2009.

Buber, Martin. *I and Thou.* Trans. Walter Kaufman. New York: Touchstone, 1971.

Bunyan, John. *The Pilgrim's Progress.* Mineola, NY: Aneko Press. 1678, 2015.

Campbell, Joseph. *The Hero with a Thousand Faces*. Novato, Calif.: New World Library, 1949, 2008.

Chesterton, G. K. *The Illustrated London News, 1908–1910* (*The Collected Works of G. K. Chesterton*. Vol. 28). San Francisco: Ignatius, 1987.

Crick, Francis and Graeme Mitchison. "The function of dream sleep." *Nature* 304 (1983): 111–114.

de Ronsard, Pierre. "Sonnet to Marie." *Sonnets to Helene*. Trans. A. S. Kline. 2004. Available at Poetry in Translation online.

Dickens, Charles. *The Adventures of Oliver Twist*. HardPress Publishing, online, 2013.

Foucault, Michel. "Dream, Imagination and Existence," in *Dream and Existence*. Ed. Keith Hoeller. Atlantic Highlands, N. I.: Humanities Press, 1993.

Frankl, Viktor. *Man's Search for Meaning*. Boston: Beacon Press, 2006.

Franklin, Benjamin. "Advice to a young tradesman" in *the American Instructor or Best Man's Best Companion*. Ed. George Fisher. Dublin, 1798.

Gikatilla, R. Joseph. *Le Secret du Mariage de David et Bethsabee*. Ed. Charles Mopsik. Paris: Editions de l'Eclat, 1994.

Ginsburgh, Yitzchak. *Body, Mind and Soul: Kabbalah on Human Physiology, Disease, and Healing*. Jerusalem: Gal Einai Institute, 2003.

———. *The Mystery of Marriage: How to Find True Love and Happiness in Married Life*. Jerusalem: Linda Pinsky Publications, 1999.

Ginzburg, Louis. *Legends of the Jews*, Vol. II. Philadelphia: The Jewish Publication Society of America, 1925, 1953.

Greenbaum, Avraham. *The Wings of the Sun: Traditional Jewish Healing in Theory and Practice*. Jerusalem: Breslov Research Institute, 1995.

Griffiths, Jay. *Pip Pip: A Sideways Look at Time*. London: Harper Collins 1999.

Hass, Robert. "Misery and Splendor," in *Human Wishes*. New York: Harper Collins, 1989.

Heschel, Abraham Joshua. *The Sabbath*. New York: Farrar, Straus and Giroux, 2005.

Hill, Napoleon. *Think and Grow Rich*. Los Angeles, Calif.: Penguin Putnam, 2005.

Hobson, Allan and Robert McCarley. "The Brain as a Dream State Generator: An Activation-Synthesis Hypothesis of the Dream Process." *The American Journal of Psychiatry* 134, no. 12 (2006): 1335–48.

Jodorowsky, Alejandro, and Marianne Costa. *The Way of Tarot: The Spiritual Teacher in the Cards.* Rochester, Vt.: Destiny Books, 2009.

Jung, C. G. *Aion: Researches into the Phenomenology of the Self (Collected Works of C. G. Jung.* Vol. 9 Part 2). Trans. Gerhard Adler and R. F. C. Hull. Princeton: Princeton University Press, 1979.

Kaplan, Aryeh. *The Bahir.* New York: Samuel Weiser, Inc., 1979.

———. *Jewish Meditation: A Practical Guide.* New York: Schocken Books, 1985.

Keleman, Stanley. *Myth & the Body – A colloquy with Joseph Campbell.* Berkeley, Calif.: Center Press, 1999.

———. *Your Body Speaks Its Mind.* Berkeley, Calif.: Center Press, 1981.

Michaelson, Jay. *Everything Is God: The radical path of nondual Judaism.* Boston: Trumpeter, 2009.

Moore, George. "Cramming more components onto integrated circuits." *Electronics* 38, no. 8 (1965).

Mopsik, Charles. *Sex of the Soul: The Vicissitudes of Sexual Difference in Kabbalah.* Los Angeles: Cherub Press, 2005.

Nachman of Breslov. *Likutey Moharan.* Trans. Moshe Mykoff. Jerusalem/Nantuet, NY: Breslov Research Institute, 1995.

Nietzsche, Friedrich. *The Will to Power.* Trans. Walter Kaufmann. UK: Vintage Publisher, 1968.

"Prayer of Saint Francis." *La Clochette.* Paris: *La Ligue de la Sainte-Messe,* 1912.

Pushkin, Alexander. "The Tale of the Fisherman and the Fish," in *Russian Magic Tales from Pushkin to Platinov.* Trans. Robert Chandler. UK: Penguin, 2012.

Raz, Simcha. *The Sayings of Menahem Mendel of Kotsk.* Trans. Edward Levin. Northvale, N.J.: Jason Aronson, Inc., 1995.

Rosenblit, Barbara Ellison. "Midrash on the Moon: In a Different Light." Available online at David R. Blumenthal's personal website.

Sarbajit, Roy, Shailendra Kumar Pandey, Vishal Kumar, Purushotam Kumar, Sudhir Kumar, Raman Kumar Mandal, Rajnish Kumar, and Deepshikha Mishra. "Ordered Complexity from Dissipative and Chaotic Systems, Including the human brain and society and the Universe; Relevance of the Second Law of Thermodynamics." *International Journal of Innovative Science and Research Technology* 6, no. 8 (2021).

Scholem, Gershom. *Kabbalah.* New York: Plume, 1978.

———. *Major Trends in Jewish Mysticism.* New York: Schocken Books, 1946.

Shainberg, Catherine. *DreamBirth: Transforming the Journey of Childbirth through Imagery*. Boulder, Co.: Sounds True, 2014.

———. *Kabbalah and the Power of Dreaming: Awakening the Visionary Life*. Rochester, Vt.: Inner Traditions, 2005.

Tales from the Thousand and One Nights. Trans. N. J. Dawood. New York: Penguin Putnam, Inc. 1954, Penguin Classics Revised Edition, 1973.

Weizmann Institute of Science. "Quantum Theory Demonstrated: Observation Affects Reality." *Nature* 391, 871–4 (1998).

Whitehead, Alfred North. *The Harvard Lectures of Alfred North Whitehead, 1924–1925: Philosophical Presuppositions of Science*. Ed. Paul A. Bogaard and Jason Bell. Edinburgh: Edinburgh University Press, 2017.

Winkler, Gershon. *Daily Kabbalah: Wisdom from the Tree of Life*. Berkeley, Calif.: North Atlantic Books, 2004.

Wolfson, Elliot. *A Dream Interpreted within a Dream: Oneiropoiesis and the Prism of Imagination*. New York: Zone Books, 2013.

Yeats, William Butler. "Kanva on Himself" in *The Academy*. Vol. 35. London: J. Murray, 1889.

Zalman, Shneur. *Tanya, the Masterpiece of Hasidic Wisdom*. Trans. Rabbi Rami Shapiro. Woodstock, Vt.: SkyLight Publications, 2010.

Zornberg, Avivah Gottlieb. *The Murmuring Deep: Reflections on the Biblical Unconscious*. New York: Schocken Books, 2009.

Learn More

I f you encounter difficulties with the exercises, the staff of certified Saphire practitioners are at hand at the School of Images to help you. Please email us at info@schoolofimages.com or call 212-627-5904. Our web site is www.schoolofimages.com.

Learning how to open dreams is difficult at first. Participating in a DreamOpening workshop online or with a Saphire teacher in person is recommended. Having a dream companion thereafter will also help to deepen the practice.

The School of Images

The School of Images (SOI) was founded by Dr. Catherine Shainberg in 1982 as a nonprofit organization and is located in New York City, where it attracts people from around the world. SOI teaches the language of imagination for instantaneous insight and transformation. The SOI teaching works to catalyze creative manifestation at all levels, and all areas of life, whether personal or professional, communal or global. If an individual chooses, the teaching may serve as the foundation for exploration of a sacred path.

Mission

The SOI mission is to teach the use of imagination for transformational purposes. Our belief is that this primary global language has the capacity to unify communities while empowering the individual. It is our goal to make this opportunity available to all people. Dreaming, visualization and revelation, the keys to the forgotten power of the imagination, are dynamic techniques that bring clarity, healing, and renewal.

Lineage

The techniques taught at the School of Images are based in the teachings of the Kabbalah of Light. The lineage dates back to Isaac the Blind of Provence, France, and Jacob Ben Sheshet of Gerona, Spain, in the thirteenth century. The last lineage holder was revered Kabbalist Madame Colette Aboulker-Muscat, who adapted the ancient methods to meet the needs of a contemporary world, and with whom SOI founder Dr. Catherine Shainberg studied for ten years and spent an additional twenty years in collaboration. Colette adopted Catherine as her spiritual daughter.

Kabbalah of Light

In the tradition of Kabbalah of Light teachings, the SOI work is experiential. There is no direct study or analysis of text, and no permutation of letters (gematria). Unlike other Kabbalistic ways, this work is pure Kabbalah, which means "receiving." It is an experience one receives through inner gazing, exploring the imaginal field using a universally understood language.

SOI International Schools

There are eight International Schools of Images in Europe, Russia, and Asia.

Index